IRISH ACES
OF THE RFC AND RAF
IN THE FIRST WORLD WAR

IRISH ACES

OF THE RFC AND RAF

IN THE FIRST WORLD WAR

The Lives Behind the Legends

JOE GLEESON

FONTHILL

Fonthill Media Limited
Fonthill Media LLC
www.fonthillmedia.com
office@fonthillmedia.com

First published in the United Kingdom
and the United States of America 2015

British Library Cataloguing in Publication Data:
A catalogue record for this book is available from the British Library

ISBN 978-1-78155-486-9

Typeset in 10pt on 13pt Sabon
Printed and bound in England

Contents

Acknowledgements

This book is not just the product of research. I have listened to—and hopefully taken on board—the advice of a large number of people who gave their time to take a call or to email suggestions to me on a whole range of matters. A bibliography cannot convey the many anecdotes and pieces of information that have helped me in my research, whether in building up a picture of a man's personality or confirming hard facts such as a casualty report or an aircraft serial number. There are a wide range of people and institutions without whom this book would be immeasurably poorer.

I am deeply grateful for the assistance of the Royal Aero Club Trust in sourcing images of the aces at the early stages of their flying careers, and I would specifically like to mention Andrew Dawrant in this regard.

The RAF Museum kindly scanned a number of casualty cards, including that of Robert Gregory, which greatly helped in settling some of the contradictory tales surrounding the deaths of several of the people mentioned in this book. Although the staff at the museum have now managed to make their entire database of scanned casualty card images available online, I have not forgotten the kind assistance provided at a time when I simply could not make another journey to London to visit Hendon.

The Imperial War Museum provided a number of images of aircraft through their prompt and courteous service. They also sourced images of Conn Standish O'Grady from their collection of papers.

The Sandhurst Collection provided an excellent service for obtaining enrolment register details of a number of cadets—and photographs of two of these—for the Royal Military College, Sandhurst and the Royal Military Academy, Woolwich. The McElroy and Molesworth images were supplied through Tempest Photography.

The image of Giles Noble Blennerhasset remains under copyright owned by the Blennerhasset family. The photograph was provided by Giles's son Brian to the Europeana project as part of a wider donation of papers and memorabilia. Copyright for the portrait of Robert Gregory by Charles Haslewood Shannon belongs to Dublin City Gallery The Hugh Lane.

The *Museo Nacional Aeronáutico Y Del Espacio* of Santiago de Chile kindly provided me with a copy of the photograph of Victor Henry Huston. I am grateful for their assistance in seeking to identify other records of relevance.

The UK National Archives have been the source of thousands of records, only a fraction of which are referenced in the text. Their online service facilitated the copying of a number of records that had not been digitised. The staff at Kew were fantastic: on one occasion I was nervously looking at my watch and recalculating journey times when a member of staff assisted in expediting the retrieval of a file that I needed.

I thank Limerick City Council for providing me with a copy of correspondence concerning David Mary Tidmarsh. The National Library of Ireland has always been informative and helpful.

The Irish military archives hold a wealth of information. For first-hand accounts of various IRA operations, including the ambushes and raids in which Robert Gregory's widow and David Mary Tidmarsh survived, the Bureau of Military History proved to be an excellent resource, although I freely admit I have not traced all operations in which Irish RAF personnel were affected, e.g. incidents to which reference was made by Henry George Crowe and so forth.

I would also like to thank Fonthill for the opportunity to have this research published, and in particular would like to thank Connie Long, my editor, for getting the text to a viable size whilst ensuring that it still remained coherent and readable.

Further, any mistakes, errors or inadequacies are wholly the fault of the author.

Joe Gleeson
February 2015

Introduction

The First World War had an enormous impact on Ireland. Over 240,000 Irishmen volunteered to serve with the Allied forces, and almost 40,000 died in the conflict. The Irish contribution to the air war, however, remains overlooked. Approximately 6,000 Irishmen served with the Royal Flying Corps and the Royal Air Force, and fewer than 1,000 served with the Royal Naval Air Service or with the naval squadrons of the RAF. Irish casualties across the flying services amounted to approximately 500 fatalities. The impact of the Irish pilots was out of all proportion to their small numbers, and naturally, this is best illustrated by the careers of the fighter aces.

The contributions of Irish aces Mannock, McElroy, and Hazell to the Allied cause were extraordinary by any standards; only a handful of aces exceeded forty aerial victories in the First World War. McElroy, Hazell, and Tyrrell were the highest-scoring pilots in their squadrons, and of the latecomers to the action, Oscar Heron was the joint-highest-scoring pilot in the second-last month of the war. The twenty-nine aces featured in this book accounted for almost 400 enemy aircraft between them.

Rationale behind the study of Irish fighter aces

An immediate challenge for anyone attempting to analyse the Irish contribution to the air war is the sheer diversity of the individuals that took part. Unlike the Irish regiments of the British Army, for example, it is not possible to group aircraftmen into a geographical location as one can when discussing the Connaught Rangers or Royal Munster Fusiliers. Similarly, although the RAF had several Training Depot Stations (TDS) based in Ireland, they were not Irish as such; notwithstanding the recruitment of some Women's RAF personnel and other support staff, the RAF TDS lacked a structure of local recruitment in the manner of an army regimental depot. In addition, the most cursory examination of the twenty-nine fighter aces featured in this book reveals just how diverse their military backgrounds were: many had served in the trenches, while others had served as observers or gunners before becoming pilots. Further, unlike the Australian Flying Corps, there were no Irish squadrons of the RFC or RAF, and unlike the 10th (Irish) Division at Gallipoli or the 36th (Ulster) Division at the Somme, there is no particular campaign associated in the public mind with Irish aviators.

Related to the problem of assessing the Irish contribution to the air war is the impact of the 'Home Rule Crisis' of 1912 onwards, the Easter Rising of 1916, and the War of Independence 1919–22, and how these affected Irish public opinion—North and South—on those in British uniform. Of the Irish fighter aces, few escaped the upheavals of the decade 1912–22. For example, Alfred Stanley Mills was a signatory to the Ulster Covenant, pledging to resist 'Home Rule' for Ireland; Herbert George Hegarty's uncle was shot by British troops in cold blood in Easter 1916; and others, such as Conn Standish O'Grady, claimed to have served with the defenders of Trinity College in suppressing the Easter Rising. In the area that was to become the Irish Free State, the upheavals of 1916-1921 led many to associate the British military with the murder of civilians, extra-judicial executions, 'official reprisals', and the destruction of property. Consequently, Irish public opinion in what was to become the Irish Free State was not receptive to accounts of Irish achievements in the wartime British armed services. Of the southern Irish fighter aces, David Mary Tidmarsh was caught up in an IRA ambush, as was bomber ace Albert Gregory Waller, as indeed was the widow of Robert Gregory. Henry George Crowe was to serve with the RAF in Ireland during this period and witness first-hand some of the violence of the era.

For those in what was to become Northern Ireland, the Irish role in the first air war also fell down the hierarchy of commemorations. For most Unionists, the narrative of the wartime sacrifice centred almost entirely on the 36th (Ulster) Division. This is understandable, as it was given to Irish unionist politician Lord Carson as a vehicle through which the Ulster Volunteer Force (UVF) could participate in the British Army; its battalions bore a direct relationship to UVF ones, and mass recruitment ceremonies were organised in many cases. This Ulster-at-the-Somme narrative did not just relegate Irish aviators to occasional references in the memoirs of army veterans, but it helped avoid the fact that, of the nine Ulster-born fighter aces, one was Roman Catholic—Oscar Heron, who joined the Irish Air Corps—and two others had distinct connections with the rest of Ireland. These were Co. Down-born Sidney Cowan, the son of a Scottish father and Mayo mother, who had a brother born in Co. Mayo and whose parents were resident in Dublin during the 1901 and 1911 census, and Belfast-born Victor Huston, whose mother was from Co. Kildare. The eight Ulster-born Protestant fighter aces are a minority like their ten Southern Protestant cousins and, on a per capita basis, form a much smaller contribution to the British war effort. Rather than look at Irish aces, it was easier for many Unionists to squint a little and just see a distinct Ulster Unionist army at the Somme, uncontaminated by these diverse elements.

The men of the flying services did not fit into the emerging political and sociocultural repositioning that took place in the newly emergent Northern Ireland and Irish Free State. One is therefore faced with thousands of individual stories of aircraftsmen, each with their own reasons for serving with the RFC, RNAS, and RAF; in examining them, it is difficult to avoid appearing subjective. As a group, the Irish fighter aces of the RFC and RAF form an objective yardstick that represents Irish aircrew personnel across all the fighter squadrons, irrespective of family provenance or religious background. By choosing to examine them particularly, I hope to illustrate just how great the acheivements of Irishmen were in the air war, relative to their small numbers.

Irishmen in the RFC and RAF

Recruitment in Ireland was voluntary, and in the absence of conscription it is meaningless to make comparisons with Great Britain's contribution in terms of manpower to the armies of the United Kingdom. However, there are some semi-official figures that may be used to give some context to Irish recruitment in the RNAS, RFC, and RAF.

A parliamentary question on 24 October 1918 from Major J. R. P. Newman MP (Enfield, Unionist) to the Chief Secretary, Edward Shortt, asked whether he would give the numbers recruited in Ireland from 1 June 1918 to 15 October 1918. The reply stated that the enlistments in Ireland between the dates in question were as follows:

Royal Navy:	626
British Army:	4,712
RAF:	4,438

This is confirmed through numerous other academic sources and shows that the recruitment rate to the RAF in Ireland was approaching 50 per cent of total enlistment in the final year of the war.

A further parliamentary question, on 18 November 1918, from a Mr Boland to the Under-Secretary of State to the Air Ministry, Major Baird, requested information on the number of men of Irish birth in the flying services at the outbreak of the war and the number who enlisted subsequently. The reply was to the effect that there were just forty-two at the outbreak of the war and 5,464 at the time the question was tabled. One may infer from the casualty rate of killed (500+), wounded (hundreds), and taken prisoner (about 100), that the overall number of Irish who had served with the aerial services over the course of the war easily exceeded 6,500.

The overall Irish casualty figure lay in the region of 40,000 from the 240,000 who served, therefore a figure of 500 losses from 6,500–7,000 who served would seem quite underweight. However, the relatively smaller Irish losses within the air services can be explained by the ratio of groundcrew to aircrew—there was a proportionately higher attrition rate among the latter. Therefore, the lower rate for the flying services (7 per cent) does not reflect the actual attrition rate at pilot and observer level. Indeed, of the twenty-nine fighter aces featured in this work, ten were killed in the war, making a casualty rate of 34 per cent.

Leaving aside relative calculations of 'head to tail' ratios, the Irish aviators were fully engaged in the air war and suffered losses at at least as great a rate as any other nationality. By the end of the war, nearly 300,000 had served in the RFC, RNAS, and RAF. Their casualties amounted to approximately 15,000 dead. Consequently the Irish attrition rate would appear to be broadly comparable. However, the Irish kill:loss ratio remains completely out of proportion to the numbers involved.

No. 24 Squadron

It is futile to attempt to identify the most 'Irish' squadron. The vast majority of the RFC, RNAS, and RAF squadrons had a prominent Irishman serve with them at some stage and personnel frequently moved between squadrons. The loss of corporate/institutional memory and the attrition rate experienced by each squadron add to the pointlessness of the exercise. That aside, of the thirty-three aces who served in No. 24 Squadron, several were Irish, including Patrick Langan Byrne, Sidney Cowan, Tom Falcon Hazell, and George McElroy. Hazell remains the squadron's highest-scoring pilot of all time and another Irish ace, David Mary Tidmarsh, was a founding member of the squadron and achieved its first aerial victory.

No. 24 Squadron accounted for 300 enemy aircraft over the course of the war, of which sixty-five were claimed by Irishmen. Towards the end of the war the squadron was commanded by the Irish ace Sydney Leo Gregory Pope, and of the ten 'A' Flight commanders during the squadron's existence, two were Irish: Hazell and Pope. Sidney Edward Cowan was probably the most famous Irishman to have served with 'A' Flight, but more of his countrymen served with 'B' Flight, which was commanded by David Mary Tidmarsh and Patrick Langan Byrne at one stage, and 'C' Flight, which had another two Irishmen, Albert Archer and George McElroy, among its commanders.

Lanoe Hawker VC, the original commander of 24 Squadron, thought very highly of his Irishmen (Archer, Byrne, Cowan, and Tidmarsh). He had served in Ireland with the 33rd (Fortress) Company of the Royal Engineers, with responsibility for searchlights at Cork Harbour; although homesick and agitating for a transfer to the RFC, it would appear that he made many friends in Ireland. Another point that should be noted is that Hawker was ferociously loyal to his men and therefore the praise heaped upon his Irish pilots was not dissimilar to that given to the other early pilots with the squadron.

No. 40 Squadron

Overall, No. 40 Squadron amassed over 300 aerial victories over the course of the war, of which almost seventy were by Irishmen. Although the focus tends to be on the high-scoring Mannock and McElroy, it was the early successes of de Burgh, Gregory, and Mulholland that helped set the standard for others to follow. Both Mulholland and Gregory are credited with several aerial victories on the F.E.8 'pusher' type, and Mulholland is credited with achieving the squadron's first aerial victory, in September 1916. Air Commodore Desmond Herlouin de Burgh was the son of Colonel Ulick George Campbell de Burgh and Anna Blance Constance Paget, of Scarva House, Co. Monaghan, but was descended from the de Burgh clan of Oldtown, Co. Kildare, who claim direct descent from Emperor Charlemagne. (The musician Chris de Burgh and his daughter, the model Rosanna Davison, are perhaps the most prominent family members from recent generations). After the First World War, Desmond de Burgh was involved in many innovations in RAF pathfinder technology, including OBOE and radar. He died in a flying accident while serving with the RAF in the Second World War. Of course, Mannock and McElroy tend to overshadow all others in terms of aerial victories, not just in No. 40 Squadron but also in the RAF as a whole.

No. 60 Squadron

There were four Irish aces who served with No. 60 Squadron, however, the two pilots most associated with it are the Victoria Cross winners Albert Ball and Billy Bishop. Consequently, other pilots are often regarded as supporting actors in the tales of these two men. However, No. 60 Squadron boasted twenty-six aces and suffered 100 casualties (killed, missing, wounded, and PoW) during the war. There were four Irish aces—Hegarty, Molesworth, Sydney Pope, and Alfred William Saunders—among the twenty-six, and a number of the others had significant Irish links—for example, Capt. 'Jack' Doyle was South African-born to an Irish father. It should also be remembered that the early commanding officers of No. 60 Squadron—the great Robert Raymond Smith-Barry and the well-liked Major Francis Fitzgerald Waldron—were Irish. Although both these 'Irishmen' were English-born, Smith-Barry inherited the stately Fota House outside Cork in the 1920s and Waldron's family lived for many years at the racing lodge Melitta House on the Curragh, Co. Kildare.

The celebrity of the First World War fighter ace

The air war was in effect fought over German-held territory, and the very nature of these offensive operations gave the RFC pilots a disadvantage when attempting to confirm a victory. A German aircraft could be seen going down 'out of control' having received several hits, but often it could not be followed so that its destruction could be confirmed. In fact, most enemy aircraft made it safely back to base with varying degrees of damage and/or pilot or observer injury. The purpose of the RFC and RAF operations was to clear the skies of enemy aircraft to facilitate British observation and reconnaissance, or to prevent German aircraft doing the same, therefore the category of aerial victory was not important to the RFC or RAF. Over the course of the war, 'forced to land' victories were dispensed with, and by May 1918, the 'out of control' aerial victories were no longer being reported in the RAF communiqués, although they were still being counted for individual pilot or observer aerial victories. In some squadrons, an aerial victory may have been awarded to either the pilot or the observer, but in recent years it has been more common to respect their contributions equally. In this regard, the number of aces in the RFC and RAF seem quite large relative to the number of French or German aces, given the differing methods of aerial victory classification. In comparison to the classification systems of later wars, many of the 'driven down damaged', 'out of control', and 'forced to land' claims would be counted as 'probables' as opposed to confirmed victories.

A further matter worth mentioning is the term 'ace' itself. It was not in common circulation in the First World War. However, French newspapers took to describing Adolphe Pégoud as *l'as* ('the ace') when he became the first pilot to have shot down several enemy aircraft. Over the course of the war the term 'ace' was applied to those who shot down five or more enemy aircraft. However, the British high command discouraged praise of individual pilots and observers. One consideration was respect for the overall contribution of airmen and groundcrew to the war effort. A related factor was the public school system, which was oriented towards honours for one's house or school colours rather than an individual claim to glory. However, medal citations often made reference to the number of kills achieved, though these were usually contextualised in terms of an overall operation in which bombing or reconnaissance are also mentioned. Pilots, however—and the commanding officers of their squadrons—were often quite score-conscious, and many died attempting to make certain a kill. Although a drip-feed of individual tales and unauthorised success stories leaked to the British public, the official discouragement caused a general lack of public awareness of individual RNAS and RFC pilot or observer achievements in air-to-air combat engagements. One unintended consequence was that Manfred von Richthofen became an American and British war hero of sorts.

In the post-war years, a whole genre of 'hell in the heavens' wartime memoirs flooded out. They were read avidly by those looking for something positive or praiseworthy in what had been a deeply traumatic four years. Of the twenty-nine Irish fighter aces only nineteen were survived the war, and of these, two were to die serving with the RAF in the inter-war years, one was to die with the Irish Air Corps, and another in a civilian flying accident. Two were also to die in the Second World War as civilian casualties. Sadly none of the Irish aces that survived contributed to the memoir genre.

Over 25,000 Irishmen and women served with the RAF, Fleet Air Arm, WAAF, and ATA in the Second World War, of which 2,000 died. Quite apart from three VCs (Esmonde, Garland, and Lord) there were hundreds of DSOs and DFCs won by Irishmen in every conceivable theatre of conflict, from the Atlantic to the Pacific, the Arctic to the Indian Ocean. At the highest echelons of the RAF there were Irishmen who had made their mark in the Second World War—Rathdowney-born Marshal of the RAF Sir Dermot Boyle for example, who served with RAF Bomber Command, and Air Chief Marshal Percy Bernard (5th Earl of Bandon). The greater number of Irish men and women who served in the RAF in the Second World War and the vast number of personal stories from that conflict have pushed the exploits of the First World War aces out of public attention. I hope that the following account of each individual Irish fighter ace will help restore the balance.

A note on selectivity

At the outset I should mention there are a considerable number of Irish pilots and observers frequently described as aces who served in bomber and corps squadrons, or the Independent Force (the forerunner of RAF Bomber Command). Unless they happen to have served in one of the squadrons in which a fighter ace features—in which case they may be mentioned—I have refrained from including them in this book, as there are at least twenty of note and it would be impossible to cover them in any respectful manner due to the constraints of space. Further, I do not cover the Irish naval aces, as the Irish involvement in the RNAS is a subject in its own right that would extend far beyond the scope of a single volume.

Given that there are a number of aces of Irish parentage who have either regularly or occasionally been categorised as Irish, I mention them if they have served in one of the squadrons in which a particular Irish ace is the subject of discussion. This will naturally give rise to some blind spots for the reader, as I could not mention every single ace that is often classified as Irish in other publications. This may prove contentious as several prominent aces of Irish parentage, including the McCudden brothers, Charles Hickey, and Denis Latimer, have not received detailed mention in this book. The reference to 'Irish', of course, also excludes Irish-Australians such as Kevin Parnell MacNamara, Irish-Americans such as Bill Geraghty, and Irish-Canadians such as 'Conn' Farrell.

1

ATKINSON,
Edward Dawson 'Spider'
(10 aerial victories)

Born: 10 November 1891, India
Died: 1953
Awards: Distinguished Flying Cross, Air Force Cross

Captain Edward Dawson Atkinson is one of four Indian-born Irish aces. He was the second son of Joseph Henry Atkinson of Calcutta and Elizabeth Mary Atkinson (née McCarthy). On his mother's side, Edward's grandfather was Charles Vincent McCarthy, C.E. On his father's side, Edward was the grandson of Miles William Atkinson and Anne Mather. Edward's great grandparents were Captain William Atkinson of Glennane, Co. Armagh, and Anne Chamney of Ballyrahine, Co. Wicklow.

Edward had four brothers and four sisters. His older brother, Charles Vincent McCarthy Atkinson, became Assistant Superintendent of the Madras Police, and another older brother, Joseph Henry Atkinson, served with the Royal Field Artillery.[1]

In the Irish census of 1901, Edward's sister Anne is reported to be living with his uncle William and three of his aunts at Sea View in Warrenpoint, Co. Down. Sadly Edward's sister is declared on the census form to be an 'imbecile'. In the Irish census of 1911, Edward's uncle and three surviving aunts are still resident in Warrenpoint, Co. Down.

Atkinson (I'll refer to all twenty-nine pilots by their surnames when talking about their military careers) arrived in France with the 40th Pathans on 2 April 1915. They marched north from Marseille and were to serve on the frontlines within days, suffering heavy casualties at Neuve Chapelle and in the Second Battle of Ypres over the course of April and May 1915. They suffered a further mauling at Aubers Ridge, but the regiment was retained for some subsidiary work at Loos. They held positions near Neuve Chapelle in August and September 1915. In December 1915 the 40th Pathans were transferred to East Africa. However, according to the Regiment's War Diary, Atkinson was wounded on 23 September 1915 and so may already have been evacuated to Ireland by the time he transferred to the RFC.[2]

On 12 December 1915 the Royal Aero Club awarded 2nd Lieutenant Edward Dawson Atkinson (40th Pathans) the Aviator Certificate No. 2145.[3] Atkinson had graduated at the London and Provincial School, Hendon. Although his address is recorded as '7 Promenade, Warrenpoint, Co. Down' it is unclear if he ever spent any significant length of time in Ireland—although some sources refer to Atkinson being raised in Ireland, he was not educated there.

Atkinson's transfer to the RFC in 1916 saw him serve with No. 1 Squadron. Indeed, the RAF Rugby Union team have a photograph on their website of Atkinson as part of the original No. 1 Squadron RFC rugby union team. During their time at Bailleul, the squadron had been equipped with two-seaters and so had a complement of pilots and observers. Atkinson would not have been unfamiliar with No. 1 Squadron, as they had flown on reconnaissance and bombing missions over Neuve Chapelle in the spring of 1915 and had directed artillery during the Second Battle of Ypres.

On 16 October 1916, Atkinson, with 2nd Lieutenant D. M. Murdoch as his observer, flew a Special Reconnaissance mission near Courtrai, escorted by three other aircraft from No. 1 Squadron. Although Atkinson and Murdoch succeeded in obtaining ten photographs, they lost one of their escort—Lieutenant C. M. Kelly became a PoW and 2nd Lieutenant T. G. G. Sturrock was killed.

No. 1 Squadron was restructured in January 1917, shedding many of its observers and groundcrew when it was re-equipped with single-seater Nieuport 17 'Scout' (fighter) aircraft. Although the traditional structure of a squadron was three Flights of six aircraft, No. 1 Squadron rarely mustered more than twelve or thirteen pilots for much of 1917. In that regard, No. 1 Squadron was closer in size and strength to a German *Jadgstaffel* ('Jasta'), rather than an RFC squadron. Atkinson was transferred from 'A' Flight to take command of 'B' Flight, and 'took to the role well'.[4] He was promoted from Flying Officer to Flight Commander (i.e. Temporary Captain) in February 1917.[5]

On 15 February 1917, the squadron's first aerial victory of the year fell to Lieutenant James Anderson 'Jimmy' Slater, an Englishman of Irish parentage. On the same day, No. 1 Squadron lost Captain James Shepherd of 'A' Flight in an encounter with Peter Glasmacher of Jasta 8. This necessitated Atkinson's return from 'B' Flight to 'A' Flight as Flight Commander. The squadron was deployed on a range of escort duties over the subsequent weeks, mainly with No. 20 Squadron.

On 25 March 1917, Atkinson recorded his first aerial victory, destroying a balloon between Warneton and Wervicq. He led a four-aircraft patrol, which had been ordered to investigate a report of an 'airship' in the Wervicq area, which turned out to be a kite balloon. He used rockets, without effect, before igniting the balloon with machine gun fire. Atkinson also fired on the winch crew as they sought to haul down the damaged balloon, and at one point he was just 50 feet above the ground.

On 7 April 1917, Atkinson and Slater, piloting two of four aircraft assigned to attack a chain of German kite balloons, came up against four enemy aircraft and broke off their attack. (The Germans were not unaware of the British tunneling operations at Messines, and their observation balloons were tasked with identifying this as much as the disposition of British troops and installations). Meanwhile, Lieutenant Robert V. Bevington, flying another of the four British aircraft, had pressed home his attack on a balloon and was bounced by six German aircraft. He survived a crash-landing and was taken as a PoW, but recovered sufficiently to serve in the Second World War as an RAF instructor.

Although the RFC did not employ mixed Flight 'circus' formations of the best pilots from each Flight, it was understood that sending small formations against well-defended targets only played into German hands, enabling them to deploy a force of overwhelming superiority. Larger formations, however, often produced better results. For example, on 22 April 1917, Atkinson led a nine-aircraft formation against a chain of German kite balloons; Lieutenant Edwin 'Stuart' Cole managed to destroy one of the balloons, but the formation became embroiled in a *mêlée* with several Albatros Scouts. Atkinson and 2nd Lieutenant E. M. Wright each drove an enemy aircraft down 'out of control', but the formation lost Lieutenant A. M. Wood, who crashed. Meanwhile, Lieutenant Cole's aircraft sustained so much damage that he crash-landed on the return journey, but fortunately he survived.

During the same month, another Irishman with No. 1 Squadron, Galway-born Tom Falcon Hazell, obtained an aerial victory. Hazell's prowess evolved over the summer of 1917, by which time Atkinson had returned to Home Establishment as an instructor.

Atkinson's rotation from frontline service arose after a series of encounters during late April and early May 1917. On 25 April Atkinson lost two of his patrol to a mid-air collision in bad weather. Both pilots—Lieutenants J. H. Mars and V. H. Collins—survived, but with serious injuries. A few days later, on 1 May, Atkinson encountered Jasta 28 and was attacked by 'an exceptionally good pilot' flying a red Albatros Scout. The German pilot was Leutnant Karl Emil Schafer, who scored his second victory of that afternoon and the twenty-fifth of his total of thirty. Atkinson was forced down behind the safety of his own lines at Elverdinghe, but his Nieuport 17 was damaged beyond repair.[6] However, the battle had not been completely one-sided; Jasta 28 suffered its first casualty of the war, with Lieutenant Alexander Kutcscher falling to the guns of Lieutenant Stuart Cole. In a letter to his parents, Cole recalled Atkinson's encounter with Lieutenant Schafer:

> The Capt. brought one down.... In turn the Capt. was shot down by one of the Hun, shots going right through his petrol tank. He came down in a spin but managed to right her before hitting the ground.[7]

In May 1917, Atkinson got to tutor a new pilot to 'A' Flight who had an interesting Irish connection: Philip Fletcher Fullard had served as an officer with the Royal Irish Fusiliers throughout much of 1915. Fullard was ultimately to become the most successful pilot with No. 1 Squadron, claiming almost forty victories between April and November 1917.

Atkinson returned to Home Establishment as an instructor on 13 May 1917 after over a year in frontline service. The squadron was to suffer heavily in the transition to new leadership; two dead and two wounded were lost on 18 May in a disastrous attack on enemy kite balloons. On 24 July 1917 Atkinson's promotion to Lieutenant in the Indian Army Reserve of Officers was gazetted, and dated to 9 April 1916.[8]

In April 1918 Atkinson returned to active service. Initially he served with No. 56 Squadron, scoring two shared victories in May 1918 with S.E.5As. He served temporarily as squadron commander with No. 56 Squadron, notionally on a frontline refresher course, but in fact he served in active combat; this was perhaps on account of his interest in experiencing frontline combat with machines of enhanced performance, better trained pilots, and improved tactics.

Atkinson transferred to No. 64 Squadron, where he scored five victories in less than a week. The squadron, which claimed over 130 aerial victories, had eleven aces serve with it at various stages, two of whom were Irish—Atkinson and Ronald St Clair McClintock MC from Carlow. However, No. 64 Squadron also had two other aces of Irish parentage: the previously mentioned James Anderson Slater MC and Bar, DFC, and Edmund Roger Tempest MC, DFC, whose mother was from Dublin. (Tempest's brother Wulstan also served in the RFC and RAF, famously shooting down the Zeppelin L31 on 1 October 1916, winning the DSO in the process, and killing the leading Zeppelin commander Heinrich Mathy; there's a Tempest Avenue and a Wulstan Park in Potter's Bar, Hertfordshire, named after Edmund's brother).

Atkinson returned to instructional duties, and on 14 August 1918 he married Nancy Rowan of Dunskaig, Ayr, in the old parish church in Ayr, Scotland.[9]

On 3 August 1918 the citation for Atkinson's DFC was gazetted:

> A brilliant fighting pilot whose flight has proved very successful under his leadership, often in combats where the enemy formation was numerically superior. Capt. Atkinson destroyed single-handed five enemy machines during May, and previously, while serving with another squadron, he brought down two enemy aeroplanes and one balloon.[10]

On 1 January 1919, Atkinson's award of the Air Force Cross (AFC) was gazetted.[11]

After the war, Atkinson served in various posts in Iraq. Although No. 1 Squadron had been disbanded on 20 January 1920, a successor squadron came into existence a few months later, equipped with Sopwith Snipes. It moved from India to Iraq in April 1921, being stationed at RAF Hinaidi, near Baghdad. In the post-war scramble for anything more than a short-service commission, Atkinson managed to continue in the RAF as a Flight Lieutenant. By September 1923, he appears to have been made commanding officer of No. 84 Squadron in Iraq.[12] This was a bomber squadron, which flew the D.H.9A, and later the Wapiti.

In January 1924 the Air Ministry included Atkinson in the list of promotions from Flight Lieutenant to Squadron Leader. Throughout the late 1920s Atkinson served as Squadron Leader of No. 1 Squadron, alternating between Iraq and RAF Tangmere, during which time he had flown a number of aircraft types including the Armstrong Whitworth Siskin.[13] Unfortunately Atkinson appears to have suffered from poor health, but his circumstances were not unique: during its time in Iraq from 1921 to 1924, No. 1 Squadron had a succession of commanding officers.

Dermot Boyle, from Rathdowney, Co. Laois—and later Marshal of the RAF, Sir D. A. Boyle, GCB, KCVO, KBE, AFC—served with No. 1 Squadron in the 1920s. Boyle makes no mention of fellow Irishman Atkinson in his memoirs, perhaps due to the latter's absence of prolonged sick leave, and indeed the much-praised Charles Lowe eventually succeeded Atkinson as Squadron Leader of No. 1 Squadron in April 1926.

Atkinson was posted to RAF Uxbridge, and in 1930 he was placed on the half-pay list.[14] He was subsequently one of a number of officers restored to full pay on 16 March 1931.[15] However, some months later, the Air Ministry announced that Atkinson had been placed on the retired list on account of ill health.[16] He retired to Scotland and died in 1953.

2

BLENNERHASSETT,
Giles Noble
(8 aerial victories)

Born: 16 April 1895, Co. Sligo
Died: 4 December 1978
Awards: Military Cross
Commemorated: Great War Roll of Honour, Cathedral of St Mary and St John,
Sligo, Ireland

Giles Noble Blennerhassett was born in Leoville, Co. Sligo, to James and Selina
Blennerhassett. Giles had three younger sisters: Kathleen, Eva, and Oonagh. His
father James was originally from Gortalea, Ballymacelligott, part of that famous
Co. Kerry family.

Leaving aside the Anglo-Norman medieval settlements and intermarriages, the
Blennerhassett family is one of the oldest English 'planter' families in Ireland. *Burke's
Irish Family Records* notes that while a small number of families descend from
English settlers in the reigns of Henry VIII and Mary Tudor (e.g. Bagenal and Cosby),
a number of prominent 'Irish' families actually date to the English plantations of
Elizabethan times (e.g. Barton, Beamish, Blennerhassett, Blood, Dobbs, Jephson,
Minchin, Ormsby, and Travers). One branch of the Blennerhassett family was granted
lands seized from the Earl of Desmond in 1590. Robert Blennerhassett was MP for
Tralee, Co. Kerry in 1613 and 1635–39, and a related branch acquired confiscated
lands in Ballymacelligott in Co. Kerry in the mid-seventeenth century. The various
Kerry and Limerick branches of the Blennerhassett families provided Ireland with
parliamentarians, peers, sheriffs, and clergymen for several centuries; up to as late as
the 1980s there was a Blennerhassett from Co. Kerry serving in the Irish Senate.

Giles's father James was an apprentice draper in Tralee, Co. Kerry, but he later
moved to Omagh, Co. Tyrone, where he studied book-keeping. He then went
to Sligo where he eventually became managing director of Henry Lyons & Co.
department store. Giles's mother was a Noble from Co. Sligo.

Giles was educated at Sligo Grammar School. He joined the Inns of Court OTC
in London and his youngest sister Oonagh became a barrister, later marrying

Justice Gardner Budd of the Supreme Court. One of their most prominent forebears from Co. Fermanagh was Chief Baron of the Irish Exchequer in 1621–25, and this office is one of the original judicial offices from which the 'Four Courts' of Dublin takes its name.

There seems to be confusion with regard to Giles's military service history. (Three of the four parts of his War Office file were destroyed in 1932). However, Giles's son Brian has recently provided his father's logbook, together with photographs and other documentation, to the *Europeana* project. This information confirms that Giles joined the Inns of Court OTC on 9 September 1915 at the rank of Private (No. 6115). He served for 267 days as a soldier of the Territorial Force in London, being discharged upon appointment as a 2nd Lieutenant in the 4th Battalion, Royal Irish Fusiliers on 2 June 1916. (The enumeration of the number of days in the OTC arose on account of service 'in the ranks' as counting at half the rate of commissioned service, i.e. Giles would have obtained 133 days of reckonable service towards retired pay at the officers' rate).

Blennerhassett fought on the Western Front from June to December 1916 with the Royal Irish Fusiliers. According to his son, Giles's experiences in the trenches gave him a great fear of rats for the rest of his life.

In late December 1916 Blennerhassett transferred to the RFC as an observer, being posted to No. 18 Squadron.[1] His logbook records a large number of target practice flights in January 1917 in FE2b 'pusher' aircraft, which were piloted by Lieutenants Faquhar, Gibbons, and Jones. On 22 January, in an FE2b (4968) piloted by Lieutenant Faquhar, Blennerhassett and Faquhar lost their patrol leader in a snowstorm while out on line patrol and had to land at Sailly-en-Bois to find their way onwards. On 24 January, Faquhar and Blennerhassett provided an escort to a photography mission.

On 4 February 1917, Blennerhassett achieved his first aerial victory as the observer in an F.E.2b (5460) piloted by Farquhar. They sent down out of control a German Albatros D.II north of Le Sars. They had also claimed a second enemy aircraft but it was recorded as being 'driven down' damaged and so was not awarded as a decisive aerial victory. They returned to the aerodrome with the main tank shot through and bullet holes in their radiator.

On 23 March 1917, Blennerhassett was 5 miles beyond Cambrai on a reconnaissance mission in an F.E.2b (4968) piloted by Lieutenant Bell when his aircraft was attacked; although he managed to bring his gun to bear on the enemy aircraft, no decisive results were observed. The next day, after photography duties with Captain Owen in another F.E.2b (5466), Blennerhassett wrote: 'Seventeen photos taken. Spaces missed as had to fire at Hun on tail'. It suggests that in this sortie, photography was the priority and that engagement with enemy aircraft was of secondary importance; experience of these types of sorties, not fixated solely on aerial victiories, worked in Blennerhassett's favour in the later war years when he got to fly single-seat scouts like the Camel.

Blennerhassett flew as observer/gunner/photographer with fellow Irishman Victor Huston on their first photography mission together on 28 March 1917 in an F.E.2b (5466), but there was no break in the clouds and they had to return after two hours.

On 5 April 1917, when flying on a photographic reconnaissance patrol as observer in Huston's F.E.2b (4969), Blennerhassett and his pilot drove down out of control two German Albatros D.II Scouts near Inchy. He recorded in his logbook: 'scrap with four Huns. Got two for certain and another doubtful'. The next day, with 2nd Lieutenant Reid in F.E.2b 5468, Blennerhassett drove down a German aircraft that had attempted to interfere with No. 18 Squadron's photographic reconnaissance. According to RFC Communiqué No. 82, 'this machine fell completely out of control and anti-aircraft report that it crashed'. In the 'Combats in the Air' report, Reid and Blennerhasset said that the Albatros made an attack but his guns jammed, enabling Reid to hit it with 60 rounds from the front Lewis gun.

Blennerhassett was also becoming skilled at aerial gunnery. RFC Communiqué No. 84 reports an engagement on 16 April 1917 in which Young and Blennerhassett, in F.E.2b A5461, take on six enemy aircraft, downing two,[2] although the fate of the second was not certain: 'I shot one down,' recorded Blennerhassett, 'and another dropped 2,000 feet but recovered and cleared off. Landed at Benguatre to have hand dressed'. It is possible that anti-aircraft or ground observers may have seen the second aircraft go down from the damage inflicted by Blennerhassett's gunfire. From his notes, this was Blennerhassett's 'eighth Hun'—a tally that does not accord with the official Wing Diaries.

While Blennerhassett was happily serving with the RFC as an observer, *The London Gazette* of 16 April 1917 reported his secondment to the RFC from 24 March 1917 with seniority from 31 December 1916.[3]

On 24 April 1917, Reid and Blennerhassett, in F.E.2b 5481, were on a photographic mission when the camera jammed after seven photos. They had to fight their way back against a formation of twenty enemy aircraft. Blennerhassett fired two drums and claimed one confirmed kill. On 30 April, again with Reid in an F.E.2b (A5474), they dropped eight bombs on Epinoy aerodrome, setting a house on fire. Blennerhassett then got to fire a drum of ammunition at a train, 'which stopped and sent up clouds of steam'.

No. 18 Squadron had a hugely diverse range of roles. On 1 May 1917, in an F.E.2b (5474) piloted by Lieutenant Reid, Blennerhassett bombed another enemy aerodrome at night. Just over a day later in, on a photographic mission in an F.E.2b (5506) piloted by Lieutenant Tolhurst, Blennerhassett exposed three photographic plates and fought in a protracted aerial combat with four enemy aircraft, one of which was sent down vertically. That night, on 3 May, Blennerhassett and Lieutenant Reid, in F.E.2b 5487 successfully bombed an enemy aerodrome.

On 23 May Blennerhassett shot down two enemy aircraft, one of which went down in flames, another crashing east of Eswars. However, engagement with enemy aircraft was not the only danger when on photographic patrol; on 21 June 1917, Blennerhassett's F.E.2b (5522) was hit in the petrol tank by anti-aircraft fire and the pilot, Captain W. A. Rough, had to make an emergency landing. On 11 July 1917, Blennerhassett flew his last mission with No. 18 Squadron, and was subsequently posted to Home Establishment.

On 26 July 1917, Blennerhassett's citation for the Military Cross was gazetted:

2nd Lt Giles Noble Blennerhassett, R. Ir. Fus., Spec. Res., and RFC

For conspicuous gallantry and devotion to duty. He has shown great skill and courage when acting as escort in attacking hostile formations. On one occasion he attacked two hostile machines, driving down both out of control. Later, he forced three other machines down.[4]

Blennerhassett was promoted to Temporary Lieutenant and was posted to the School of Aeronautics on 9 August 1917 for further training. From Reading he was then posted to No. 198 Depot Squadron at Rochford on 25 September. His logbook records a number of dual control flights in September and October 1917 in an Avro 504 (5940) with a Lieutenant Bruce. By late October 1917, Blennerhassett was flying solo and effecting landings. He put a variety of Avro 504 trainers (8578, 5940, 8511, 8514) through their paces, with minor mishaps such as a buckled strut on 14 October 1917 and an emergency landing on 19 October due to engine failure. By late October 1917 it was the turn of the B.E.2e training aircraft (8703, 2952, 3656, 7233, 3670, 3652) to take their punishment. Managing some cross-country flights, Blennerhassett struck a ditch on one occasion. However, he was improving all the time: on a return journey from Goldhanger aerodrome on 22 November 1917, Blennerhassett managed to land without incident three times when seeking his bearings in dense fog.

On 3 December 1917 Blennerhassett graduated from the Central Flying School at Upavon, being awarded Certificate No. 9070. He was assigned to No. 78 Squadron upon appointment as Flying Officer that month. At this time, No. 78 Squadron was based at Sutton's Farm (later called RAF Hornchurch), with a detachment stationed at Biggin Hill. The squadron's role was to intercept German airships and Gotha bombers in the defence of London. Throughout December 1917, January 1918, and early February 1918, Blennerhassett flew a number of examples of the Sopwith Pup (6246, B5907, 6153) single-seat scout aircraft, attempting formation flying and other test flights to and from Rochford.

On 8 January 1918 he married Kathleen Maud Curry from Newbridge, Co. Kildare, at Aldershot in Hampshire. As mentioned earlier, Blennerhassett had a sister named Katherine Maud Victoria who was known as 'Kathleen', so the new Kathleen Maud Blennerhassett may have needed to spell any additional middle name in correspondence in order to disambiguate from her sister in law.

In January 1918, in the half-yearly promotion lists, Blennerhassett was promoted to Flying Officer. However, *The London Gazette* Supplement of 4 March 1918 records him as being 2nd Lieutenant with effect from 2 December 1917 in the Special Reserve of Officers. It would appear that his temporary acting rank in the RFC and his home position in the Royal Irish Fusiliers were somewhat out of sync.

Blennerhassett was shuffled around quite a lot while various home defence squadrons were restructured and reorganised. He transferred from No. 78 Squadron to No. 112 Squadron, which was stationed on home defence duties but in the middle of transitioning from Sopwith Pups to Sopwith Camels when Blennerhassett joined. On the night of 19/20 May 1918, No. 112 Squadron sent all available aircraft up to intercept twenty-eight Gotha bombers. Major C. J. Quentin-Brand, a South African who had served in No. 1 Squadron with Atkinson and Hazell, brought down a Gotha in flames over the Isle of Sheppey. He flew Sopwith Camel D6423, with Blennerhassett also flying a Camel (D6465) that night.

The tale of Irishmen on Home Defence duties is primarily one of the RNAS rather than the RFC; the Westgate/Manston seaplane and scout stations had a number of interesting Irishmen based there, like James Garvey Farrall, Cecil Henry Fitzherbert, Leonard Graeme Maxton, James Alexander 'Ally' Shaw, and so forth. Apart from Gotha-hunting, Irishmen of the RNAS also hunted submarines and Zeppelins, but as already outlined in the Introduction, their contribution to the RNAS is beyond the scope of this book.

Quentin-Brand took a Flight from No. 112 Squadron into the newly formed No. 151 Squadron, which was sent to France on night fighter/interceptor duties. Blennerhassett, however, transferred from No. 112 Squadron to No. 152 Squadron on 12 October 1918, but was attached to No. 61 Squadron on occasion. No. 152 Squadron was formed in October 1918 as a night-fighter unit, flying Sopwith Camels. Blennerhassett returned to France with 152 Squadron on 22 October 1918, and was made Acting Captain in November.

Blennerhassett had a number of crashes during his time with No. 152 Squadron. On the night of 8 November 1918, in Camel H745, he overshot the runway, ran onto a road and overturned on landing. The same night another Sopwith Camel (D9571) crash-landed, with Lieutenant G. H. Williams also surviving. Blennerhassett was due to fly Camel B2402 on the night of 11 November 1918 but it was not in a fit condition for night flying. A Lieutenant Wykes crashed a younger Camel (E5168) that night in strong crosswinds.

Blennerhassett served beyond the end of the war with No. 152 Squadron, but on 3 March 1919 he was transferred to 11th (Irish) Group, based at RAF Baldonnell. He stayed there until 1 April 1919 when he was transferred to the 6th Brigade. He was notionally with 49th Wing and No. 153 Squadron in May 1919. Blennerhassett relinquished the rank of Acting Captain with effect from 1 May 1919. Following a series of re-assignments in May 1919 Blennerhassett served with No. 143 Squadron from 6 June 1919 onwards. This squadron was disbanded on 31 October 1919.

A qualified pilot, in October 1919 Blennerhassett was granted a short service commission as Flying Officer by the Air Ministry. On 1 November 1919 he was transferred to the notional strength of No. 39 Squadron, but over the course of November and early December 1919, he is variously described as being with Home Defence Wing, 1 Group, 10 Aircraft Acceptance Park, amd Nos 39 and 143 Squadrons.

On 18 December 1919, however, he was posted to RAF HQ India, as a corps observer rather than pilot, and was assigned to No. 48 Squadron in India on 12 January 1920. This squadron had recorded distinguished service in France during the First World War but was scheduled for disbandment on 1 April 1920. It was merged into No. 5 Squadron at Quetta for Army Air Co-operation on the North-West Frontier. On 30 April 1920, Kathleen Maud Blennerhassett and their son Brian sailed from Liverpool to Bombay on the SS *City of Calcutta* to join Giles in Karachi.

Blennerhassett duly served with No. 5 Squadron but his medical record indicates that on 16 August 1920 an assessment recommended that he be granted six months leave. On 14 October 1920 he was placed on board the ambulance transport ship HMHS *Vita*, leaving Bombay on that date. A further assessment on 23 November 1920 recommended four weeks' leave with a requirement to report on 21 December 1920 for further assessment.

Blennerhassett resigned his RAF Short Service Commission and was granted the rank of Captain with effect from 22 January 1921.[5] By December 1921, he had relinquished his commission in the Royal Irish Fusiliers.[6]

Giles and Kathleen's son Brian served with RAF Bomber Command in the Second World War, reaching the rank of Squadron Leader. Blennerhassett remarried in 1932 to a Dorothy Margaret Pinnock, in Edmonton, Middlesex. Giles was a lay representative for the Church of Ireland and donated the Bishop's Throne at Sligo Cathedral in memory of his father James. Giles died on 4 December 1978.

3

BYRNE,
Patrick Anthony Langan
(10-11 aerial victories)

Born: 12 November 1894, Clogherhead, Co. Louth
Died: 17 October 1916
Awards: Mentioned in Despatches, Distinguished Service Order (DSO)
Commemorated: Arras Flying Services Memorial, France; Great War Memorial,
Drogheda, Co. Louth, Ireland; Clongowes Wood College Great War Memorial
(commemorated as 'Langan Byrne')

Captain Patrick Anthony Langan Byrne was born near Drogheda, Co. Louth.
Patrick's father was Dr John V. Byrne, a medical practitioner, and his mother was
Harrietta Rose Byrne (née Langan). Dr Byrne was from Drogheda but Harriett Rose
Langan was English-born, from London, though Patrick's aunts, Maud Langan and
Margaret Teresa Langan, were born in Co. Meath. The Irish census of 1901 records
Dr Byrne and Harrietta being resident at St Laurence's Street, Drogheda, Co. Louth.
By 1911, Patrick was a student at Clongowes, Co. Kildare, and his parents and his
brother (Francis Joseph) were still living on St Laurence's Street.

Byrne was granted a commission on 9 October 1914 as a Temporary 2nd
Lieutenant with the Royal Field Artillery.[1] Two days later, on 11 October, he was
assigned to the 16th Division Artillery, and from 24 October he joined the 241st
Battery. By 2 January 1915, Byrne was training at Ballincollig, Co. Cork, for various
courses of instruction. On 21 April, he was transferred to 37th Division Artillery,
and posted to the 126th Battery of the RFA. On 28 July 1915, Byrne sailed to
France with the British Expeditionary Force (BEF).

Byrne was appointed Temporary Lieutenant with effect from 31 January 1916,[2]
and was subsequently granted a permanent commission as a 2nd Lieutenant with
the RFA, starting 4 March 1916. Byrne served with the 129th Battery, 30th Brigade,
prior to his transfer to No. 5 Squadron of the RFC on 15 March 1916.[3] On 24
March 1916, he was admitted to No. 24 General Hospital, Etaples, with a contused
head wound, but was transferred to England on the hospital ship HMHS *Cambria*
on 6 April 1916. He soon recovered to begin training with the RFC.

Byrne was posted to Oxford on 23 May 1916. He transferred to No. 2 RS on 3 June 1916, and subsequently trained with No. 10 RS in July and August 1916. On 11 July 1916, Byrne was awarded Royal Aero Club Certificate No. 3211, flying a Maurice Farman biplane at the Military School, Brooklands.

On 11 August 1916, Byrne rejoined the BEF, this time with No. 24 Squadron, commanded by the great Lanoe Hawker VC. Byrne was assigned to 'B' Flight, which was commanded by a Limerick man, David Tidmarsh. On 16 August, Byrne survived a crash-landing when his D.H.2 (5991) suffered a broken connecting rod shortly after take-off. This aircraft had been subjected to a hard landing by a 2nd Lieutenant J. N. Holtom a week previously, so perhaps it was badly repaired, or an early example of the legendary 'hangar queen' or 'problem child' aircraft so hated by maintenance crew.

On 31 August 1916, Byrne, flying a D.H.2 (6010), forced an enemy aircraft to land near Bapaume. Most of Byrne's claims were 'forced to land' and other 'soft' or essentially moral victories, which were granted in the early years of the war but not after 1916. Byrne fought bravely, however, though somewhat recklessly, according to some accounts:

Langan-Byrne, a dashing Irishman, dived into the middle of every hostile formation he saw, shooting left and right, scattering the German machines by his impetuosity. Only the limited performance of the D.H.2 and his lack of training prevented him from piling up a much larger score of victories.[4]

RFC Communiqué No. 52 of 1916 records Byrne's victory as attacking, driving down, and damaging a hostile machine on 31 August. On 2 September, Byrne was involved in another encounter in which the claim was deemed to be an 'out-of-control' victory rather than a confirmed destruction:

Lt Byrne attacked ... firing 20 rounds at 50 yards range. The hostile machine banked steeply, offering a good target, and Lt Byrne fired the remainder of his drum at very close range. The German machine side-slipped, and went down in a very steep dive towards Beaulencourt. Owing to the continued fighting, Lt Byrne was unable to see whether it reached the ground.[5]

Byrne also features in RFC Communiqué No. 54, which states that on 15 September 1916 he was in the thick of the action:

Lieutenants Byrne, Mackay and Nixon, of 24 Sqdn, while on offensive patrol near Morval, encountered 17 hostile aeroplanes at various heights. They dived into the middle of the hostile formation and attacked. Lt Byrne got to very close quarters with one machine, which burst into flames and was seen to crash. He then attacked a second machine, which was driven down and crashed in a field.[6]

Byrne was only credited with one victory from this incident. In many of these cases several pilots can often see the same stricken plane crash after disappearing down through clouds, imagining it to be the one they had engaged in combat. The common perception is that the RFC granted claims massively in excess of actual German losses, but the above communiqué shows that often pilots were awarded one victory from several claims arising in a combat incident. Byrne went back to the aerodrome for more ammunition and set out on offensive patrol later that day, then joining Lieutenant Wilkinson for ground strafing operations.

On 16 September 1916 Byrne accounted for another enemy aircraft, though he was probably overshadowed in the squadron mess by the success of fellow Irishman Sidney Cowan, who had brought down two German aircraft on that day.

Also on 16 September, there was a significant development in the arrival of the first batch of new German aircraft, the Albatros D.I, for *Jagdstaffel 2* (Jasta 2), a new hand-picked fighting unit led by the great German ace Oswald Boelcke. The Germans had begun to organise their single-seat fighters into attacking units, or *Kampfeinsitzer Kommandos* (KeK), to great effect, and then into hunting squadrons, or *Jagdstaffeln*. On Jasta 2's first mission they intercepted a British bombing raid on Marcoing Railway Station and shot down three of the formation. From this date onwards the pilots of No. 24 Squadron frequently reported combats with 'very fast enemy scouts'.

On 22 September, Byrne forced enemy aircraft to land on two separate occasions, near Velu in the morning and at Grandcourt in the evening. Byrne's 'forced to land' victories should not be taken as some sort of act of chivalry; frequently the aircraft were strafed on the ground.

On 23 September 1916, Byrne, flying his usual D.H.2 (7911), was badly shot up. According to Hawker:

> Four HA concentrated their fire on him at thirty yards, and shot through his engine, a tail boom and the main spar. His machine gun, ammunition drums and undercarriage were shaken off, and his D.H.2, out of control, drifted towards our lines with two German machines on its tail. Tidmarsh dived to the rescue and drove the Germans off, but Langan-Byrne was observed to crash in our trenches, and great was the sadness in the squadron that evening. However, that night he turned up smiling at what he considered a great joke.[7]

On 13 October 1916 Byrne was appointed to succeed Limerick man David Mary Tidmarsh as commander of 'B' Flight, due to the latter's transfer to No. 48 Squadron.

At 3.15 p.m. on 16 October 1916 Byrne, in his regular D.H.2 (A2542), led his Flight on an offensive patrol from Bertangles aerodrome, their objective being to cover the Fourth Army Front. Just north of le Transloy their patrol was attacked by Jasta 2. Byrne was shot down by Oswald Boelcke, marking the latter's thirty-fourth victory. Oswald Boelcke's diary, of which several translated versions of varying quality are in existence, records the combat in the following terms:

On October 16th, in the afternoon, I got into a fleet of six Vickers' machines. I had a fine time. The English leader came just right for me, and I settled it after the first attack. With the pilot dead, it fell, and I watched till it struck, and then picked out another. My men were having a merry time with the other Englishmen. One Englishman favored me by coming quite close to me, and I followed him close to the ground. Still, by skillful flying, he escaped.[8]

It would therefore appear that Byrne was 'the English leader' and that another aircraft had been involved in various manoeuvres at a lower altitude when escaping Boelcke. (Note that the Germans referred to all 'pusher' types as 'Vickers' in the belief that they were variations on the Vickers F.B.5 Gunbus.) However, that entry was recorded on 19 October and was one of a series of entries addressing aerial combats of the preceding days. Another entry deals with an RFC aircraft falling in flames, and Boelcke's increasing absorption in the cult of the ace:

On the 16th I got Number 35 ... I saw six Vickers over our lines. These I followed ... Lieutenant Leffers attacked one and forced him to earth (his eighth). The others were all grouped together in a bunch. I picked out the lowest and forced him to earth. The Englishmen did not try to help him, but let me have him, unmolested. After the second volley he caught fire and fell.

It is peculiar that so many of my opponents catch fire. The others, in jest, say it is mental suggestion; they say all I need do is attack one of the enemy and he catches fire or, at least, loses a wing.

Another Irishman who fell to Boelcke's guns was the famous pre-war racing driver, Leslie Vernon Porter of No. 45 Squadron, who was killed on 24 October 1916.

In correspondence home Hawker lamented the loss of Byrne:

I am feeling very depressed as I hardly know anyone in my own squadron now. Three of four went home for a rest, including two flight-commanders. I had two good lads to replace them, but one was taken for another squadron as I told you, and I got a stranger instead. The other however, was a splendid fellow—just got the DSO, a charming Irishman and brave as a lion. He had done more in two months than most of my people did in six months, and I relied on him to found the 'New 24'. Unfortunately he was shot down two days after he was made Flight-Commander, and I haven't recovered from the blow of losing him, he was such a nice lad as well as the best officer I have ever met.[8]

Byrne was the 'splendid fellow' who was as 'brave as a lion'; Tidmarsh was one of the two Flight Commanders mentioned, and Cowan, who had been promoted to Flight Commander in No. 29 Squadron, was one of the 'good lads' taken from Hawker. The 'New 24' that Hawker mentions refers to a plan to create 'scout' squadrons grouped together into a wing, but the idea was yet to be put into action.

Hawker himself was dead just days after Byrne had been shot down. He was killed in a 35-minute duel against the legendary von Richthofen—the 'Red Baron'—in which Hawker's obsolete D.H.2 could do little but continuously manoeuvre in the slim hope of getting on the Albatros's tail or escaping from the twin guns and 1,000 rounds of ammunition it bore.

On 27 October 1916, 2nd Lieutenant W. E. Nixon wrote from the 2nd Southern General Hospital, Southmead, Bristol, to J. R. Long, No. 24 Squadron, regarding the fate of Byrne, stating that he thought Byrne must have been killed.

Byrne's DSO citation was gazetted on 14 November 1916:

2nd Lt Patrick Anthony Langan-Byrne, RA and RFC

For conspicuous skill and gallantry. He has shown great pluck in attacking hostile machines, often against large odds. He has accounted for several. On one occasion, with two other machines, he attacked seventeen enemy machines, shot down one in flames and forced another to land.[9]

Given the large number of 'forced to land' victories credited to Byrne, it is ironic that the medal citation includes a 'forced to land' aerial victory that was not actually awarded to him. However, a DSO is an award for distinguished service and is not a gallantry award in the same manner as the Military Cross or (from 1918 onwards) the Distinguished Flying Cross. For such a young and junior officer to receive the DSO is a good indication of the esteem in which the early aces were held.

Byrne's official status as 'missing' gave rise to some unnecessary distress and confusion on behalf of the Byrne family. On 18 June 1917, the C.2 Casualties Records Section of the Army Council wrote to Mrs H. Byrne—then of 'Sunningdale', 41 Eglinton Road, Donnybrook, Dublin—to state that the Army were proceeding to conclude that Patrick was dead. On 4 July 1917, from London, Harriett Byrne wrote 'I have not received any further news of my son Captain P. A. Langan Byrne DSO RFA & RFC but I still hope he may be a prisoner. Might I ask you not to do anything in the matter for a few months longer.' This prompted a more frank response from C.2 Casualties:

In deference to your wishes no further action will be taken at present to proceed to the official acceptance of his death. At the same time I am to say that the Council consider it only right to inform you that so far as the evidence in their possession goes ... they are not in a position to hold out any hope that Second Lieutenant P. A. L. Byrne, DSO, is alive.[10]

On 22 September 1917, from Cowslip Lodge, Drogheda, Co. Louth, Harriett Byrne wrote to accept the inevitable.

I feel I am not justified in waiting any longer—I am a widow and as he and my younger son [2nd Lt F. J. Byrne RFA, then serving in France] are my only means of support I must request that you will allow me the compensation usual in a case of this sort.

Mrs Byrne nominated J. H. McCann Solicitors of Lawrence St, Drogheda, to handle the winding up of Patrick's affairs and to accept the insignia of the DSO.

However, Patrick's mother had not quite let go of the matter. Years later, and since remarried, Mrs H. R. Humphries, with an address at the 'Standard Hotel, Dublin', wrote to the War Office at Whitehall regarding second-hand information concerning hospitalised airmen in Germany. Mrs Humphries wrote on 8 May 1931 and also made a series of telephone calls. On 15 December 1932 the Air Historical Branch wrote politely but firmly to extinguish any false hopes:

I am to state that the impression that among the officers or soldiers of the British Army remaining in hospital there are any who are unidentified is a mistake and is entirely without foundation. Among those remaining under care for mental troubles there is not one who has not been identified, and his condition and location notified to his relatives or registered next-of-kin.

I am to add that since the War every possible avenue of enquiry ... has been explored, and any information forthcoming communicated at the time to the relatives. There is no reason to suppose that any officer or soldier whose name now appears in the records of the dead or missing is still alive.[11]

Mrs Humphries' address by this stage was the Regent Palace Hotel, London W1. It may therefore be assumed that Patrick's mother was encountering war veterans in London and becoming increasingly willing to believe any tale that could provide even a glimmer of hope—for example, a throwaway comment about hospitalised airmen with memory loss.

Byrne was one of Ireland's first aces, but by the aerial victory standards of the later war years, just over half his ten or eleven victories would not have counted. However, Byrne was a pilot who showed what could be acheived in aerial combat and his acheivements should be viewed in context. The Airco D.H.2 was a 'pusher' aircraft— i.e. the engine was behind the pilot—and Byrne's score is the joint-highest achieved on this type. The D.H.2 was quite unstable, with a tendency to spin easily and to stall. This contributed to the aircraft's manoeuvrability, and although it was useful in ending the 'scourge' of the Fokker EIII Eindecker, with the introduction of the Halberstadt D.II and Albatros D.I, the D.H.2 was completely outclassed. Several notable pilot who survived the early war engagements using the D.H.2, James McCudden VC being one, went on to remarkable achievements on more advanced types. Like VC-winner Lanoe Hawker, Bryne was unfortunate to be caught in the transitional period between the development of British and French types relative to German aeronautical advances.

4

CAIRNES,
William Jameson
(6 aerial victories)

Born: 10 July 1896, Co. Louth
Died: 6 June 1918
Commemorated: Arras Flying Services Memorial, France; Great War Memorial, Drogheda, Co. Louth, Ireland; Roll of Honour, St Peter's Church of Ireland, Drogheda, Co. Louth, Ireland

Captain William J. Cairnes was born at Stameen, Co. Louth, to William Plunket Cairnes and Alice Jane Algar. He was one of three brothers—Tom, Francis, and William—all born in Stameen, which is on the boundary between counties Louth and Meath. All three brothers were educated at Rugby College, and both Tom and Francis went to the Royal Military College at Sandhurst.

Major Francis Herbert Cairnes served with the Royal Field Artillery in the First World War. Thomas Agar Elliott Cairnes also served in the RFC, rising to the rank of Lieutenant-Colonel in the RAF in the Second World War. Tom had been a cavalryman with the 7th Dragoon Guards from 1905, who had only one eye as a result of a pre-war polo injury. Tom served as an observer with No. 15 Squadron, as Flight Commander with No. 27 Squadron (scoring two aerial victories in April and May 1916 with the dreadful Martinsyde G.100 'Elephant'), and as commanding officer of No. 32 Squadron from July 1916.

In the Irish census of 1901, William was recorded as living with his parents, two brothers, an uncle, and six servants at Stameen. Unlike his Sandhurst-trained brothers, Cairnes served with the Junior Division of the OTC while at Rugby, reaching the rank of Sergeant by August 1914. Capt. H. H. Hardy, Officer Commanding, Rugby School Contingent, Junior Division, OTC, reported that Cairnes was 'a very capable and sound NCO, well fitted to take a Territorial Commission at once'. He wrote a separate reference to recommend Cairnes strongly for a commission.[1]

On 22 September 1914, Cairnes's promotion from cadet to 2nd Lieutenant, 5th Battalion, Leinster Regiment was gazetted, and in April 1915, he was confirmed in this rank.[2] The 5th Battalion of the Leinster Regiment had its origin in the Meath Militia and retained the name 'the Royal Meaths' in much of the military correspondence and documentation. Throughout much of 1914 and early 1915, the 5th Leinsters served on garrison duties in Great Britain and Ireland. They embarked from Southampton on 19 May 1915 for duty on the Western Front. The 5th Leinsters fought in a series of minor but costly actions on the Western Front. Further, several draughts from the 5th were used to replenish the 2nd and 7th Battalions. Consequently, the Western Front service history of the Royal Meaths is fragmentary in nature. (Readers are advised to consider Kevin Myers's *Ireland's Great War* for a detailed examination of the subject.) On 27 November 1915, after six months on the Western Front, Cairnes embarked on HT *Transylvania*, arriving at Salonika on 14 December 1915.

Cairnes fought in the Salonika campaign until January 1916 when he was medically evacuated to Malta. He was transferred to 27 Infantry Base Depot at Sidi Bishr, Alexandria, in March, but his respite was short-lived, and he rejoined his battalion at Salonika on 1 April 1916.

Cairnes transferred to the RFC in August 1916, arriving at Alexandria on 23 August 1916. He was attached to No. 21 RS, Heliopolis, on 23 September. His training with the RFC was not uneventful: on 10 October Cairnes was admitted to the Military Hospital at Ras el-Tin, Alexandria, with injuries to his head, hands, and knees. However, he was fit to resume duties at Aboukir on 23 October 1916.

Cairnes was appointed Lieutenant (Flying Officer) with effect from 6 November 1916. On 28 November 1916 he embarked on HT *Minnewaska* from Alexandria for Home Establishment. In January 1917 Cairnes trained with 'C' Squadron at the Central Flying School and at the School of Aerial Gunnery before being briefly posted to No. 62 Squadron in February 1917. He was transferred to No. 19 Squadron, entering France with them on 21 February 1917.[3]

Both Nos 19 and 23 Squadrons were equipped with the French-built SPAD fighter in February 1917. These squadrons had a reputation for drunken excess and contained some maverick characters, but they also had a good record in air-to-air combat and in their ground strafing operations during the Arras offensive. The eccentric Anglo-Irishman Major Hubert Dunsterville Harvey-Kelly became the commanding officer of No. 19 Squadron in February 1917. He was the first RFC pilot to land in France in 1914 and had achieved the RFC's first aerial victory on 25 August 1914. Cairnes was not personally part of any hard-drinking clique.

On 19 March 1917, following an engagement with enemy aircraft over Cambrai, Cairnes suffered a forced landing near Glinchy, with his SPAD (A312) being wrecked. No. 19 Squadron was still based at Fienvillers aerodrome at the time, and although engaging in the occasional line patrol, the priority had been familiarisation with the SPAD S.VII. The squadron moved to Vert Galand on 2 April 1917 for frontline combat operations. Over the course of 'Bloody April', the squadron was to lose several high profile pilots, including Major Harvey-Kelly.

On 19 May 1917, Cairnes achieved his first two victories in SPAD S.VII B1565, destroying an Albatros C east of Croisilles and an Albatros D.III north of Vitry. After scoring two further victories with No. 19 Squadron, Cairnes was returned to Home Establishment in July 1917 to serve as a flying instructor with No. 56 TS. For a short period, his time in the squadron overlapped with that of Dublin-born Arthur Lionel Gordon-Kidd, a pre-war 4th (Royal Irish) Dragoon Guards cavalryman. Flying two-seaters, Gordon-Kidd had been recommended for the Victoria Cross for one bombing mission against an enemy troop train. Like Harvey-Kelly, Gordon-Kidd was to not to last very long in the single-seat fighter capacity, scoring two confirmed aerial victories before being killed on 27 August 1917.

Cairnes was appointed Flight Commander in February 1918, transferring to No. 74 Squadron on 14 March 1918 with the rank of Temporary Captain. This was the much-vaunted 'Tiger Squadron', about which Ira 'Taffy' Jones sought to build so many myths. The squadron did have a good kill:loss ratio, achieving over 200 aerial victories for less than 40 losses (killed, wounded, and PoW). However, it was a squadron formed with many experienced pilots among its ranks. It also flew the excellent S.E.5a for the duration of the war. Accordingly it is difficult to make a like for like comparison with other squadrons that had to endure the 'Fokker scourge' of 1915 or 'Bloody April' of 1917. However, in its favour it had New Zealander Major Keith 'Grid' Caldwell as its commanding officer, a celebrated figure from No. 60 Squadron. The squadron also had Edward 'Mick' Mannock from No. 40 Squadron as one of its Flight Commanders, who alone accounted for nearly 40 enemy aircraft during his time with No. 74 Squadron.

Mannock's 'A' Flight had experienced combatants like Lieutenant Benjamin Roxburgh-Smith, and he was to mentor the likes of 'Swazi' Howe, Henry Dolan, and 'Clem' Clements to develop his Flight into a formidable force. Capt. W. E. Young commanded 'B' Flight and Cairnes was appointed to take charge of 'C' Flight.

Cairnes's Flight included Lieutenant Giles, a battle-hardened veteran who was wounded at the Somme with the Somerset Light Infantry and had served as an observer with No. 43 Squadron; Lieutenant Birch, who had been an instructor; Lieutenant Charles Skeddon, a sombre but enthusiastic Canadian-born, American-raised former infantryman; Lieutenant Sydney Begbie, a Londoner who had served with the East Surrey Regiment; and 'Taffy' Jones, an experienced observer who was to become a famous fighter ace who served in both world wars. Jones was Welsh nonconformist and Skeddon was Presbyterian; both were strict teatotallers, which would probably have suited Cairnes, notwithstanding the fact that his family owned a brewery. In any event, the eighteen pilots of the squadron would have fraternized as a whole, and with Caldwell and Mannock present it would not have fallen to Cairnes to be responsible for morale.

On 30 March 1918 the squadron moved to France, but 'C' Flight did not have the most auspicious start. Cairnes experienced engine trouble, firing a white flare, requiring the Flight to land at Rochford. Then Lieutenant Birch had engine trouble shortly after leaving Lympne. Eventually 'C' Flight reached Petite Synthe, the home of a former naval bomber squadron, No. 211 Squadron. Of the ex-RNAS pilots to greet and dine with them was the Irishman Thomas Netterville 'Teddy' Gerrard, nephew of Eugene Louis Gerrard, the famous pre-war flying Royal Marine. No. 74 Squadron moved to Tetengham to take over the aerodrome from No. 208 Squadron, the ex-RNAS 'Naval Eight', one of the most highly decorated Camel units of the war. (Just over a week later No. 208 Squadron was to suffer the embarrassment of having to destroy fifteen Sopwith Camels on the ground at La Gorgue aerodrome, as they were unable to evacuate due to heavy fog).

On 7 April 1918, Cairnes led 'C' Flight on a line patrol. In the absence of enemy aircraft he took them over the enemy positions between Dixmude and Nieuport to give the Flight some experience of anti-aircraft fire. Unfortunately Jones's aircraft was hit by 'Archie', which ripped a large hole in the linen fabric of the fuselage behind his cockpit. Jones had Contact, the squadron mascot, in a locker behind him and was fearful of the dog falling out. The mutt survived Jones's hard landing, in which the aircraft suffered further damage.

On 11 April 1918, No. 74 Squadron finally got into offensive action. Cairnes won the toss as to which Flight would get to carry out the first offensive patrol. Unfortunately Jones's worship of Mannock does not leave much room for any praise of Cairnes:

> Cairnes is a topping fellow, but he does not strike me as being a good patrol leader. In our practice flights against A and B Flights at London Colney he rarely saw our opponents soon enough. Mick always huffed him. From my experience as an observer, I know how important eyesight must be to a leader. He must shield his Flight from surprise attacks; otherwise casualties will occur and the morale of his Flight will drop. We are hoping for the best however.[4]

There's much to dispute with Jones' view as to who should be the 'eyes' in a formation, particularly if bounced in a surprise attack from above and behind the patrol leader. However, 12 April 1918 was to prove a tough one for 'C' Flight. Cairnes led Giles, Birch, Begbie, Skeddon, and Jones over the lines between Forest de Nieppe and Merville. Cairnes is the subject of criticism for leading the patrol at a height of 6,000 feet, well below the cloud cover and thus facing the twin dangers of being in the range of anti-aircraft fire from below and a height disadvantage in any potential air-to-air engagement from above. Cairnes's Flight was broken up by an enemy formation. No Germans were shot down, and Jones's S.E.5a made a hard landing at the aerodrome after being badly shot up.

On a later patrol Jones's S.E.5a (C1786) was written off in a crash-landing. Jones recorded the incident:

> We were between Armentières and Lille, at 17,000 feet. Suddenly there was a cloud of smoke and the machine quivered. Slowly my propeller stopped, and so,

I might also say, did my heart. What a plight I was in! Far over enemy lines, while all around were bags of hungry Huns! Cairnes and the Flight protected me until I crossed the lines. It was an uncanny business…. On my way down I tried to think what I had done to deserve all this bad luck…. Grid [Caldwell] says I'm a hoodoo. Mick [Mannock] goes even further. He says that the sooner I'm shot down in flames the better.[5]

Over the course of that day Mannock led his Flight to several aerial victories, including one that he declared to be a shared between his entire Flight. On the other hand, Clements' S.E.5a (C1079) crashed on landing back at base, so the losses of the squadron's aircraft were not unique to 'C' Flight.

On 21 April 1918, Cairnes's Flight experienced the squadron's first fatality. In a confused battle in which Cairnes and Skeddon each claimed an Albatros sent down out of control, Birch and Jones followed Cairnes and Skeddon into the attack, while Begbie and Giles provided top cover. Before they had time to properly reform, the Flight became embroiled in a further scrap, and Begbie went down in flames. Skeddon's S.E.5a (D269) was forced to land at Marie Cappelle. Later, in the mess, it was discovered that von Richthofen—the Red Baron—had been brought down that day. A toast was proposed to him but there is a much-quoted retort from Mannock that he hoped von Richthofen went down in flames, i.e. the toast should exclusively have been for Begbie. On that topic, Mannock is said to have asked Cairnes what his final thoughts would be in the event of his aircraft going down in flames. Cairnes did not answer, but Mannock, attempting a joke, said, 'the last thing to go through my head would be a bullet!' He would rather blow his brains out than endure the pain.

On 6 May 1918 Cairnes had a lucky escape: his Very pistol discharged accidentally, burning through the longeron of his S.E.5a (C6385).

In early May 1918, all three Flights of No. 74 Squadron were to suffer losses: Cairnes's 'C' Flight lost Skeddon; 'B' Flight ceased to exist in its original guise, losing Bright and Stuart-Smith, with Lieutenant Piggott shot down but surviving; and even Mannock's 'A' Flight lost Henry Dolan on 12 May 1918. In that encounter Jones was hit several times in the petrol tank by an Albatros. As on 12 April, it was up to Cairnes to extricate Jones from the situation, allowing him to effect an emergency landing at Proven Aerodrome. Some of the replacement pilots did not last long either: from Cairnes's Flight a Lieutenant Leigh Morphew Nixon was killed on 17 May and a Lieutenant Henry Eyre O'Hara, from a Glaswegian Irish family, was shot down on 25 May 1918. Jones describes Nixon's death:

Nixon's end was a sad affair. Terribly keen to do his first show, he implored me to ask Cairnes if he could come up with C Flight on our 8.30 show. Cairnes agreed, and asked me to look after him…. At 9.15 Cairnes gave the signal to attack. I went up alongside Nixon … and led him into the fray…. What the devil actually happened, I don't know; but when I had finished my zoom and had steadied myself to look for Nicky on the Hun's tail, I saw to my horror quite the reverse picture. The Hun was pumping lead into Nicky, who was diving in a straight line away from him. Before I could help, my dear old machine with my mascot [a black cat logo] and poor old Nicky was enveloped in flames. Why have we no parachutes, for God's sake?[6]

Jones's point was that the new pilots, no matter how inexperienced, were repeatedly told not to dive away from an enemy but to keep turning, put the machine into a vertical bank and keep circling. Overall there were at least thirty serious casualty incidents involving No. 74 Squadron in April and May 1918. However, Cairnes's 'C' Flight had managed some innovative tactics when engaging in balloon strafing; on 19 May 1918 Jones succeeded in bringing down a kite balloon in flames.

On 31 May 1918 the squadron got to celebrate the award of a bar to Mannock's DSO and the asward of the Military Cross to Jones. According to Jones, 'Cairnes made a very witty speech. I did not know he could be so funny, but I suppose every Irishman has Mark Twain's baton hidden somewhere on his person.'

The following day, on 1 June 1918, Cairnes was shot down by Lieutenant Paul Billik of Jasta 52. Jones witnessed the kill and reported that Cairnes' S.E.5a (C6443) had lost a wing in the engagement, north-east of Estaires:

A determined Pfalz got to within 25 yards of him and gave him the gun. His right wing was suddenly seen to break up, the nose of his S.E. dipped viciously, then downwards he spun at a terrific rate.

I watched him for a short while, sickness overcoming me. It is a terrible thing to see a pal going to his death. Then I saw red, and went for everything in sight, but my aim was bad. I got nothing in revenge ... Cairnes was a great gentleman, and we are all very cut up ... I cannot imagine why we have no parachutes.[7]

Cairnes's service record, dated 1 June 1918, reports him as 'Missing', and on 14 November 1918 this is updated to 'Prisoner of War'. Eventually, on 9 December 1919, his record was amended to read 'death accepted for official purposes on or after 1.6.18'. It is unclear as to whether it was a genuine error in recording Cairnes as missing and/or a prisoner of war. In some military services it is possible for the families to benefit from a measure of pay while the MIA is described as being a PoW. However, the Cairnes family would have wished only for certainty on William's fate, so it is likely that bureaucratic caution was being exercised.

CALLAGHAN,
Joseph Cruess
(5 aerial victories)

Born: 4 March 1893, Co. Dublin
Died: 2 July 1918
Awards: Military Cross
Commemorated: Contay British Cemetery, France

Major Joseph Cruess Callaghan was one of three brothers killed while serving with the RFC and RAF. The volumes of *Ireland's Memorial Records* actually record four Cruess-Callaghan brothers as casualties, this arising from an erroneous duplication of 'Eugene'. The youngest of the three, Owen, appears as 'Eugene Owen' on the War Memorial, Belvedere College Dublin, and as 'Owen' in the 1937 Reading Room of Trinity College Dublin.

Joseph was born in 1893, the eldest of six children to Joseph and Croasdella Callaghan. The Irish censuses of 1901 and 1911 record the family as being resident at Stillorgan, Co. Dublin, together with a governess and two servants. Joseph Senior came from Co. Roscommon, while Croasdella came from Dublin. The actual name of the house was Ferndene, on the Deansgrange Road, Stradbrook, Blackrock, Co. Dublin.

Five of their six children were boys, three of whom joined the RFC or the RAF. Joseph, Stanislaus and Eugene Owen are recorded variously as 'Cruess Callaghan' and 'Creuss Callaghan' in *The London Gazette* and on their service records. Their niece, Consuelo O'Connor, wrote a memoir which touches on the origins and use of the 'Cruess' part of the name.

As time went on, my grandmother added her mother's maiden name ... to that of Callaghan. In a book signed in 1905 she describes herself as Croasdella Cruess Callaghan.[1]

Joseph was educated at Belvedere College in Dublin and later at Stonyhurst. There is some dispute as to whether he attended Trinity College Dublin, but Callaghan certainly attended the Royal Veterinary College of Ireland. He was known to be quite a gambler. However, the Cruess-Callaghan family in Ireland are more closely associated with industry: Frank Cruess-Callaghan became the owner of a number of cast iron and metalwork companies, e.g. farm machinery suppliers Pierces and Springs engineering, and Waterford Stanley became a successful brand of cast-iron cooker manufacturers. But Cruess-Callaghan descendants also ventured into politics and public affairs: Carmencita Hederman was a Lord Mayor of Dublin and a senator in the Irish Houses of the Oireachtas, while Consuelo O'Connor was a prominent environmentalist and conservationist, being a founder member of the heritage body *An Taisce*.

Joseph was living in Texas at the outbreak of the war, returning home to enlist with the Royal Munster Fusiliers in December 1914.[2] He passed a medical examination at Portobello barracks on 23 December 1914.

He subsequently joined the RFC from the 7th Battalion of the Royal Munster Fusiliers. The 7th Munsters had served in the Mediterranean theatre, at Gallipoli and the Dardanelles, as part of the 10th (Irish) Division. However, over the course of the war, Callaghan applied for a permanent commission in the 2nd Battalion, i.e. to remain in a service battalion of the Munsters following the standing down of any reserve battalions and/or the conclusion of his secondment to the RFC. Confusion can therefore arise as to his actual service with the Royal Munster Fusiliers.

Upon transfer to the RFC, Callaghan was initially posted to Norwich on 1 September 1915. On 25 January 1916 he transferred to the Central Flying School. On 1 February 1916 he joined No. 18 Squadron, at the time still persevering with the Vickers FB.5 'Gunbus' before re-equipping with the F.E.2b. The F.E.2b was a 'pusher', with the engine in the rear, propelling the aircraft forwards. Although Callaghan did not become an ace with this squadron, he was not the only Irish ace to have served with them: Belfast man Victor Huston became an ace with No. 18 Squadron, as did Giles Blennerhassett from Sligo. Later, when it converted from a multifunctional role to being a bomber squadron, equipped with the D.H.4, Galway man Albert Gregory Waller was also to 'make ace' with the squadron.

Callaghan's first aerial victory was claimed on 26 April 1916, a Fokker E.III Eindecker. According to No. 18 Squadron's 'Combats in the Air' submissions to the Wing and Brigade levels, Callaghan was flying F.E.2b (5232) with a Sergeant Mitchell as his observer when they encountered four Fokkers. Callaghan describes the action as follows:

I turned sharply towards them. The Observer got off half a drum at the first. The rest of the drum he fired at the second Fokker. Some of these last shots hit the front of the machine.

I then turned towards our lines to allow the Observer to load. Just then the third Fokker, firing at us from the rear, put the engine out of action. I put her nose down towards our lines. The other two Fokker had turned and were again firing at us from the rear. I told the Observer to crouch down. Their shooting was most accurate: bullets kept tearing past me on both sides. Some of the shots took away my elevator controls and left me without any fore and aft control. Over the lines the firing stopped. I looked into the front seat and saw the Observer lying over to the right of the nacelle with a ragged bullet hole through his skull. In crouching down he had evidently put his head on the right side of the nacelle and it was one of the shots that passed beside my right arm that killed him.[3]

He crash-landed near Château de la Haie on account of the damaged controls. Callaghan's squadron commander, G. I. Carmichael, would appear to have written in pencil, '1 Fokker brought down, fight broken off'—that was one way of putting it. He also notes that observers on the ground may have seen one of the Germans go down, the second Fokker being hit with half a drum. Generally speaking an aircraft will not be in great flying shape after taking a half drum of Lewis gun ammunition! The Fokker E.III Eindecker frame had steel-chrome alloy tubing instead of wood, i.e. it was akin to a flying bicycle. However, the Eindecker had no ailerons on its wings, instead relying on wing-warping to control roll. Consequently, any damage to control wires or bracing wires could have catastrophic consequences. But it is entirely possible that one of the Germans suffered battle damage and limped home from the fray in a controlled descent. (The Germans do not record a fatality, but this does not preclude a damaged aircraft made serviceable.) Apparently, the German attackers were Leutnant Max Ritter von Mulzer, Leutnant Österreicher, and an unnamed pilot of FA26.[4] They were not awarded an aerial victory for the stricken F.E.2b, however, Mulzer was to become one of Bavaria's highest scoring aces of the war. (He should not be confused with the other great Bavarian, *Orden Pour le Mérite* 'Blue Max' winner, Leutnant Max Ritter von Müller.) Callaghan's observer was a fellow Irishman, 2nd Lieutenant James Mitchell, from Cappa, Kilrush, Co. Clare. He had previously served with the 5th Canadian Infantry Brigade, and prior to that had been in the Royal Navy.

Given the range of aerial photography, bombing, escort, and fighting duties assigned to No. 18 Squadron at this point in the war, Major Carmichael and the relevant officers at Wing and Brigade level would not have been particularly concerned as to the precise categorisation of an aerial victory.

On 5 June 1916 Callaghan was promoted to Captain (Flight Commander). He was wounded on 31 July 1916.[5] I cannot identify a corresponding casualty report. However, as this was the height of the Battle of the Somme it's likely that it could have been a landing accident following one of the numerous missions flown by Callaghan that day or night. Callaghan's Log Book contains a reference that day to a lengthy bombing and reconnaissance mission undertaken against railway, transport, and recently dug entrenchments.[6]

However, Callaghan's medical board assessment includes an admission from him, dated 12 August 1916, that he suffered from malaria. Callaghan applied for a permanent commission in the 2nd Battalion of the Royal Munster Fusiliers, but with continuing secondment to the RFC. In support of this application on 17 August 1916, Major G. I. Carmichael penned a hand-written note, 'I certify that Captain J. C. Callaghan received an education fitting to an officer holding a permanent commission in the regular force—Trinity College Dublin.' Of course, Carmichael's 'certification' of Callaghan's education avoids Callaghan having to produce any evidence for it. He is not included in the University of Dublin Roll of Honour.

On 27 August 1916, his brother Eugene Owen was killed in action serving with No. 19 Squadron. His B.E.12 (6545) was one of five to accidentally descend on an enemy aerodrome after a bombing raid, mistaking the aerodrome for their own advance landing ground. Three were killed and two were taken prisoner. According to the Stonyhurst War Record, Eugene (known as 'Owen'), was 'a serious, thoughtful and religious boy,' and his CO regarded him as 'one of the most popular youngsters in the mess, and we all miss him very much.'[7]

Notwithstanding his own wounding and his brother's death, Callaghan returned to No. 18 Squadron. In an RFC Communiqué No. 57 of October 1916, for example, Callaghan is credited with a night bombing attack. According to his own account, on 9 October 1916 Callaghan crossed the lines at Gueudecourt at 11.55 p.m. and followed the road from Bapaume to Cambrai.

> Had a good look at Cambrai and found a train with steam up in station on East side of the town. At 12.25 a.m. dropped three 20-lb Hales HE on train. A beauty. Hit train just behind engine. All lights immediately went out and AA guns and searchlights became very active. We ... dropped the remaining three bombs on railway line which is on the West of the station running parallel. The AA fire was hellish. A strong searchlight played on us from Sailly on the Northern side of the Cambrai–Arras road, so we dived on him and I gave him a drum of the best. The searchlight then went out and another one got on us.[8]

Callaghan managed to continue to engage hostile searchlights while effecting their escape, even though they accidentally used tracer ammunition at one stage and so drew fire on themselves as they had given away their location.

Callaghan was granted the rank of Temporary Captain, with seniority, on 4 October 1916. On the night of 9/10 November 1916 Callaghan, with Sergeant Ankers as his observer, led a bombing mission on the German aerodrome at Villers, inflicting some damage and driving off an enemy aircraft that attempted to intercept them.

> As we hovered over the aerodrome to drop our remaining bombs a machine was wheeled out of a hangar and took off into the wind. We followed him and ... kept him in sight. We were getting quite close to him (we were at 4,000 feet and he was

at about 1,500 feet) when he turned sharply and we turned to get on top of him. He was drawing away from us so I opened fire on him and gave him a drum. He then went down out of sight.[9]

The bombing of the German aerodromes was a tactic deployed in the face of the superiority of the Albatros fighter over the D.H.2 and F.E.2b 'pushers'. However, presumably the Albatros pilot wouldn't risk being hit by his own AA fire in a nighttime dogfight and so flew away to safety. The following night Callaghan and Sgt Ankers bombed Valencinnes train station, causing fires to break out there.

Callaghan was posted to Home Establishment on 16 November 1916. A medical board examination of 20 November reported him as unfit for general service for two months, this assessment being re-confirmed on 29 December 1916. Callaghan was duly declared fit in an assessment of 6 February 1917.[10] However, it diagnosed 'nervous strain and ague'. Obviously the latter could be attributed to malaria but the former was found to have arisen on account of '10 months flying'. This was still the era of 'shell shock' rather than PTSD, but the Medical Board still recorded physical symptoms such as raised blood pressure and irregular heartbeat. The initial examination in December 1916 had stated that Callaghan 'is suffering from enfeebled heart action, accentuated by overuse of tobacco.' But the subsequent examination recorded 'three cigarettes per day,' so a diagnosis of 'nervous strain' was made on a step-by-step basis to prepare Callaghan and the RFC for the possibility of an ongoing lack of fitness for active service.

On 13 February 1917 Callaghan's Military Cross citation was gazetted:

2Lt (Temp. Capt.) Joseph Cruess Callaghan, R. Muns. Fus. and RFC

For conspicuous gallantry in action. He displayed marked courage and skill on several occasions in carrying out night bombing operations. On one occasion he extinguished a hostile searchlight.[11]

On 22 February 1917, Callaghan was posted to the No. 2 School of Aerial Gunnery, subsequently transferring on 25 October 1917 to the No. 1 School. Callaghan was known for his hair-raising aerial stunts when serving as the aerial gunnery instructor there. Apparently, while based there he flew back to Ireland—on three separate occasions—to visit his mother!

His brother Stanislaus was killed on 27 June 1917 in a flying accident when training in Canada. Stanislaus's training in wireless telegraphy had seen him posted to No. 5 Squadron, and he fought at the Battle of Ypres, being brought down twice and suffering burns. In Easter 1916 Stanislaus was captured by the forces of the Irish Republic and held prisoner in the Four Courts for a week. (In the trial of Edward Daly, CO of 1st Battalion, there is no witness statement from Stanislaus Callaghan, though a number of other former prisoners testify). In early 1917 Stanislaus was appointed to Camp Borden in Canada as part of a wireless deployment, and was killed in a crash within a fortnight of his arrival there.

On 4 January 1918 Callaghan was gazetted as Temporary Major (Squadron Commander), dated to 21 October 1917. On 1 February 1918 he was briefly assigned to No. 54 TS, before being allocated to No. 87 Squadron on 27 February 1918.

It was with No. 87 Squadron that he excelled as the 'Mad Major', flying with a combination of recklessness and bravery. He was granted the full rank of Squadron Commander with effect from 1 February 1918. The squadron flew the Sopwith Dolphin, in which Callaghan scored four victories in May and June in the same aircraft (D3671). Commanding officers were not supposed to engage in patrol duties, and to some extent Callaghan reminds one of Victor Beamish in the Second World War.

Callaghan's Sopwith Dolphin (C4168) was decorated with a shamrock logo on the fuselage that's over one foot in height.[12] There is no certainty that Callaghan's personal shamrock marking appeared on D3671, however.

On 2 July 1918 Callaghan's luck ran out, when he was caught within the killing range of a formation of as many as twenty-five German aircraft on a patrol of No. 60 Squadron. Callaghan attacked the formation single-handedly with his Sopwith Dolphin (D3671), presumably in an effort to scatter and cause confusion. He was shot down in flames by the German ace Leutnant Franz Buchner of Jasta 13, the latter's seventh of forty victories he would achieve in the war.

A member of No. 87 Squadron described the fight:

> Captain Maxwell in No. 56 Squadron saw one machine fighting about twenty-five Germans, but the machine was hit before he could arrive close enough. I am afraid there is no doubt as to who was the pilot of that machine. He was so absurdly gallant and so absolutely without any idea of fear, that he would cheerfully take on any kind of odds. We had all implored him not to go about by himself and run such risks, but I don't think he realized that he could ever find a Hun or any number of Huns that he wasn't a match for.
>
> We have lost in him one of the finest squadron commanders, and one of the finest fighting pilots on the Western Front today, and as such he cannot be replaced. But to us his loss is even more irreplaceable. We feel that we have lost a great stout-hearted friend, always ready to help anybody out of trouble, a gallant companion in a fight, and a sportsman to the backbone.[13]

The letter to next-of-kin from RAF 3rd Brigade HQ conveyed similar sentiments:

> I cannot possibly express to you in these few lines the sympathy which all of us who knew him feel for you. He was one of the most gallant officers I ever met, and had that wonderful power of infusing those that served under him with the same spirit. His squadron worshipped him, and we all fully realise the terrible loss he will be to you.[14]

According to the Stonyhurst War Record, Callaghan was a devoted a Catholic:

> 'Casey', for so he was called by all his friends … was a man of not only extreme
> physical courage, but also great moral courage. Here is an illustrative episode
> related to his mother by his greatest chum, a Protestant: The first night when the
> squadron flew out to France there was no accommodation for its members, and
> all the officers of the squadron slept in one large hall. 'It was the bravest thing I
> ever knew Casey to do. He knelt down and said his prayers, and not one dared to
> jeer or sneer. It was a thing unheard of.'

Joseph Callaghan is commemorated at Contay Cemetery, without any corresponding
Irish memorial, but his brothers, Owen and Stanislaus, are commemorated on the
War Memorial at Belvedere College. Ken Kinsella's excellent history of the various
South Dublin families who served in the First World War contains a poignant poem
written by Louise Cruess Callaghan for her three uncles.[15]

Callaghan's surviving brother, Cedric, kept the family's war relics, its interest in
aviation, and indeed that maverick streak:

> Cedric never spoke of his three older brothers who were killed in the First World
> War. He must have had memories of them because he was aged ten when his eldest
> brother, Joseph, was killed. He always kept three wall plaques inherited from his
> mother on the drawing room mantelpiece in his home … He rode to hounds with
> the Bray Harriers and flew his own light airplanes, flying once to Genoa in Italy …
> Frank [Consuelo's brother], a champion pole vaulter, was keen to attend an
> athletic event in Cork but was refused permission by his boss to take the day off to
> travel to Cork. Uncle Cedric came to the rescue, flying him down to Cork, landing
> in a field … and Frank made it to the sports meeting in time.[16]

6

COWAN,
Sidney Edward
(7-8 aerial victories)

Born: 23 August 1897, Downpatrick, Co. Down
Died: 17 November 1916
Awards: Military Cross with Two Bars
Commemorated: Cagnicourt British Cemetery, France

Captain Sidney Edward Cowan was one of two brothers to die in the war while serving in the RFC. He was one of the earliest aces of the war and one of the most highly decorated. A note of caution, however, should be sounded in respect of awards to aviators in the early stages of the war: Cowan's early aviation exploits, exceptional at the time, became more routine as the war continued. However, it is nevertheless quite an achievement to win the Military Cross three times, let alone over the period of just a few months, and at only nineteen years of age. Furthermore, Cowan helped establish just what was possible in the exercise of air power generally and in the specific performance of particular machines.

Cowan's father was actually from Scotland. Peter Chalmers Cowan served in a number of senior engineering positions in Counties Mayo and Down, having worked in a number of roles in railway engineering throughout Canada and the USA. In 1886 he was appointed County Surveyor of South Mayo. He met his future wife, Marion (née Johnston) of Westport, Co. Mayo, while serving there. They married in 1888. Their first son, Frederick Alex, was born in Co. Mayo in 1889. Peter served as Consulting Engineer to the Piers and Roads Commission. He was responsible for the completion of the Achill viaduct and swing-bridge. In 1889 Cowan was promoted to County Surveyor of South Down, later being responsible for the entire county.[1] Cowan's position as Chief Engineering Inspector for the Local Government Board of Ireland led to his professional opinion being sought in Parliament, and he appears in Hansard on numerous occasions.

Sidney's sister, Hilda Marion, was born in Belfast in 1894. His older brother, Philip Chalmers, was born in Belfast in 1896. Sidney was born at Downpatrick, Co. Down. As one may expect from all the movement around Ireland, it is difficult to refer to the family as being from any particular locality. However, the Irish censuses of 1901 and 1911 both record Peter Chalmers Cowan and his wife Marion as being resident at Ailesbury Road, Dublin.

Sidney was educated at Castle Park, Dalkey, Co. Dublin, and later at Marlborough College, Wiltshire. The UK census of 1911 records him as resident there as a student with his older brother Philip. Both Sidney and Philip were also educated at Trinity College Dublin.

Cowan was a founding member of No. 24 Squadron when it formed in Hounslow on 1 September 1915.[2] In fact, three of the original twelve members of the squadron were Irish-born: 2nd Lieutenant S. E. Cowan with 'A' Flight, 2nd Lieutenant David Mary Tidmarsh with 'B' Flight, and 2nd Lieutenant Albert Erskine Carson Archer as Flight Commander of 'C' Flight. We generally think of the early squadrons as three Flights of six aircraft, but they were frequently under strength. No. 24 Squadron retained an unusual 'Irish' dimension throughout the various phases of the air war, notwithstanding the enormous turnover in personnel over the years.

In February 1916, when No. 24 Squadron was in the course of moving to France, Cowan's D.H.2 was blown over by high winds. Given that there were no ferry pilots in those days it was up to the squadron's pilots to find their own way over the Channel and use railways, rivers, and other navigational aids to locate the specified landing grounds. Cowan did not have to cross alone, however, as 2nd Lieutenant J. O. Andrews had also suffered a mishap on the way between Hounslow and Kent. However, the squadron's problems began in earnest at Bertangles, with several fatal crashes, one of whom was the Dublin-born 2nd Lieutenant A. E. C. Archer.

Even though the D.H.2 'pusher' had a tendency to spin, like many rearward propulsion craft, Cowan was seen as an innovative early experimenter with the capabilities and limitations of the machine.

> A certain amount of trouble was caused at first through the ease with which these machines used to 'spin'—a manoeuvre not at the time understood—and several casualties resulted. Lieutenant Cowan did much to inspire confidence by the facility with which he handled his machine. He was the first pilot to really 'stunt' this machine, and gradually the squadron gained complete assurance.[3]

On 4 April 1916 the Limerick man, David Mary Tidmarsh, opened No. 24 Squadron's account, crashing an Albatros over Grandcourt. Cowan was involved in several aerial engagements over the course of that month. On 24 April 1916 Lieutenants Andrews, Cowan, Manfield, and Wilson of No. 24 Squadron escorted five B.E.2s of No. 15 Squadron in D.H.2s. The IV Army Commander sent a special message of praise to them in successfully breaking up the German attack. The days of the Fokker Eindecker scourge were nearing an end, although the squadron did not record a decisive aerial victory against their attackers.

On 25 April 1916, Cowan had a further indecisive encounter with a number of Fokkers. Cowan's No. 24 Squadron was on escort duty to No. 27 Squadron, who were acting as the British IV Army's reconnaissance and artillery ranging aircraft. No. 27 Squadron succeeded in ranging a 12-inch howitzer on the Comines railway station. The work of the aces should often be seen in the context of the success of the Army Cooperation units rather than whether or not an enemy aircraft was shot down in the encounters: aerial superiority was the priority.

However, in a later encounter that day, Cowan was in D.H.2 5925 escorting a B.E.2c of No. 9 Squadron on a reconnaissance mission when an aerial combat occurred. There has been much speculation as to whom Cowan faced in this encounter; his description of the aerial combat is as follows:

> When at 9,000 ft over Flers I was attacked from behind and above by a Fokker ... I did an upward spiral following the Fokker and when about 100 feet below him, I pulled the nose of the de Havilland right up, training my gun on him and fired half a drum ... although my engine was missing badly I was able to reach his height. After some manoeuvering I got behind his tail, about two lengths away: finishing the first drum, I changed drums ... meanwhile, I had got still nearer and was able to fire this drum right into him, though my aim was erratic, as the back draught of the Fokker bumped the de H about. The Fokker dodged wildly but could not get away. He then suddenly put on vertical bank and side-slipped down about 500 feet. The sideslip developed into a nose dive, which he did not come out of until low down. While he was diving I was able to get another drum in, I then picked the BE2c again and finished the escort.[4]

Major Lanoe Hawker, a VC-winner with No. 6 Squadron and Cowan's CO at No. 24 Squadron, was sufficiently incensed to send a report to the Brigade Commander, Brigadier-General E. B. Ashmore, on account of the damage to Cowan's aircraft being such that they thought the enemy aircraft had been using illegal incendiary or explosive munitions.

One likely candidate with whom Cowan might have sparred was the great German ace, Leutnant Max Immelman, who was wounded that day. Cowan was not awarded an aerial victory for the encounter. However, it's more likely that Immelman was wounded by Lieutenants Andrews and Manfield in the earlier encounter, as his own letters home to family make reference to two attackers and it would be unlikely in the extreme that the sheep-like B.E.2c could be described as a second attacking aircraft. Cowan obtained his first confirmed victory on 4 May 1916, flying an Airco DH.2 (5966). For his exploits in May 1916 he was awarded the Military Cross:

2Lt Sidney Edward Cowan, RFC (Spec. Res.)

For conspicuous gallantry and skill. He dived onto an enemy machine in the enemy's lines and drove it to the ground, where it was smashed, and then circled round and fired at the pilot and observer as they ran for shelter. Although forced to land through his engine stopping he contrived to restart it and got back under heavy fire.[5]

RFC Communiqué No. 36, of 4–21 May 1916, recorded that Cowan's thumb switch had jammed and would not come on again, forcing Cowan to land not far from where he had strafed the crew of the German aircraft. However, the jolt of the forced landing released the spring and the engine restarted. Cowan crossed the lines at only 500 feet, under heavy fire.

On 30 June 1916 Cowan and Prothero are credited with driving off a number of German aircraft that were attempting to ascertain the disposition of British troops. On 1 July 1916 Cowan was involved in a series of aerial engagements. Illingworth's official history of No. 24 Squadron credits Cowan with two aerial victories, with a third disallowed as an undecided, 'observer apparently hit' outcome.[6] However, other sources only credit Cowan with one aerial victory.[7] Cowan's combat report itself is quite detailed:

> When over Curlu with rest of Patrol, I saw a hostile machine over Peronne, and attacked, firing half a drum at about 150 yards. He turned and dived eastwards. When over Pys about 10 minutes later, I saw 2 H.A. Type A coming west over Bapaume ... I dived at the hindmost machine and fired half a drum, passed him, and fired the rest of the drum into the other machine. The observer in this machine ceased fire and collapsed into the nacelle, so I climbed up and having changed drums, again attacked the first H.A., which had attacked me from behind. I fired several bursts into him at close range and he suddenly did a side slip tail slide and fell into a cloud, apparently out of control and was seen to crash. About five minutes later, while regaining my height, somewhere over Achiet-le-Grand, I saw another H.A. Type C approaching from the north east. He opened fire at about 400 yards and turned back. I managed to get within about 200 yards and as I was unable to catch him, fired about 20 rounds. He dived east and I rejoined the patrol.[8]

This was the opening day of the Somme offensive, so the ranging of artillery by the Corps squadrons was of paramount importance. The classification of aerial victories was well down the list of priorities for the 4th Brigade HQ, notwithstanding the fact that pioneers such as Cowan were developing offensive and defensive tactics in aerial combat.

RFC Communiqué No. 45 of 1916 reported that, on 27 July, Cowan engaged five enemy aircraft, which were attacking a B.E. between Le Sars and Martinpuich. 'All the hostile machines were driven off.' Once again, a decisive aerial victory was not awarded to Cowan, although the outcome was decisive insofar as the B.E. was able to continue with its work.

On 29 July 1916 Cowan attacked a Roland C.II over Morval. It went down in a nose dive, with the wreckage subsequently identified just west of Bois de Vaux. Just days later, on 3 August, Cowan achieved further success in aerial combat. RFC Communiqué No. 46 of August 1916 records that Cowan engaged several enemy aircraft in combat in several different encounters:

On the IV Army front four de Havillands of No. 24 Sqn ... encountered 7 hostile machines near Flers ... Lt Cowan drove one down near Sailly, and pursued two others, driving them down at Velu aerodrome. Returning, he encountered another machine at which he fired several bursts from above and behind. The machine ceased fire and began to manoeuvre wildly. Lt Cowan saw the observer hanging head downwards over the side of the fuselage. After he had fired a few more rounds it commenced to spiral, gradually descending more steeply and faster. Lt Cowan did not see it reach the ground, as he was engaged with another machine which he also drove away east.[9]

For this particular engagement Cowan was credited with an 'out of control' victory over the German LVG 2-seater, as the other three were 'driven down' at Sailly and Velu but were not decisive aerial victories.

On 9 August 1916 Cowan was slightly wounded, being temporarily blinded by wooden splinters after emptying a drum into an LVG over Bapaume, but he was back in action shortly thereafter. On 16 September 1916 he sent down a German two-seater in flames over Sailly-Saillisel. Cowan was flying D.H.2 5964, in which he had recorded some of his earliest victories. One account credits Cowan with aerial victories on 16 and 17 September, but Illingworth records one of these combats as being a 'driven down, damaged' outcome.[10] On 30 September 1916 Cowan and Lieutenant Robert Saundby combined to save a Lieutenant Roche, whose D.H.2 (6000) crashed near Meault. Saundby—who later shot down the Zeppelin L48—rose to rank of Air Marshal in the post-war era. However, the squadron were beginning to take casualties from the 'fast scouts' of Oswald Boelcke's new Jasta 2.

No. 24 Squadron suffered the loss of its three best Irishmen in the course of October 1916, with David Mary Tidmarsh being transferred to command a Flight in the newly founded No. 48 Squadron, Cowan being promoted to Flight Commander to take charge of a Flight in No. 29 Squadron, and Patrick Anthony Langan Byrne being killed on 17 October 1916. Even in early October 1916 Major Lanoe Hawker VC was despairing at the loss of Cowan:

Awful blow yesterday [1 October], as my best pilot was promoted and moved to another squadron. He came to me in Sept. 1915, so had been with me over a year. A nice boy and an extremely clever pilot—he got the MC last May and a bar to it this month.

Dreadful loss as I am moving two of my three Flight commanders [Wilkinson and Tidmarsh] home for a rest and was counting on him [Cowan] to replace one of them.[11]

The award of a bar to the Military Cross was gazetted on 20 October 1916:

2Lt Sidney Edward Cowan, MC, RFC, Spec. Res.

For conspicuous gallantry and skill. He has done fine work in aerial combats, and has shot down four enemy machines. (The Military Cross was awarded in *The London Gazette* dated 31st May 1916.)[12]

The award of a second bar to the Military Cross was gazetted on 14 November 1916:

2Lt (Temp. Capt.) Sidney Edward Cowan, MC, RFC, Spec. Res.

For conspicuous gallantry in action. He fought a long contest with seven enemy machines, finally bringing one down in flames. He has displayed great skill and gallantry throughout. (The Military Cross was awarded in *The London Gazette* dated 31st May 1916. The 1st Bar was awarded in *The London Gazette* dated 20th Oct 1916.)[13]

Cowan was transferred to No. 29 Squadron. On 27 November 1916 he drove down a Halberstadt D.II out of control, but when maneuvering for a further kill he collided with another British pilot, William Spencer FitzRobert Saundby.

Cowan was mentioned in articles in *The Irish Times* of 16 November 1916 and the *Weekly Irish Times* of 2 December 1916, in the former in respect of the bar to his Military Cross and in the latter as being missing in action. *Flight* magazine of 26 April 1917 and *The Irish Times* of 2 May 1917 carried fine obituaries, the latter of which stated that 'a letter from an officer at the Front, also a Marlburian, states that he came across the grave of his schoolfellow in an old graveyard at Ablainzevelle, 12 miles south-east of Arras.' The actual correspondent was 2nd Lieutenant H. A. Freeman, Royal Welsh Fusiliers.

It is in very good condition with a rail round it and a cross at the head on which is written in German: 'In memory of a gallant English Officer, Captain S. E. Cowan, killed in air combat'... Hoping I have not made a mistake or taken too great a liberty.[14]

Cowan's War Office service records file contains a copy of the correspondence from 2nd Lieutenant Freeman, which is dated 20 March 1917.[15] It triggered a series of bureaucratic wrangles between the War Office and the Casualties Branch; for instance, in May 1917 one official noted that 'as this evidence only points to a location of a grave and no confirmation of burial is obtainable, it is not considered sufficient on which to render a report of death.' However, accepting the date of death as being on 17 November 1916 had other advantages, i.e. although a gratuity of £158 under Article 497 (Pay Warrant and Army Order 406 of 1915) did issue to Cowan's father in October 1917, it was made the subject of a deduction of £11 for pay that had been advanced to Cowan, which had covered up to 30 November 1916—a period to which Sidney had not actually survived. However, Cowan's father soon had greater concerns: Sidney's brother Philip was killed on 8 November 1917. Philip's S.E.5a (B4883) was one of three that No. 56 Squadron lost that day, though he was the only fatality, most likely to have fallen to the guns of Leutnant Hans Gottfried von Häbler of Jasta 36.

7

COWELL,
John J.
(16 aerial victories)

Born: 1889, Limerick
Died: 30 July 1918
Awards: Distinguished Conduct Medal, Military Medal with Bar
Commemorated: Longuenesse (St Omer) Souvenir Cemetery, Pas-de-Calais, France

Sergeant J. J. Cowell is one of Ireland's most accomplished aces, yet receives so little recognition. He obtained fifteen of his sixteen aerial victories as an observer rather than as a pilot—but then, observers were gunners, not some exotic passenger burden on the pilot. Too many German pilots underestimated Cowell, and it is unfortunate that so many of his countrymen did the same.

One of ten children, he was born to Michael and Kate Cowell at Carey's Road in the city of Limerick. Some details of his childhood are unclear, e.g. the Irish census of 1911 only records seven of the nine children as being resident with the parents at Carey's Road, while the Irish census of 1901 does not record any of the family as being in Limerick.

Unfortunately, as Cowell did not serve with an Irish regiment, his early wartime service history is difficult to trace, given the forename-surname combination, and on account of Cowell being given a new service number upon transfer to the RFC. However, from a reconciliation of the duplicate medal card index entries and service records it's clear that Cowell initially served as a sapper with the 12th Field Company of the Royal Engineers. They were based at Moore Park, Fermoy, Co. Cork, at the outbreak of the war, as were the 16th Brigade of the 6th Division. They paraded through Ballynahoun, Co. Cork, on 13 August 1914, though they were still missing much of their bicycle equipment, and a large number of sappers had refused to avail of voluntary inoculation. They left Fermoy for Queenstown on 19 August 1914 and travelled on the SS *Maidan* to Liverpool, from which they joined the 6th Division at Cambridge. They departed for France from Southampton on 8 September on the SS *Oxonion*, but their vehicles had to be lowered in vertically down the hatches, so presumably there was a small advance party at St Nazaire to help with the customisation of any equipment needed to disembark men and material. The medal card generated in respect of his service with the Royal Engineers records that Cowell (under the service number 21018) was eligible for the Mons Star from 8 September 1914. According to the War Diary for the 12th Field Company, they disembarked at St Nazaire on 10 September, so Cowell might have been part of an advance party.[1]

Unfortunately the War Diaries do not name sappers and 'other ranks', but the 12th Field Company were engaged in a series of marches and deployments in support of a number of overstretched British positions; for example, on 23 September they were attempting to repair the pontoon bridges at Vailly and were the subject of German shelling. By 24 September the 12th Field Company were laying wire entanglements by day in front of the King's Shropshire Light Infantry, and by night digging trenches for the Leicestershire Regiment and improving trenches and other support works for the Buffs (East Kent Regiment) at Maison Rouge. In theory there were supposed to be two Field Companies attached to each Division of the BEF, but it soon became obvious that much more support was needed. It would be impossible to cover the range of tasks that men like Cowell experienced in the campaigns of 1914–1916 but, to give an example of the dangers faced, on 3 October 1914, a consignment of barbed wire that had been due to arrive at 10 p.m. only arrived at 3.30 a.m. The sappers nevertheless set to work as originally planned, and as the dawn mist thinned the Germans became aware of their presence. The shelling consequently killed Sapper G. H. Byrne (23758), whose body was retrieved by his comrades that night, and burried at Vailly British Cemetery. But everything is relative—of the other constituent units of the 6th Division, the Leinsters suffered an unmitigated mauling on 20 October 1914.

Over the course of the winter of 1914, and throughout 1915 and 1916, the 12th Field Company endured a steady rate of attrition. In October 1916 Cowell was awarded the Military Medal as a Sapper (Acting Corporal) in the Royal Engineers.[2] This award is sometimes confused with that of another J. J. Cowell (14627), of the Royal Dublin Fusiliers, who was awarded the Distinguished Conduct Medal that same week.

John J. Cowell married on 20 December 1916 in Limerick. His wife's address was recorded as '2 Ahern's Row, Athlunkard Street, Limerick'. Upon transferring to the RFC, he was initially posted to No. 20 Squadron as an air mechanic (2nd Class) on 26 March 1917. Although the RFC was still a branch of the Army, Cowell is recorded under a new service number, 78171, from this time onwards. There is a suggestion that Cowell served briefly with No. 46 Squadron, but I have found no concrete evidence of this.

No. 20 Squadron was one of the most successful squadrons of the war, operating a variety of two-seater aircraft over the years. Of the Irish-born members of the squadron there were three who 'made ace'—John J. Cowell, H. G. Crowe, and A. S. Mills—but many more who became casualties, mainly observers.

Cowell became an observer/gunner in April 1917. On 1 May 1917 in a F.E.2d (A6359) piloted by 2nd Lieutenant Reginald E. Condor, they survived a forced landing due to a propeller malfunction. The F.E.2d was a 'pusher'-type aircraft, which looked a little like a flying bedframe, the engine mounted behind the pilot and propelling the contraption forward much the same way that a ship's corkscrew operated, and a propeller malfunction could see the aircraft part company with the booms that attached the tail. Although the F.E.2 had officially been withdrawn from offensive operations following the slaughter during the 'Bloody April' of 1917, it was still formidable. Like in most 'pushers', the observer sat in front of the pilot and thus the aircraft had a wide angle of attack. There was also a rearward-firing gun available to the observer, but it required him to stand up in the nacelle and reach over the pilot behind him in order to operate it. There was no harness for the observer and the act of attempting to use this gun restricted the pilot's view. (The pilot also had a Lewis gun to operate, which was controlled by a 'Bowden' cable.)

On 5 May 1917 Cowell obtained his first aerial victory in a F.E.2d (A6539) piloted by 2nd Lieutenant Reginald Conder. Throughout May 1917 Cowell secured several victories against a variety of types, including the much-vaunted Albatros D.III; the victories were against German fighters and not their artillery observation and reconnaissance aircraft. In the build-up to the Battle of Messines, the RFC stepped up the aerial offensive. Some squadrons received the new Sopwith Camel, which helped tilt the balance in the Allies' favour.

Cowell was promoted to Sergeant on 5 June 1917.[3] The next day he and 2nd Lieutenant Conder were to survive being brought down near Abeéle by British anti-aircraft fire. Their F.E.2d (A6480) was wrecked and Conder was badly shaken, but Cowell was soon back in action.

RFC Communiqué No. 91 indicates No. 20 Squadron were quite prepared to use the F.E.2d on offensive patrols. Cowell was observer to Lieutenant R. M. Trevethan in F.E.2d (A6480) when they took on eight Albatrosses, sending one down in flames.[4]

Cowell was awarded the DCM, which was gazetted on 18 July 1917.

78171 Sgt J. Cowell, RFC

For conspicuous gallantry while assisting as an aerial gunner during bomb raids. He showed remarkable skill and judgment in the eight combats in which he has been engaged, and on several occasions has shot down hostile aircraft.[5]

With the exception of the Victoria Cross, which was available to all ranks, officers received crosses, and NCOs and other ranks received medals, hence Cowell receiving a DCM.

In July 1917 Cowell accounted for seven of the Luftstreitkrafte's new Albatros D.V, including a double-victory over Polygon Wood on 17 July, sending one of his victims down in flames. It is unclear if Cowell took part in a celebrated incident involving No. 20 Squadron on 27 July 1917. They were used as 'bait' east of Ypres, and in the running battle that followed No. 20 Squadron accounted for nine of the thirty German machines brought down on that date.

Cowell was sent on a pilot training course in August 1917, around which time No. 20 Squadron was re-equipped with the Bristol F2.b two-seater fighter. While on training Cowell received the bar to the Military Medal, gazetted in September 1917.[6] Initially Cowell was posted to No. 31 TS, and subsequently to No. 35 TS in December 1917.[7] Upon the creation of the RAF in April 1918 Cowell was re-graded to the rank of Sergeant Mechanic. Cowell briefly trained at the school of aerial gunnery in May 1918 and at wireless training school in June 1918.

Upon completion of pilot training he re-joined No. 20 Squadron as a pilot on 24 July 1918. Flying the Bristol F2.b Fighter (E2471) he scored his only pilot victory on 29 July 1918, being shot down the next day by Oberleutnant Friedrich 'Fritz' Ritter von Roth of Jasta 16, the latter's seventeeth of twenty-eight victories during the war. Sergeant Cowell and Corporal Hill's 'Brisfit' was seen to burst into flames at 10,000 feet and disintegrate. The pieces were scattered near Locre but Cowell's body was not recovered.

CROWE,
Henry George 'Hal'
(8 aerial victories)

Born: 11 June 1897, Co. Dublin
Died: 26 April 1983
Awards: Military Cross (26 July 1918); Commander of the Order of British
Empire (8 June 1944); Cloud and Banner Decoration with Special Cravat (25 June
1946)

Air Commodore Henry George Crowe was one of the more remarkable Irish
aviators of the First World War: he survived being shot down six times in eleven
days in April 1918.

Crowe was the son of John Joseph and Florence Helen Crowe. His family lived
at Simmonscourt, Donnybrook, Dublin, as recorded by the Irish censuses of 1901
and 1911. In the latter census Francis Howard and Cecil John were still living
with the parents, but Henry was listed in the UK census of 1911 as a boarder at
Mydon, Colwyn Bay, Wales. Crowe subsequently went to school at Cheltenham,
then studied at Trinity College Dublin, where he joined the OTC, continuing to
Sandhurst upon the outbreak of the war.

Crowe enrolled in the Royal Military College (Sandhurst) in November 1915.
Although Crowe was interested in aviation at an early age and arranged his first
Flight in the pre-war years—on a Maurice Farman at Farnborough—Crowe
served with the Royal Irish Regiment for some months until he managed to secure
secondment to the RFC.

On 18 July 1916 Crowe graduated from the Royal Military College (Sandhurst)
with a commission as a 2nd Lieutenant with the Royal Irish Regiment. Initially,
Crowe was posted to the Reserve Battalion in Dublin. However, the Royal Irish
Regiment was badly mauled at the Somme, and in September 1916 Crowe was
sent to the 6th Battalion near Kemmel. This battalion was under the command of
Lieutenant-Colonel Roche-Kelly, who had a son flying with No. 24 Squadron.

Crowe fought in the Battle of Messines in 1917. There's a passing reference to 2nd
Lieutenant Crowe in the Battalion War Diary on 27 March 1917, but only in relation

to the rotation of responsibilities with another junior officer.[1] During Crowe's time with the battalion the most politically sensitive death it suffered was that of Major Willie Redmond MP, on 7 June 1917. His death prompted the East Clare by-election, which resulted in a victory for Éamon de Valera of Sinn Féin in July 1917.

Crowe's posting to the RFC came through on 5 September 1917. Crowe had been lucky to have survived a year on active service at the Front, as the average life of a second lieutenant was a matter of days at certain stages of the Western Front campaigns of 1916 and 1917. Crowe was seconded to the RFC as an observer pending assessment of his suitability for training as a pilot. Crowe's initial training was at the School of Military Aeronautics at Reading, then the School of Aerial Gunnery at Hythe.

Crowe was assigned to No. 20 Squadron in November 1917, based at St Marie Cappel near Cassel. Crowe cherished his observer's badge.

> The observer's flying badge, 'the flying 0', was almost a decoration. Before one could wear it one had to complete so many hours' war flying; have had at least two successful air combats; and pass a viva exam in memorising a map of enemy aerodromes etc. in a large area. I remember a lady asking me 'have you ever been up' as she examined my wing. And was I annoyed![2]

Crowe scored his first victory on 13 January 1918 in a Bristol F2.b piloted by 2nd Lieutenant Thomas Colvill-Jones. Just over a week later, in an F2.b piloted by 2nd Lieutenant Douglas Cooke, Crowe achieved two further victories on 22 January 1918, one of which was an Albatos DV that went down in flames.

On 21 February 1918 Crowe's appointment as a Flying Officer (Observer) was gazetted. The German offensive in the spring of 1918 required all squadrons to engage in fighter, reconnaissance, ground-attack, and Army support roles. In March 1918 Crowe was engaged in dropping bombs and machine-gunning the advancing enemy. On one occasion they were hit by ground fire and had to make a hard landing near Marieux Aerodrome, but were fortunately in a position to benefit from the services of a tank fitter from among the retreating ground forces, who was able to repair their damaged radiator and enable them get back to St Marie Cappel. In the confusion they had been posted 'missing'. On 27 March, in a Bristol F2.b (B1191) piloted by the South African ace, 2nd Lieutenant Ernest Lindup, they sent down a Fokker triplane out of control over Albert when they were badly shot up. Their crippled aircraft made it back to Bruay but was so badly damaged it was stuck off the squadron's strength. On 29 March, in a new Bristol F2.b, Crowe was badly shot up again with a damaged oil tank, and they were forced to land.

On 2 April 1918, he was shot down by anti-aircraft fire when out on evening patrol.

> Suddenly a German anti-aircraft shell burst just below us and close enough for black smoke to be smelt. It was a lucky shot but German gunners were good and

had good predictor instruments. We were at once covered in petrol, both tanks having been ripped open.

The pilot switched off and we did a steep dive combined with violent turns and made it to our side of the lines with a barrage of AA shells following us. We crash-landed among shell holes near a battery. Neither of us were hurt in the crash and we got out with the Lewis gun in double quick time, dashing to the shelter of the battery. German artillery had seen our landing and got the range, accurately destroying the aeroplane in minutes.[3]

The Flight Commander was Major J. A. Dennistoun; the Bristol F2.b (A7240) was indeed destroyed on the ground. Crowe had now been shot down several times during this period. On 12 April 1918, Crowe was observer to a Bristol F2.b (C4605) fighter piloted by Captain Douglas Graham Cooke when they crash-landed at Boisdinghem after evacuating there at night from St Marie Cappel (which had by that stage fallen within German artillery range and was being shelled). However, throughout March, April, and May 1918 Crowe achieved a string of aerial victories against Fokker Dr.I and Albatros D.V fighters.

On 22 April Crowe was promoted from 2nd Lieutenant to Lieutenant. By May 1918, Crowe's six months as an observer had been completed. His Commanding Officer, Major Johnson, acceded to his request to return to England for pilot training, which was facilitated through being sent back as a patient at Étaples to the RAF hospital at Hampstead. Crowe's citation for the Military Cross was gazetted on 26 July 1918:

Lt Henry George Crowe, R. Ir. Regt and RAF

For conspicuous gallantry and devotion to duty when taking part in many low-flying bomb raids and reconnaissances as an observer. On every occasion he brought back very accurate and valuable information. On three occasions his machine was shot down by enemy fire, but he continued his work, and his great fearlessness and fine spirit have been an invaluable example to others. He has taken part in several air combats and been responsible for the destruction of many hostile machines.[4]

In August 1918, Crowe was posted to the Aircraft & Armament Experimental Establishment at Orfordness while awaiting his place on the pilots' course at Reading. At the time Lewis guns was the subject of various four-gun experimental mountings, but none of Crowe's experiences were to have led to an operational version being adopted.

In September 1918 Crowe started pilot training at Reading. He learned Morse code for artillery observation purposes, but during his time there radiotelephony was being developed. By the time Crowe undertook training on the armaments course at Ealing the war was over.

In December 1918 Crowe was transferred to RAF Collinstown (the site of the present-day Dublin Airport) for flying training on the Avro 504 biplane. In March 1919 the IRA raided Collinstown, cutting telephone wires and making off with arms and ammunition. Crowe escaped censure, as he had turned out the guard correctly at 11 p.m. before retiring that night. Collinstown was abandoned shortly thereafter, and flying training was transferred to RAF Baldonnel. At the end of April 1919 Crowe was posted to No. 106 Squadron, one Flight of which was based at Fermoy, Co. Cork. Crowe was re-seconded for a two-year period as Observer Officer, effective from 1 August 1919. There are several widely-published photographs of Crowe in a D.H.9 at Fermoy in 1920.

Crowe was awarded Royal Aero Club Aviator's Certificate No. 7911 on 25 November 1920. His address in Ireland at the time was 'Carahor' (now known as 'Marlfield'), Shrewsbury Road, Dublin. This was designed by Richard Caulfied Orpen, brother of Sir William Orpen, renowned for his wartime paintings, including those of RAF aces such as the Canadian Reginald Hoidge and the Anglo-Welsh Arthur Rhys-Davids.

The British Army medal rolls index cards record 'No. 2 Squadron, RAF, 11 Irish Wing, Fermoy, Co. Cork' as Crowe's address on 11 January 1921. Crowe was based at Baldonnel from April 1919 to November 1921. No. 106 Squadron had Flights at Oranmore, Co. Galway, Castlebar, Co. Mayo and Fermoy, Co. Cork. Crowe's time in Fermoy entailed daily dropping of mail bags at Army and police detachments and barracks, dropping baskets of carrier pigeons to police posts, passenger flights for VIPs, reconnaissance of road and railways for signs of damage, dropping British propaganda leaflets and acting as escort to road convoys.

If the Auxiliaries and 'Black and Tans' consisted largely of mercenary forces, the RAF in Ireland was also quite unsettled at this time, with many long-serving veterans awaiting demobilisation:

> We were a cheery bunch of officers who came and went, some to be demobilised, others to return to their homelands in Canada, Australia and South Africa. I was the only one with a Regular Army Commission and I wanted to follow this up with a permanent commission in the RAF which I was granted later. There was much discontent after the war at the slowness of demobilisation. There were mutinies at aerodromes abroad and in England but at Fermoy we only had a refusal to go on parade which was quickly withdrawn when we officers paraded wearing our revolvers.[5]

Crowe recalls instances of local girls' hair being shorn off for fraternising with RAF officers. During his time with the RAF in Fermoy, Crowe had occasion to go on an operation with British troops.

> I had to give lectures at various times to the Army on air cooperation. One lecture was given in Cork Barracks and after it I went with the troops on a raid ... We left

the barracks ... in a column of open vehicles with armoured cars as escort. After 3 a.m. we debussed and marched several miles across country ... Police with troops crept up to a house which was just visible in the darkness ... men were running away from the back of the building. We gave chase but lost them in the bushes. If we had had tracker dogs we might have caught them. It grew light as we advanced across the hills in open order ... Then quite suddenly we came under machine gun fire. ... I went over a high bank like a Grand National winner! It was in that burst of firing that we had three officers killed. But we could see columns of black smoke in the valley and thought another part of our forces had found a rebel hideout ... We found later that by pure chance the rendezvous for our transport had been fixed just where the rebels had set up an ambush. It was our cars we had seen burning. We found the drivers' dead bodies lined up by the roadside. If the Army had asked for air cooperation from dawn this operation might not have ended so disastrously.[6]

Crowe perhaps failed to recollect that many military operations were notionally in aid of the civil power—the Auxiliaries, for instance, were there in support of the police, not the military. Over time martial law was declared but for long periods the war was fought out with the military in a quasi-policing role, combined with extra-judicial killings by British forces—notably of the Lord Mayor of Cork, Tomás MacCurtain— and unofficial reprisals, as part of a terror campaign to subdue the local population. Predictably enough, this inflamed the local population and also alienated many of those who would otherwise have supported the retention of the link between the UK and Ireland. Crowe recalls a rampage by British troops in Fermoy, in which windows were smashed and shops looted on foot for the kidnapping of a hapless British officer, Brigadier-General Lucas, while he was out fishing.

I went into the town in mufti to see what would happen ... The soldiers walked down into the town from barracks with their officers in mufti and we followed. Then someone shouted, 'Put that bloody light out.' A brick shattered a street lamp, then it started. The troops ran into the town square. They threw bricks at shop windows shattering the plate glass with a noise like shrapnel ... Then the soldiers started looting. Some stole from grocers' shops; some threw trays of trinkets from jewellers' shops into the river; some threw cycles into the river ... Some tried to set fire to draperies in the town centre while the owner watched from an upper window. The situation was now completely out of control ... I went back to camp. It really was a disgraceful affair. Every shop window smashed, and nearly every store looted.[7]

Fermoy was a garrison town, and the destruction meted out to those areas of Ireland in which a substantial proportion of the population supported the Crown was disastrous for the prospects of the UK's survival. James Burke Roche, 3rd Baron Fermoy, Princess Diana's great-great-grandfather, took to living in London until his death in November 1920. What Crowe neglects to mention is that in September 1919 the IRA had ambushed men of the KSLI on their way to church services in the town. The intention had been to seize weaponry, but a soldier was killed and three were wounded for just 13 rifles. It should have been a propaganda disaster for the IRA, but was turned into a minor recruitment tool when the British military were granted an unofficial rampage, smashing shop windows and attempting to set fires. Although it had none of the menace of the more structured reprisals in which civilians were shot, it alienated the local population still further from British rule.

British military history tends to record the number of British military personnel deaths as being in the region of 200 or so for the period of the Irish War of Independence, while Irish newspapers of the period record at least 500 British military deaths (excluding Auxiliary troops), all these dead being quite apart from Irish servicemen in the British Army, Royal Navy, or RAF who died of wounds or from pneumonia, influenza, and so forth. Some deaths that occurred in Cork at the time Crowe was stationed in Fermoy relate to soldiers based there. In October 1920 two artillery officers stationed at Fermoy, Lieutenants Bernard Loftus Brown and David Alfred Rutherford, were killed when apparently off-duty, on a motorcycle trip to Killarney. In reality both men had previously engaged in reconnaissance work in conjunction with the security forces and therefore the IRA executions were probably on sounder ground than many of the more spurious killings in Cork, but it is unlikely that the men were on a spying mission: their trip coincided with the funeral of Terence MacSwiney, Sinn Féin Lord Mayor of Cork, who had died after seventy-four days on hunger strike. They may have simply been at the wrong place at the wrong time. Similarly, an Army Educational Corps officer and probable British Intelligence Officer, Captain Seymour Livingston Vincent, was captured near Fermoy by the IRA and executed, his body not being reinterred to Glenville, Co. Cork, until the late 1920s. (Vincent had apparently a notebook on his person with details of various local Protestant families, and it was therefore suggested that he was engaged in intelligence-gathering, or at least attempting to engage local families in an intelligence network.) There was quite a grim tally outside regular ambush combat in Cork, and Crowe was lucky to avoid becoming an IRA target. That is not to say that Crowe's sojourn in Cork was entirely uneventful: he crashed a Bristol Fighter (H1590) at Fermoy on one occasion.

On 14 October 1921, Crowe's continued attachment to the RAF as Flying Officer for a two-year period with effect from 1 August 1921 was gazetted. Crowe was transferred from Fermoy to No. 39 (Bomber) Squadron at Spittlegate, Grantham, in Lincolnshire. On 13 January 1922 Crowe was granted a permanent commission as Flying Officer, to take effect from 17 November 1921.[8] He later transferred to Farnborough for training in air photography.

Crowe was promoted from Flying Officer to Flight Lieutenant with effect from 30 June 1922. Crowe transferred from No. 39 Squadron (Inland Area) to School of Photography (Inland Area) on a supernumerary basis, with effect from 19 October 1922. At the end of 1924 he was posted to Air HQ in Baghdad. Crowe was subsequently assigned to HQ Iraq on 27 February 1925. His photographic reconnaissance was largely undertaken in D.H.9As, often flying in support of the work of geologists in the oil exploration business. Although Crowe once contracted sandfly fever, his time in Iraq seems to have been a happy one, with weekend shooting parties in the ruins of Babylon, and visits to Damascus and Beirut.

Crowe subsequently moved to Amman, Jordan, for similar photographic reconnaissance duties. Overseas tours of duty with the RAF at this time entailed either five years in India, or two in Iraq plus three in Egypt or Palestine. Crowe's time in Jordan was served with No. 14 (Bomber) Squadron for a three-year period. Crowe was serving with them at the time of the death of fellow Irish ace George McCormack, but he makes no reference to McCormack's death in 1928. During his time in Jordan, Crowe flew bi-weekly sorties to assist in the monitoring of Wahabi raiders from Saudi Arabia. This work brought him south to Aqaba regularly and so he was quite fortunate to visit Petra twice. With the RAF being kept on ready alert, they had to alternate between Amman and Ramleh due to adverse weather conditions.

> The Wahabis were planning to raid Jordan and so we increased our patrols of possible routes and wells that might be used ... we did a desert patrol from Ramleh without seeing anything unusual ... we were all in the ground floor ante-room of Ramleh Mess having a pre-lunch aperitif with windows open and sun beating down on the lovely gardens when, with no warning sound, the pictures came off the walls and the whole place shook ... in a few seconds we had all gone through the windows to end up in the garden with our drinks still in our hands, looking at a great column of dust from Ramleh village where the earthquake had wrecked native houses killing a large number of people. Buildings at the aerodrome were not really damaged but aircraft in hangars had moved, damaging wing tips.[9]

In January 1929 Crowe transferred to Staff College Andover for staff training. Another Irishman (and a future Air Vice-Marshal), William Munro Yool, was also sent on this course. Several papers were in fact generated by Crowe at this time— 'An Account by Course Students of War Experiences', for example.[10]

On 8 January 1930, Crowe was promoted from Flight Lieutenant to Squadron Leader. He married Alicia Nora Jarratt in Knaresborough, Yorkshire, in 1931, and commanded the 'Demon' fighters of No. 23 (Fighter) Squadron from Biggin Hill for 'Northland' in the annual air exercises in July 1933, and again in 1935. In the Abyssinian crisis of 1935 Crowe was posted to command No. 74 (F) Squadron at Malta, flying Hawker Demons. This squadron—the 'Tiger Squadron' of 'Taffy'

Jones and 'Mick' Mannock—also flew the Hawker Hart. Crowe was promoted from Squadron Leader to Wing Commander in July 1936.

Wing Commander Crowe was assigned to Director of Operations, Department of Air Member for Supply and Organisation (AMSO), with effect from 10 September 1936.[11] Crowe was given a temporary promotion from Wing Commander to Group Captain with effect from 1 January 1940. His role was as Deputy Director of War Training and Tactics, which is sometimes referenced as Assistant Director Air Tactics ('ADAT').

Crowe served in command of No. 1 (Indian) Wing at Kohat, but returned to the Air Ministry by June 1940. In some accounts Crowe was party to the interminable discussions in October 1940 on the viability or otherwise of the 'Big Wing' advocated by Bader.[12] Group Captain Crowe's responsibility is recorded to have been in the Air Defences branch. On 10 June 1941 the Air Ministry announced that Crowe was promoted from (Temporary) Group Captain to (Temporary) Air Commodore, with effect from 1 June 1941. Crowe became Director of Allied Air Cooperation and Foreign Liaison.

As Director of Allied Co-operation and Foreign Liaison (DAFL) Crowe faced a diplomatic battle: in the Levant, the Free French 'Alsace' Flight did not have sufficient groundcrew to maintain itself. General Valin wanted replacements from the groundcrew of No. 340 Squadron, which was notionally the RAF's 'Free French' squadron. However, Sholto Douglas would not accept Valin's request, believing that he had been misled into supporting the establishment of an Anglo-French force when there was insufficient personnel to support it.[13] Although Douglas had worked with the similarly-structured No. 313 (Czechoslovak) Fighter Squadron, he felt that to facilitate French pilots with British groundcrew would be at the expense of another RAF squadron. On 22 January 1942 Crowe had to relay a diplomatic version of Douglas's refusal, instead offering General Valin that the French pilots from the Middle East—*Groupe de Chasse N°1 'Alsace'* included—could have the opportunity to join RAF squadrons. However, General Valin was adamant that he decided on the deployment of Free French forces and that No. 340 Squadron should be dissolved if necessary to allow for French naval air mechanics to be released for other exclusively French units. Crowe kept this dysfunctional show on the road, but by November 1942 his successor at DAFL, Frank Beaumont, and Sholto Douglas managed to repopulate the squadron groundcrew in the character of an ordinary RAF squadron, while retaining the nominal French appellation. This balancing act would hold until the new French unified command could be established from among the former Vichy and Free French units. Eventually, the *Première Escadrille de Chasse* (E.F.C. 1)—or *Groupe de Chasse N°1 'Alsace'*—became No. 341 Squadron of the RAF, a solution which suited everyone.

Crowe was stationed in RAF HQ in India from 27 October 1942, initially at AHQ Delhi. Crowe was made a Commander of the Military Division of the Most Excellent Order of the British Empire (CBE), which was gazetted on 8 June

1944. Another Irishman, Air Vice-Marshal William Tyrrell, was made Knight Commander (KBE) on this date. Tyrrell's brother, like Crowe, had been an ace in the First World War.

On 5 October 1944 Crowe was appointed Commanding Officer of 223 (Composite) Group at Peshawar, India, which had formerly been Air HQ Far East. It was in effect a re-named 1 (Indian) Group. Crowe was decorated by the Chinese for his wartime service in the Far East with the Order of the Cloud and Banner with Special Cravat.

> The KING has granted unrestricted permission for the wearing of the under-mentioned decorations conferred upon the personnel indicated in recognition of valuable services rendered in connection with the war:
>
> CONFERRED BY THE PRESIDENT OF THE NATIONAL GOVERNMENT OF THE REPUBLIC OF CHINA.
> Order of the Cloud and Banner.
> Special Cravat.
> Air Commodore Henry George CROWE, CBE, MC, RAF (Ret'd)[14]

Crowe served as a Justice of the Peace following his retirement in 1946. For a man who had on several occasions been able to walk away from aircraft in which he had been shot down or crashed, it was always likely that he would engage with services for less fortunate airmen and for servicemen's welfare generally. Crowe was involved in the RAF Association and Benevolent Fund. He died on 26 April 1983 at Thornton-le-Dale, North Yorkshire.

9

GREGORY,
Robert William
(8 aerial victories)

Born: 20 May 1881, London
Died: 23 January 1918, Padua, Italy
Awards: Military Cross, Chevalier of the Legion of Honour
Commemorated: Padua Main Cemetery, Italy

Major Robert Gregory is the subject of numerous myths and legends. He was the subject of four poems by William Butler Yeats, the most famous of which—'An Irish Airman Foresees His Death'—involves a person wholly unrelated to the character or beliefs of Gregory. The actual manner of Gregory's death has been the subject of so much repeated misinformation it is often difficult to re-assert the facts without making at least a passing reference to the myths, e.g. the claim that he was shot down in a 'friendly fire' incident by an Italian pilot. Gregory scored no more than eight confirmed aerial victories, yet the family often quoted a figure three times higher, and Yeats's poem—'Reprisals'—claims nineteen German planes.

Robert's family published a slim 40-page volume on the centenary of his birth, which repeats many of the foregoing misinformation, but it is nevertheless an excellent reference for Robert's paintings, theatre sets, and other artistic and cultural engagements, such as book illustrations, bookplate designs, woodplates, and stonework.[1]

Robert was born on 20 May 1881 to the playwright Isabella Gregory (later styled Augusta, Lady Gregory) and—according to most sources—Sir William Gregory. However, there's a tale that the father was actually a young local blacksmith named Seanín Farrell, who had been approached to sire the child and was then helped to emigrate. Gregory was born in London, and not Galway as often stated, though the family home was at Coole and he was brought up there. He was christened William Robert though he was generally known as Robert Gregory to distinguish him from Sir William.

The Gregory family was in many respects quite typical of the Anglo-Irish landlord class, and Unionist politically. Although they regarded themselves as good landlords they had opposed Gladstone's initial attempts at land reform in Ireland, i.e. they were hostile to the land courts system, which—when established—found almost invariably that tenants were being subjected to excessively high rents. Robert was sent to Park Hill boarding school at Lyndhurst, Sussex, in April 1891. On 6 March 1892 Sir William died after a long period of bronchial and pulmonary difficulties. His will was something of a shock to Lady Gregory, with various mortgages, bequests to potential former mistresses, and so forth. Robert, however, was to inherit the estate at Coole, and his mother was granted the right to reside there for the rest of her lifetime.

Robert started at Elstree School in North London in the autumn of 1893. He won a classical scholarship to Harrow on the strength of his Latin and started there in May 1895. By the summer of 1896 Robert had established a cricket team at Coole, composed of tenants and employees of the estate. Robert's first partridge shoot in August 1897 at Coole took precedence over his declared interest in learning Irish, though Lady Gregory's acquaintance with Douglas Hyde provided Robert with a unique opportunity to discuss Irish language, culture, and folklore with the foremost expert. Later Robert was to produce stage sets for Hyde's *Nativity Play*. In the artistic and literary circle Lady Gregory had gathered around herself Robert must nevertheless have been somewhat alienated. His mother had also taken it upon herself to subsidise the poet W. B. Yeats.

However, Robert was moving towards the more orthodox political views of the Anglo-Irish ascendancy class. In 1899 he expressed his support for the Conservatives and Unionists over the Liberals in the forthcoming elections. Robert was introduced to William Peel, who put Robert's mother in touch with Sir Archibald Milman, but Robert was too young for a clerkship of the House of Commons (or perhaps just too unsuitable) and Milman refused to nominate him.[2] Robert went to Oxford instead in the autumn on 1899 to read Classics. During the breaks between college terms Robert sketched with Jack Yeats at Coole. William Yeats addressed St John's College Essay Society in Oxford on 18 May 1902, and Robert, who was a student at New College, reported: 'his visit and lecture were I think a great success, though a large part of the audience at the latter were rather unappreciative, and the dons who asked questions were terrors.'[3]

However, in the winter of 1900 and spring of 1901 many tenants had exercised rights under the Land Acts to rent arbitration. The Gregory family forced many tenants through the rigors of the entire process, damaging much local goodwill. Nevertheless the tenants arranged bonfires and flags on the road from Gort to Coole in June 1902, when Robert turned twenty-one. In March 1903 Robert was given an opportunity through William Yeats to produce some designs for the set and costumes of *The Hour Glass*. He contracted chicken pox in 1904 but was also still labouring under the fearsome Henry Tonks at the Slade School of Art in London that year. Unsurprisingly, when Lady Gregory had a portrait commissioned of 'Robert as an artist', the portraitist Charles Haslewood Shannon painted Robert with his eyes shut, his brushes clean, and his paint tubes unopened. In 1905 Robert designed the costumes and sets for Lady Gregory's *Kincora* and *The White Cockade*, the latter an occasion in which his artistic efforts were deemed more praiseworthy than hers.

Robert graduated from the Slade School of Art in the summer of 1906. Jack Yeats's sketch of Robert on 'Sarsfield' at Gort Show, in September 1906, is often cited as inspiration for William's later poem and tribute to Robert as an accomplished horseman. On 26 September 1906 Robert married a fellow art student, Lily Margaret Graham Parry, in London. Robert's cousin, Hugh Lane (the noted collector of Impressionist art), supplied the engagement ring. In transferring some stocks, shares, and bonds to the couple, Lady Gregory secured informally the right to continue to reside in and manage Coole, while Robert and Margaret spent time between Chelsea and Paris.

Robert produced a unicorn image for the Dun Emer Press (and later the Cuala Press), which was first used for Yeats's *Discoveries* in 1907. However, there was much dissent within the Yeats family. Elizabeth 'Lolly' Yeats resented her brother imposing the use of Robert's designs. Lolly asserted that she need to keep 'some control over my own press. I don't want Robert Gregory's masterpieces.'[4]

In January 1907 J. M. Synge's *Playboy of the Western World* sparked riotous scenes at the Abbey Theatre. Unfortunately the Dublin Metropolitan Police made little distinction between peaceful protesters (for instance, Patrick Collumb, father of the poet Padraic Colum) and the bizarre array of agitators, which ranged from Sinn Féin activists (namely Piaras Béaslaí, the English-born IRA activist)—who regarded the play as anti-Irish Paddywhackery—to Catholic fundamentalists. Robert's letter to Yeats seems to regard the outcome as a political victory.

> We have won a complete victory over the organised disturbers—Sinn Féin men to a great extent. It was quite necessary that someone should show fight and we are the only people who have done it. Judge Ross said to my mother last night 'You have earned the gratitude of the whole community—you are the only people who have had the pluck to stand up against this organised intimidation in Dublin.'[5]

It was positive for the Abbey Theatre to resist censorship but Robert allegedly used his boxing skills in the course of ejecting protesters from the theatre, breaking a golden rule for a boxer to refrain from the use of one's fists against an untrained opponent. In the spring of 1907 Robert accompanied his mother on a tour of Italy; they were joined by William Yeats.

In March 1908 Margaret became pregnant with Richard, the first of their three children. Robert was at the studio of Jacques-Émile Blanche in Paris, but he and Margaret also toured Italy briefly. However, their artistic activities were not self-supporting. Robert's landscapes of Ireland were reasonable, and his stage set for *The Rogueries of Scapin* well regarded. Robert and Margaret sub-let their Paris apartment and returned to Coole in the summer of 1908 for the remainder of the pregnancy. Robert and Margaret accepted Lady Gregory's role as *de facto* manager of the estate, but had difficulty with the reality of William's arrival for several months of the year, during the summer and autumn. He behaved like the head of the household when there, but Lady Gregory had indulged him for a decade at Coole since Sir William's death.

Robert was quite erratic in his dealings with William Yeats. In February 1908 Yeats had to engage Charles Ricketts for the set designs for the Abbey's production of *The Well of Saints*, as Robert had vacillated on the matter then let William down. Perhaps it was his way of reclaiming something from William's apparent control over Lady Gregory. However, in February 1909 Lady Gregory suffered a cerebral haemorrhage, which brought William Yeats closer to the Gregory family. Robert continued to design sets for the Abbey Theatre.

The Land Courts were having an effect on the earning potential of Coole. The Land Act 1909 had also introduced a compulsory purchase option to the operations of the Congested Districts Board, which resulted in Robert making the decision to sell Coole. William Yeats's 'Upon a House Shaken by the Land Agitation' was inspired by the endgame at Coole, with an unfortunately patronising tone towards the peasantry. 'Ancestral Houses', however, is a little more critical of Robert, with the great house 'sinking away through courteous incompetence'. A journal entry of William Yeats in 1909 seems to mirror the terminology:

> I thought of this house, slowly perfecting itself ... and then of its probably sinking away through courteous incompetence, or rather sheer weakness of will, for ability has not failed in young Gregory.[6]

At least he used the phrase 'courteous incompetence' rather than 'weakness of will' in his poem! In the summer of 1910, Margaret had William Yeats removed from the master bedroom of Coole to more modest quarters. However, Robert and Margaret were still sufficiently close to him in October 1910 to give him an honest opinion of the early draft of *The Player Queen*, which gave rise to his deciding on a total rewrite. The Gregorys began to sell the land piecemeal to tenants rather than the estate in its entirety to the Congested Districts Board. However, Coole was an estate in which there was tenanted and untenanted land, and also land upon which the Gregorys employed hired labour to harvest crops and tend to livestock. Lady Gregory mediated between various parties and offered a shilling in the pound towards a shortfall to Robert in a rent reduction in favour of the tenants, rather than let her brother, Frank Persse, seize the tenants' cattle.[7] Robert and Margaret's second child, Augusta Anne, was born on 13 September 1911.

There was a major falling out between Robert and William Yeats over the matter of the Civil List pension awarded to the latter. This was not on any matter of political principle, as Robert would have been indifferent to whether William became a stuffed animal in an establishment trophy room; rather, it was a deeply personal row over how Lady Gregory had been treated. Lady Gregory sought to use her influence in William's favour—she had lined up a whole range of the 'great and the good' of the Anglo-Irish establishment—only to find that it was spurned by Sir Edmund Gosse, who had privileged access to the Asquiths and other political players. Robert demanded that William express his disapproval to Gosse of how Lady Gregory had been discarded so lightly, but instead William engaged in much internal hand-wringing over what to do. William composed many imaginary apologies to Robert over how his mother was treated, and although he wrote a suitably angry letter to send to Gosse, none of the correspondence was actually issued.

Robert produced a ram and goat design for the cover of his mother's play, *The Full Moon*, in 1911. This simple image, of two animals squaring off under the moon and stars, was used on the covers of all the Putnam editions of her plays. In June 1912 Robert had an exhibition, at the Baillie Gallery in London, which mainly entailed paintings of Galway landscapes. In 1912 his abilities in cricket saw him capped for Ireland. In a first-class match against Scotland on 29 August 1912 at Rathmines in Dublin, he took 8/80, an impressive bowling average for first-class cricket.

The Congested Districts Board made an offer to Robert for Coole in December 1912, but the combination of cash and Government stock was not sufficient. Robert declined the offer.

In 1913 Margaret was expecting their third child, and Lady Gregory 'bought' her a house near Newquay on the Finvarra peninsula in Galway Bay, which was named 'Mount Vernon' after George Washington's summerhouse. It was actually a house owned by the Persse family. William Persse and George Washington had corresponded with each other. On 21 August 1913 Catherine was born. William Yeats was not made welcome that summer, and upon his offer to visit in October 1913 Robert asked him to bring his own wine. In September 1913 Robert and Margaret asked George Bernard Shaw to be Catherine's godmother, but Shaw firmly but playfully rejected the offer, saying that 'if I undertook to see to her religious education, I should do it; and then where would she be?'

In June 1914 Robert had a further successful exhibition, at the Chenil Gallery in London. Several paintings were sold, although Hugh Lane indulged the Gregorys a little through the purchase of 'Coole Lake' for the Municipal Gallery. Following protracted negotiations for the sale of Coole, Robert eventually accepted an offer from the CDB for the tenanted and untenanted lands—approximately 5,000 acres in all—while retaining the 1,300-acre house and demesne lands. Thus, they would attempt the transition from landlords to farmers.

In January 1915 Robert succeeded in getting 'The Island' exhibited at the New English Art Club. But Hugh Lane died in the sinking of the *Lusitania* on 7 May 1915, and this gave Lady Gregory several years of legal difficulties in trying to give effect to Hugh's signed-but-unnotarised codicil to his will, which donated thirty-nine pictures to the National Gallery in Dublin. The collection had been held at the London National Gallery, who had come to regard it as their own. William Yeats made an attempt in June 1915 to have Robert fill Hugh Lane's vacancy as Director of the National Gallery; however, the vacancy was filled by Robert Langton Douglas, the father of Sholto Douglas, who in turn was to have a significant link with Ireland through the establishment of many Irish airfields—Aldergrove, Collinstown, and Baldonnell among them.

From late 1914 onwards Robert had an affair with the artist Nora Summers, who had also been a student of the Slade Art School. She had married fellow student Gerald Summers in September 1912. It is difficult to ascertain whether Nora and Robert had any deep connection from their student years, or whether it was just some short-lived extension of artistic expression. The marriage of Nora and Gerald was unaffected, and they went on to have five children. (Their second youngest child, Caitlin, married Dylan Thomas.) However, although a devastated Margaret had tolerated some aspects of the affair, a visit of the Summers to Coole in June and July 1915 resulted in a scandalous scene involving Nora and Robert which left Margaret humiliated.[8] She had a miscarriage in 1915.

Robert joined the 4th Battalion of the Connaught Rangers on 24 September 1915. This battalion has its origins in the Galway Militia, and had been the subject of a minor controversy when in July 1912 Dr O'Dea, Bishop of Galway, refused permission for the chapel in Renmore Barracks, Co. Galway, to accept the colours. According to some accounts, Robert told William Yeats, 'I joined out of friendship.'[9] On 14 September 1915, a captain in the Coldstream Guards gave Robert a character reference, and Robert was appointed on 15 November 1915.[10]

At the outset there's reference on his file to seeking a transfer to the RFC, and so he did on 10 January 1916, reporting initially to the School of Instruction in Reading. In April 1916 Robert was serving at Swingate Down. The Easter Rising of 1916 accelerated the exodus of Anglo-Irish landlords from Connacht, for which the fear of agrarian rather than political violence was the driving force. This did not affect the Gregorys personally.

According to Robert's children, his training was arduous. His logbook records several incidents in a fortnight in May 1916, in which struts were broken and wheels damaged on landing.[11]

On 19 June 1916 Robert was appointed Flying Officer and assigned to No. 40 Squadron in July 1916—the first unit to fly the F.E.8, a 'pusher' aircraft. By August 1916 Robert was stationed at Bruay with No. 40 Squadron. His commanding officer was Robert Loraine, the pre-war aviator celebrity and well-known actor. Loraine had come close to being the first man to fly across the Irish Sea in a heavier-than-air Flight but came down just off the Irish coast. From his years as an actor, Loraine had become a close friend of G. B. Shaw, and a steady stream of praise for Robert's abilities was to reach Lady Gregory via Shaw and Yeats which went beyond polite admiration.

Although it was a glamorous squadron, with a celebrity in command and many artistic or cultural figures keen to laud its successes, it was—at the outset—quite an 'Irish' squadron in many respects. Apart from Robert Gregory there was Lieutenant (later Captain) Denis Osmond Mulholland, a fellow 4th Battalion Connaught Ranger. Mulholland actually recorded the squadron's first aerial victory, on 22 September 1916. Another noteworthy pilot from the squadron's early months was Co. Monaghan, born Desmond Herlouin de Burgh, later an Air Commodore. He was Robert's friend, and was also to become Mick Mannock's sparring and debating partner.

On 25 September 1916 Robert survived when his F.E.8 (6383) had its propeller shot away by anti-aircraft fire. On 9 November 1916 Robert scored his first victory, over a Roland while flying a F.E.8. His victim may have been from Jasta 2. By January 1917 he had been promoted to Flight Commander.

The debut performance of G. B. Shaw's play *O'Flaherty VC* in February 1917 involved de Burgh performing the role of Mrs O'Flaherty, with Robert taking on the part of Tessie the Maid and Mulholland taking the lead character role.[12] For such a risible play it is amusing to note just how many decorated Irishmen of No. 40 Squadron featured in its debut performance. Mulholland was known as 'Little Mull' and would have been quite a comical contrast to the tall, angular de Burgh. Sadly, despite Shaw's socialist credentials, although he sent Robert *O'Flaherty VC* he complied with a request to send another play for the 'other ranks'. Sending the one-act play *The Inca of Perusalem* in tandem helped preserve the Upstairs/Downstairs order of the squadron when it came to matters of fraternisation. Apparently, their theatre was an abandoned Red Cross hut, which they moved onsite.[13] Robert and Loraine dined with Shaw on 31 January 1917 at Tirancourt.

On 9 February 1917 Robert obtained a further aerial victory, over an Albatros C, while flying a F.E.8 (7606). He followed the German down from about 9,000 feet to 4,000 feet, firing a full drum at 100 yards range. The Albatros dived steeply and was last seen at 500 feet, a height from which it would be reasonable to conclude the survival prospects were slim.

In March 1917 Robert scored two further victories, on 6 March and 30 March 1917. The first of these was obtained with an F.E.8 (6384), against a Halberstadt. He fired a short burst at about 30 yards, then closing to 15 yards and firing 25 rounds into the German aircraft's fuselage. It is suggested that his victim may have been Leutnant Hans-Georg Eduard Lübbert, who was wounded on that date. No. 40 Squadron had clashed with von Richthofen's elite Jasta 11. Lieutenant Benbow brought down von Richthofen himself in the clash, puncturing the Red Baron's petrol tanks. Lübbert, Robert's apparent victim, was the only other Jasta 11 loss in the encounter. He was one of two brothers to serve with von Richthofen. Lübbert was known as *Kugelfang* (the 'bullet-catcher') on account of the number of times he'd been hit. It was Robert's last success on a 'pusher' aircraft.

However, the conversion to the Nieuport was not without incident. On 23 March 1917 Robert was shaken when his Nieuport (A6669) overturned after the rudder jammed on take-off. However, the arrival of this excellent French-built fighter was to change the fortunes of the squadron considerably.

The victory on 30 March 1917 was probably once again over Leutnant Hans-Georg Eduard Lübbert. 'Eddy' Lübbert was killed flying an Albatros DIII, but many Allied pilots mistook the wing shape of the Albatros DIII for the Halberstadt. Lübbert went down over Bailleul, not far from Arras, which is where Robert claimed his victory. The No. 40 Squadron 'Combats in the Air' submission to the Wing states that Robert, in a Nieuport (A6680), was a 12,000 feet on line patrol when he saw two Halberstadts flying among clouds south of Vimy.[14] Robert got on the tail of one German and fired a full drum at close range: he started firing at 40 yards and finished at 15 yards. The German turned over and was last seen side-slipping into a cloud near Bailleul. The engagement concluded at 5,000 feet. It's not an unusual occurrence for pilots to find themselves in aerial engagements against previous opponents: von Richthofen, for example, had brought down Flight Sergeant Sidney Herbert Quicke twice in March 1917, fatally on the second occasion.[15]

On 13 April 1917 Robert made a forced landing, luckily in friendly territory, near Chocques. His petrol tank had ruptured when on offensive patrol. His Nieuport (A6680) overturned and was wrecked.

Several publications have covered in detail the aerial victories of No. 40 Squadron.[16] Robert is credited with having forced down an Albatros C-Type when flying a Nieuport. On 6 May 1917 Robert, in Nieuport (B1448), forced an Albatros D Scout to land. Robert had attacked the aircraft from underneath, a tactic made popular by the great British ace Albert Ball. (It was also the principle behind the German night-fighter tactics of the Second World War; with the *Schräge Musik* 'Jazz Music' upward-firing guns being used to attack the vulnerable underbelly of the British bombers.) Robert had to swerve to avoid the Albatros as it spun downwards and to clear a stoppage in his gun. He lost sight of the Albatros in this manoeuvre, but other Nieuports on the patrol saw the German spin downwards. Owing to heavy anti-aircraft fire they could not follow the Albatros down, but it was not seen to crash.

On 10 May 1917 he drove down another enemy aircraft, and finally, on 26 May 1917 he claimed his last victory with No. 40 Squadron. According to No. 40 Squadrons 'Combats in the Air', Robert was flying a Nieuport (B1548) at 19,000 feet when he observed three Albatros Scouts at 15,000 feet, with a fourth aircraft flying above at 17,000 feet. He dived on the first aircraft, getting to within 20 yards before firing half a drum. The Albatros stalled, nose-dived, entered a spin, and then stalled again. It fell through the formation of other German aircraft, and was last seen spinning downwards.

However, there is some information on Robert's time with No. 40 Squadron that survived in the letters of William Bond to his wife Aimée, which appears in some editions as *An Airman's Wife* and in others as *My Airman Over There*. In the latter version the names are fictionalised; there's an 'Air Hog', an 'Odd Man', and so forth. Robert is 'Romney'. But the use of a pseudonym for Robert was pointless, as Bond makes explicit reference to Robert's artistic background.

I am more than content to be in this squadron. There are some awfully good fellows in it: good fellows both as pilots and personally.

My Flight Commander, Captain Romney, came out eight months ago and is a great Hun Strafer. Several years before the war he was an art student in the *Quartier*.

He leads our patrol, and I need not assure you how closely I follow his lead. We have tremendous confidence in him.[17]

Bond's first victory comes after a month on the frontline. It was one of a pair of German aircraft claimed by Bond and Robert. In a later patrol, Robert got to claim one exclusively:

Romney, who goes in for getting right up to his Hun before firing, approached to within 40 yards of the first one and then fired ten rounds. The Hun did an Immelmann turn and came out on Romney's tail. Romney did the same, got off another burst and the Hun dived away ... In the afternoon Romney got one again. There were four of us out, but he got so close to the Hun, a two-seater, and sat so persistently under his tail that we could not get near and dare not fire. Ultimately the Hun went down burning, and that was confirmed from the ground.[18]

In one instance Bond credits Robert with persuading the CO that he should not be required to go on balloon strafing exercises on successive occasions. Bond recalls he and Robert having a catty exchange regarding 'the haystack expert', an unfortunate pilot who'd crashed once too many. It is sometimes cited as a conversation about Mannock. However, this is quite wide of the mark: Mannock collided with a haystack on 20 August 1917, in a Nieuport (B3554), and by that stage Robert had returned to Home Establishment and Bond had been killed in action. Mannock is actually 'Kelly' in Bond's letters to Aimée. The actual 'haystack expert' was Lieutenant J. L. Barlow, who ran into a haystack on 20 May when attempting to take off in Nieuport B1647; and days later, he ran Nieuport B1519 out onto a road, when he misjudged a landing. Barlow actually became an ace with No. 40 Squadron, but was killed—perhaps unsurprisingly—in a non-combat flying incident on 23 September 1917.

When Robert got to leave the squadron Bond praised him highly:

Tonight we are having a special celebration dinner. Romney, who has been out here a long time, and has brought down many Huns, is going home tomorrow.

We expect he will get a squadron and his majority [rank of Major] in addition to his MC, and Croix de Guerre.

He is an awfully dear fellow and absolutely the stoutest-hearted I have ever met.[19]

Another Irish ace, Edward 'Mick' Mannock, had encountered Robert in No. 40 Squadron. It is possible that Robert had signed one of the facing pages of Mick's diary with the line 'don't let your wires sing' on 27 May 1917, a reference to the likelihood of an early warning of an aircraft disintegrating.

In June 1917 Robert got to return to Home Establishment. Robert served with the Central Flying School at Upavon, Wiltshire, for three months, although this was only a temporary instructor role. In June 1917 Robert was awarded the *Légion d'Honneur* by the French Republic, and in July the Military Cross:

> On many occasions he has, at various altitudes, attacked and destroyed or driven down hostile machines, and has invariably displayed the highest courage and skill.[20]

On 16 October Robert was ordered to France, in command of No. 66 Squadron—he had been promoted to Major by this stage. On 22 November No. 66 Squadron were sent to Italy. By 4 December, Robert was stationed at Grossa. That month, a major Austrian offensive had incited a corresponding Allied counter-attack, while at home Margaret had another miscarriage.

On 23 January 1918 Robert was killed in an aircraft crash. It appeared that Robert had been shot down by mistake by an Italian pilot, a story that his family repeated for many years. However, Italian records prove that there were no aircraft active in the area that day. No. 66 Squadron's record book for the day records that Major R. Gregory was flying a Sopwith Camel (B2475) on a test exercise at 11.45 a.m. when reported killed, the machine wrecked. Robert had been inoculated shortly before his final flight and may have suffered an adverse reaction. The RAF casualty card for Robert states that he was

> ... last seen at 2,000 feet near Monastiero. Went into spin and crashed to ground with engine full on. Investigation fails to discover cause of accident.

Despite his posturing as an artist Robert actually carried a considerable amount of wealth on display on his person. The RFC's inventory for next-of-kin included a gold wristlet watch, which was engraved on the back, two silver wristwatches, and a gold tie-pin. (First World War aviators had been early proponents of the merits of the wristwatch over the pocket watch.) Margaret was no stranger to Robert's apparent materialism; her correspondence to the War Office requested that the valuables be forwarded to her sister—Mrs Green—in London and not to Coole Park in Galway.[21] Curiously, Robert's service records several times categorise him as 'killed in action', which does not accord with the official account of his death. Indeed the casualty card records one version of this death but the telegram to his family actually refers to 'killed in action'.

Flight magazine of 7 February carried a short obituary, followed by a lengthy obituary on 21 February 1918:

He was educated at Harrow, where he took the first classical scholarship of the year, and went on to New College, Oxford. Afterwards he studied painting in Paris under Blanche, who declared that his work 'had reached the highest level of artistic and intellectual merit.' He exhibited at the New English and other galleries paintings of West Irish landscape. The Abbey Theatre in its earlier days owed much to the beautiful scenes painted and designed by him.[22]

William Yeats wrote a eulogy for *The Observer* on 17 February 1918.

I have known no man accomplished in so many ways as Major Robert Gregory ... His very accomplishment hid from many his genius. He had so many sides: painter, classical scholar, scholar in painting and in modern literature, boxer, horseman, airman ... that some among his friends were not sure what his work would be. To me he will always remain a great painter in the immaturity of his youth.

There were numerous artistic and sporting publications that carried appreciations of Robert's life, for instance the *Illustrated Sporting and Dramatic News* of 23 February 1918:

He was also an all-round sportsman. A good shot, a fine boxer, and excellent slow-breaker bowler, and a fearless horseman and point-to-point rider. He belonged to the Authentic Co. Galway and Phoenix Cricket Clubs ... At Oxford he was chosen as light-weight boxer against Cambridge, and in Paris as a candidate for the amateur championship of France. One of the leading members of the 'Galway Blazers' writes: 'A gallant fellow, one of the very best ... for a more fearless horseman never rode over this country.'[23]

The *Harrow Memorials of the Great War* contained praise from his colonel and several Flight commanders: 'a really fine airman, and a dead game man,' 'he always did more than was asked of him,' and was 'always out to do as much work as anyone else ... and, though officially not supposed to go over the lines, he came with us nearly every day.'[24]

G. B. Shaw reassured Lady Gregory that, when he visited Robert in February 1917,

... in abominably cold weather, with a frostbite on his face hardly healed, he told me that the six months he had been there had been the happiest of his life. An amazing thing to say considering his exceptionally fortunate and happy circumstances at home, but evidently he meant it. To a man with his power of standing up to danger—which must mean enjoying it—war must have intensified his life as nothing else could; he got a grip of it that he could not through art or love. I suppose that is what makes the soldier.[25]

However, William Yeats's knowledge of Robert—combined with Lady Gregory's determination that her son should have a greater legacy than the unrealised potential exhibited fleetingly in some stage props or paintings—resulted in his writing four poems for the Gregory family. Ostensibly they were written about Robert, but in many respects were about Lady Gregory's anguish and William's coming to terms with the loss suffered by a family he knew so well. 'Shepherd and Goatherd' deals primarily with Lady Gregory's grief, but the question of Robert's legacy is one which remains elusive:

> Shepherd. You cannot but have seen
> That he alone had gathered up no gear,
> Set carpenters to work on no wide table,
> On no long bench nor lofty milking-shed
> As others will, when first they take possession,
> But left the house as in his father's time
> As though he knew himself, as it were, a cuckoo,
> No settled man. And now that he is gone
> There's nothing of him left but half a score
> Of sorrowful, austere, sweet, lofty pipe tunes.

Interestingly, the poem most associated with Robert, 'An Irish Airman foresees his Death', ignores Robert's views on the Irish in the service of British Empire, while also attempting to bestow an apolitical individuality on Robert's motivations to become an aviator:

> Those that I fight I do not hate
> Those that I guard I do not love
> ...
> Nor law, nor duty bade me fight,
> Nor public men, nor cheering crowds,
> A lonely impulse of delight
> Drove to this tumult in the clouds;

Yeats apparently had quite some difficulty in composing 'In Memory of Major Robert Gregory', as there were numerous interventions by Lady Gregory regarding the content of many of the stanzas. He had started composing the poem in April 1918 when visiting Coole, but it has the feel of a compromise or collaboration by a committee. It attempts to present Robert as a Renaissance man, with a regular refrain of 'soldier, scholar, horseman, he', yet overall it is closer to portraying Robert as the everything-to-everyone in the manner of the German phrase '*eierlegende Wollmilchsau*'—the wool-bearing, egg-laying, dairy-producing pig.

'Reprisals' makes reference to nineteen aerial victories by Robert, but the poem is largely concerned with using Robert as a stick with which to beat the British authorities over the lawlessness of their campaign of subjugation in Ireland. The Troubles had affected the Gregorys' part of Galway badly: Robert's cousin, Frank Shawe-Taylor, was murdered on 3 March 1920. As in so many of these cases, the precise motivation behind the killing was unclear. Ironically, Shawe-Taylor had been instrumental in tenants' rights and the redistribution of land: his proposals to George Wyndham for a Land Conference resulted in the 1902 conference chaired by Lord Dunraven that eventually gave rise to the Wyndham Land Act 1903.

However, among Robert's erstwhile colleagues in the Connaught Rangers, a mutiny occurred in June 1920 in India, partially as a consequence of British military and paramilitary policies in Ireland.

Lady Gregory's brother, Frank Persse, was forced to abandon Ashfield after shots were fired through the window and doors in one attack. Frank Persse arranged the sale of Coole demesne in October 1920 on behalf of Lady Gregory and Margaret, to a group of former tenants, for just £9,000.

Whereas the British media focused on Irish 'anarchy', Lady Gregory's journals record the other side of the story. On a journey home from the Burren on 27 September 1920, she noted the following:

> I had been told that Feeney's house in Kinvara had been burned in the night ... and we passed by the ruined walls in the town. A little farther, at the cross roads, there was another ruin, McMerney's the smith. His house had also been burned down in the night by soldiers and police. He and his family had found shelter in the cart shed. It seemed so silent, we had always heard the hammer in the smithy and seen the glow of the fire.

On 27 September 1920 two lorries of soldiers drove into Gort, firing live rounds randomly, searching people and raiding houses. At least one house was burnt. On 1 November 1920 Ellen Quinn, the young, pregnant wife of one of Robert's former tenants, Malachi Quinn, was killed by random gunfire from Black and Tans. On 14 November 1920 Fr. Michael Griffin was killed by the Auxiliaries and his body dumped in a bog near Barna, in an effort to show that the Catholic clergy bore guilt for the death of Protestants and would be silenced accordingly. Similarly so was the abduction and murder of two young local men—Patrick and Harry Loughnane—by the Black and Tans near Shanaglish in late November 1920. One of the Loughnanes was actually in the IRA, and had participated in an ambush at Castledaly on 30 October 1920. However, much of the violence by Crown forces was against innocent civilians, with the death of an IRA activist being coincidental. Willaim Yeats's poem urges Robert to 'rise from your Italian tomb' and stay,

> Till certain second thoughts have come
> Upon the cause you served, that we
> Imagined such a fine affair:
> Half-drunk or whole-mad soldiery
> Are murdering your tenants there.
> Men that revere your father yet
> Are shot at on the open plain.

Of those shot on the open plain, further north in Co. Galway, near Tuam, a Michael Moran of Carramoneen was 'shot while trying to escape', as was a Jim Kirwan of Ballinastack, Corofin, when working in a field with his father. However, the vast majority of incidents that occurred entailed the destruction of property and possessions, life-threatening events to small tenant farmers but not necessarily in themselves fatal. There were dozens of incidents on almost a daily basis.

However, if 'Reprisals' had little to do with Robert, the man himself had left a bitter legacy for his family in his will, dated 14 September 1916, which stated that he wished to leave everything to his wife. However, it also stated that 'I wish her to have the fullest freedom in the upbringing of my children and the management of my house and estate.' That sentence was a near-impossibility to apply to the situation as it prevailed at Coole: Lady Gregory had been the manager of the house and estate, and had spent considerable sums of her own money on Coole, while Robert and Margaret had lived between London and Paris. However, Lady Gregory and Margaret reached a compromise, notwithstanding Robert's odious link between conferring responsibility with the upbringing of his children with the management of his house and estate. By May 1918 the overall value of Robert's estate, including Coole (its furniture and effects, and family heirlooms of Sir William), amounted to £31,960 8s—not an inconsiderable amount for such a debt-ridden estate.

The situation was not been helped by the Yeats family: William's sister Lily regarded Margaret as 'just a little suburban minx ... in the suburbs they like to move every three years.' It conjures up images of Alan Clark's damning of Michael Heseltine as 'a man who bought his own furniture.' Some of Lily's remarks were not unfounded: Margaret had living-room curtains and other fixtures and fittings stripped from the house, even as Lady Gregory resided there in her final stages of breast cancer. Conversely, Lady Gregory regarded William's wife Georgiana with disdain, noting she 'has money, though perhaps not so much as he was led to believe.'

Margaret was the sole survivor of an IRA ambush on 15 May 1921, in which the local District Inspector of the RIC, Captain Cecil Blake, was killed, together with his pregnant wife Eliza 'Lily' and two British officers, Captain Fiennes Cornwallis and Lieutenant Robert McCreery of the 17th Lancers. Captain Cornwallis was the son of a former Conservative MP for Maidstone in Kent. Blake had been a vet with the RSPCA before the war, and had served with the RFA during it. These men would have perceived themselves as combatants, and the reports cite multiple wounds. They were leaving a tennis party at the Bagot house at Ballyturin near Gort. (Ballyturin House was abandoned by the Bagot family and now lies in ruins.) The IRA had in fact been hoping to decapitate the British Auxiliary leadership in southern Galway, District Inspector Biggs being among their intended targets in this ambush.[26]

An attempted break-in in May 1922 brought home to Lady Gregory the seriousness of the situation, and evidence of her class's precarity was undeniable. The Goughs' residence at Lough Cutra was unofficially requisitioned by one faction of Irish Government 'Irregulars' to serve as a hostel for Catholic refugees from the Belfast pogroms, though it was eventually restored to the family by a rival faction. The Persses also lost Roxborough, from which they were burnt out in 1922, ending an association with the area which dated back to grants of confiscated land in counties Galway and Roscommon in the 1670s. Ultimately Coole was sold to the Department of Agriculture for forestry in March 1927, thus severing Robert's final legacy of it as a hunting, fishing, and shooting resort for a wide circle of British and Irish civilian and military friends, as well as his children's link with Ireland. On 8 September 1928 Margaret remarried to the Gregorys' neighbour, Guy Vincent Hugh Gough of Lough Cutra.

In truth the four poems in which Robert features are not representative of his life or death. Even Robert's grave at Padua has been a source of contention. Lady Gregory recounted that it was marked with a wooden cross 'made with love' by members of his squadron from aeroplane parts, until this was replaced in 1923 with a stone 'just the same as every other stone, made by contract.'[27]

10

GRIBBEN,
Edward
(5 aerial victories)

Born: 10 September 1890, Co. Down
Awards: Military Cross

Edward Gribben was born at 'Avondale', Cultra, Hollywood, Co. Down. The Irish census of 1901 records Edward as resident at Ballycultra with his widowed mother Isabella, his aunt Mary Coutes, and his sister Isabella, and the census of 1911 as still living with his mother and sister in Hollywood, along with a servant. Gribben is described as an 'Engineer, Motor Works Manager'. His service record cites his civilian occupation as being with Chamber Motors Ltd, University Street, Belfast, from 1906 to 1914.[1]

Gribben joined the 5th Battalion of the Royal Irish Rifles on 4 August 1914. He was appointed 2nd Lieutenant with effect from 15 August 1914.[2] However, I have been unable to locate a reference to Gribben in the battalion's War Diaries.

He transferred to the RFC in 1916, and on 18 August 1916 was sent to the No. 1 School of Aeronautics, transferring to the No. 2 School on 24 August 1916. On 3 October he was transferred from No. 5 RS, subsequently moving to No. 34 RS on 10 November 1916.

On 12 January 1917 Gribben was appointed Lieutenant (Flying Officer) with effect from 24 December 1916.[3] On 15 February 1917 Gribben joined No. 46 Squadron, which flew a variety of Sopwith and Nieuport two-seaters. On 6 March 1917 in a Sopwith 1½ Strutter (A882), Gribben and his obsever, a 2nd Lieutenant R. A. Manby, were brought down by enemy fire, suffering a forced landing in a field but ultimately crashing into a house. Gribben was transferred on 8 March, subsequently moving to No. 70 Squadron on 28 March 1917.

On 31 March 1917 in a Sopwith 1 1/2 Strutter (A954), Gribben and his observer 2nd Lieutenant N. Mellor experienced a hard landing, wrecking the undercarriage of the aircraft—not the most auspicious start to his time with No. 70 Squadron. On 4 May Gribben and 2nd Lieutenant N. Mellor flew a Sopwith 1½ Strutter (A996) on a reconnaissance mission to Tournai. They were flying at 11,500 feet over Lille when they encountered engine trouble and were obliged to turn back for home. However, they were attacked by an Albatros, which had the advantage in speed and armament. 2nd Lieutenant Mellor fired two-and-a-half drums of ammunition during one of the enemy aircraft's approaches. The Albatros 'suddenly turned off and went down steeply eastwards in sideslips, but apparently under control.' Gribben and Mellor had escaped, but one half of the main petrol tank had been shot through. In the early war years such claims against the Albatros may have been entertained, but by 1917 would no longer count as decisive aerial victories.

No. 70 Squadron was to amass 290 aerial victories over the course of the war, but the vast majority of these were from the time it was equipped with the Sopwith Camel. Gribben survived the final few months of the squadron's use of the Sopwith 1½ Strutter, which could no longer hold its own at this late stage—a matter about which Gribben would have been well aware from his exploits with No. 46 Squadron. No. 70 Squadron's over-achiever was the Irish-Canadian, Frank Granger Quigley, who alone accounted for over thirty of the squadron's total. There were eighteen aces in all who served with the squadron, with Gribben and Oscar Heron being the two Irishmen.

By July 1917 No. 70 Squadron had converted to Sopwith Camel single-seaters. On 17 July Gribben scored his first confirmed aerial victory, over an Albatros D.V south of Gheluvelt. Gribben was part of a five-man offensive patrol, which was led by the English ace Noel William Ward Webb and included Belfast/Glasgow man Charles Service Workman, a protégé of Webb's who had recently transferred to No. 70 Squadron. Their formation had crossed the line south of Zillebeke Lake and was about 4 miles into enemy territory when it encountered thirty to forty enemy aircraft. The melee started at 15,000 feet and concluded at 9,000 feet. Although the Camels had attempted to concentrate their attack on a single enemy, this proved impossible. Their formation was broken up, with only Captain Webb and Lieutenants Smith and Grosset managing to stay together in a defensive combat, until they were split up as the fight progressed. Their survival prospects were increased when a mixed formation of D.H.5s, S.E.5s, and Sopwith Triplanes joined the frenzy. Gribben hit an Albatros, which emitted smoke and dived vertically from the combat, but was unable to follow it down to confirm its fate as he was constantly under attack. His guns jammed and he left the combat, landing at La Lovie Aerodrome. Workman, Gribben's fellow Ulsterman, was last seen isolated from the other Camels, engaging several enemy aircraft. Workman crashed behind German lines and died in a German hospital from his wounds. He was not the only casualty from the five-Camel patrol: Lieutenant W. E. Grosset was taken PoW, his Sopwith Camel (B6332) wrecked on landing.

If Gribben's first confirmed aerial victory had come in a traumatic and costly encounter, his next aerial engagements were not straight-forward affairs either. On 21 July Gribben was flying a Camel (B3813) as part of a large formation on a bombing run when he began to experience engine difficulties. Gribben returned at

3.55 p.m. and went out again in an attempt to pick up the formation. He couldn't find them but proceeded to patrol from Ypres to the sea for about an hour. On his journey back he climbed to 18,000 feet and found an Albatros two-seater about 500 feet above in the vicinity of St Omer. Gribben fired several bursts from underneath the Albatros, after which the observer ceased firing (though I cannot find a corresponding match to a dead or wounded German observer for the date and location). Although slower than the Camel, the Albatros had a better rate of climb and continued to ascend in a running fight that was only broken off when Gribben had found himself over a mile behind enemy lines. A claim could not be awarded for an encounter of this nature, though undoubtedly Gribben had prevented an aerial reconnaissance mission from being completed and in all likelihood had drawn blood.

On 24 July 1917 Gribben was on offensive patrol in his regular Camel (B3813) as part of a Flight led by Captain Webb. They had only crossed the lines south of Ypres when they encountered two separate formations of German aircraft— 'Albatros Nieuports', as Gribben described them—about ten in all, approaching at different altitudes.

> One E.A. dived on me from right front. As he crossed my bows I opened fire and saw the pilot fall sideways and forward towards me. His machine went down out of control. Another E.A. came across my front from the same direction. I turned into him and fired straight into his engine. He appeared to fall out of control and went down. I then circled round after the other Camels. I saw an E.A. diving on Capt. Laurence who was below me. Capt. Laurence turned to the right and I turned to the left. As E.A. came on I turned round onto his tail and as he dived I fired into him. I could see tracers going into his fuselage, close to cockpit. He went on and seemed to be out of control. At this time another E.A. was on my tail. I disengaged, by turning downwards, and met E.A. coming 'head-on'. His guns must have jammed as he did not fire. I fired a short burst and ran out of ammunition, and made for home.

This combat sequence continued into another, with Gribben being chased over Polygon Wood by ten German aircraft, his wing planes hit. Gribben vouched for Captain Webb apparently destroying a red Albatros—which was not credited to him but only regarded as 'driven down'—but there was no corresponding verification that any of the four aircraft that Gribben had hit had actually met a decisive fate. In the end, one Albatros DIII was credited to Gribben as going down 'out of control'. Captain Frederic Hope Laurence had survived the encounter thanks to Gribben, and was ultimately to become an ace with No. 70 Squadron, whereas Lieutanant H. D. Tapp's Camel (B3825) was badly damaged and he was taken PoW. Tapp's victor was Oberleutnant Ernst Frieherr von Althaus of Jasta 10; Tapp was his final victory before handing over the command of Jasta 10 to the legendary Werner Voss.

On 26 July 1917, flying his usual Camel (B3813), Gribben got involved in another large-scale combat, on this occasion at 14,000 feet over Polygon Wood. However, as there were S.E.5as and Camels of different squadrons Gribben was reduced to a peripheral attack, firing several rounds at 200 yards. Captain Ward claimed an Albatros D.V, which Gribben confirmed had descended, its wings coming off, in a flat spin. The German ace Lieutenant Otto Brauneck of Jasta 11 was killed in the encounter.

On 28 July Gribben had another indecisive aerial victory. His Camel (B3813) had experienced some engine trouble, so he ended up having to break from formation but north of Ypres, near Menin, Gribben encountered a battle between a five enemy aircraft and some D.H.5s. Gribben helped to force a German two-seater to land, south of Langemarck. By this stage of the war 'forced to land' aerial victories were no longer awarded. Gribben's Flight suffered in his absence, with No. 70 Squadron losing two other Camels near Roulers that day, with 2nd Lieutenant Joseph Cecil Smith (B3874) being killed and 2nd Lieutenant R. C. Hume (B3824) taken PoW.

On 29 July Gribben experienced yet another indecisive encounter. He was part of a five-Camel offensive patrol over Roulers. They were over the Forest de Houthulst when they met an equal number of German aircraft. Gribben wrote that both he and Collett put a few good bursts into one E.A., but although it spun down it flattened out at 6,000 feet. Lieutenant H. O. MacDonald's Camel (B3780) was damaged in the encounter, but he managed to land safely, and was taken PoW. (He was in fact a rookie Canadian pilot, Hubert Orr MacDonald, and not the South African ace Hector Omdurman MacDonald, who served with No. 84 Squadron.)

On 10 August 1917 Gribben finally got his third and fourth decisive aerial victories. He was part of an offensive patrol, some 15,000 feet over Roulers, Menin, and Courtrai, flying Camel B3840 when they encountered a formation of five enemy aircraft on line patrol. A German two-seater observation aircraft flew close to Gribben's formation, presumably as bait. Then another formation of fifteen German aircraft appeared, which they duly attacked. In the confused battle that followed Gribben was credited with the destruction of one Albatros DIII, with another regarded as having been sent down out of control. Gribben and Webb worked well together:

One E.A. dived down and flattened out, in front of me. I got on his tail and fired a long burst with both guns. I saw tracers going all round the pilot. He turned over and went down in successive spins. I followed him down some way and saw him crash. I then climbed to rejoin my formation and saw two E.A. on Capt. Webb's tail; one behind the other. I closed onto the rear one from his left, and fired two burst at him. The second burst went right into his engine, and observed one bullet ricochet off the machine. He then put his nose down and did 'S' turns for the ground.

Capt. Webb and I then dived on another E.A. Capt. Webb spiraled round his tail, but he disengaged and I followed him. My pressure gave out, and then the

E.A. got on my tail. Capt. Webb came up and drove him off. I then came home with Capt. Webb.

No. 70 Squadron was experiencing an attrition rate of an aircraft a day in July and August 1917, but the RFC could afford this rate; neither could the Germans. RFC Communiqué No. 100 of 1917 makes reference to Gribben in an important battle on 10 August 1917.[4] On 13 August, Gribben 'made ace', claiming his fifth kill on an offensive patrol near Roulers. He was at 15,000 feet in the same Camel he'd flown previously (B3840), accompanying Capt. Webb when they encountered three German two-seaters. Gribben overshot one but managed to pull up from his dive and riddle the two-seater from underneath, hitting its fuselage as it passed over him. Gribben then caught up with another two-seater, a DFW, further northwards. Gribben's opening shots killed the observer. He kept firing

... until he suddenly nose-dived into the ground NE of Dixmude. I observed him with his nose in the ground, which was marshy, and his tail in the air.

Gribben returned to the aerodrome to find that Webb and Hudson had been credited with the three DFWs from the first encounter near Dixmude. However, Gribben could not have been disappointed, as four of his five victories had come against Albatros Scouts, and several of these were in dangerous melees.

Gribben was transferred to Home Establishment on 3 September 1917, from which he was assigned to No. 44 (Home Defence) Squadron. He mainly flew night operations in the defence of London. The squadron used the Sopwith Camel. On 26 September the award of the Military Cross to Gribben's was gazetted, although the citation was not actually published on that date. On 30 November 1917 Gribben was transferred to Aero Experimental Station at Ipswich.

On 8 January 1918 Gribben's citation for the Military Cross was gazetted:

Lt Edward Gribben, R. Ir. Rif., Spec. Res. & RFC

For conspicuous gallantry and devotion to duty on offensive patrols. In every combat he has been most conspicuous, continually attacking superior numbers of the enemy, destroying some and driving others down out of control. He fights with great dash and skill, and whenever any machine of his formation is in difficulties, he is invariably at hand to render assistance.[5]

Gribben was appointed Temporary Captain (Flight Commander) with effect from 1 January 1918. Gribben appears on the Air Force List of May 1918 as a Lieutenant (Temporary Captain) with effect from 1 April 1918.

On 23 September 1918 he was transferred from the Aero Experimental Station to No. 41 Squadron. No. 41 Squadron was sent to the Front in October 1918, having been re-equipped with the S.E.5a. Gribben was wounded on 4 October 1918, just days after returning to combat duties. According to Franks *et al* in *Above the Trenches*, Gribben's S.E.5a was badly shot up by a Fokker D.VII, causing him to crash-land with a wounded arm. However, another report shows Gribben's S.E.5a (F5494) being shot up, with the engine—and not Gribben—taking the bullets. Gribben was initially treated at Brighton throughout the month of October 1918, subsequently being transferred to Belfast on 13 November 1918. He was not discharged until 7 December 1918.

The War Office announced on 14 February 1919 that Gribben was to be promoted to Captain with the 5th Royal Irish Rifles, with effect from 16 March 1917, but would not be entitled to pay or allowances other than for the period for which he was acting at that grade. Gribben was to remain seconded to the RAF.[6]

A Medical Board examination of 20 February 1919 declared him unfit for twelve weeks. On 24 March 1919 Gribben returned to the Aero Experimental Station, though he was reporting to Cambridge for medical assessment. He was back on experimental machines on 13 July 1919. On 18 July 1919 Gribben, in a D.H.9A (E748), with a Mr Mitchell as observer, experienced a hard landing at Farnborough, wiping off the undercarriage. (This particular aircraft was later reconditioned and ended up being landed—on its nose—onto the deck of HMS *Argus* at Spithead in August 1921 by a Flying Officer J. H. Bryer, who survived the incident.)[7] On 4 October 1919 Gribben was assigned to 86 Wing of 186 Group, based at Farnborough. On 15 October he was injured in an aeroplane accident and admitted to Cambridge Military Hospital, Aldershot. Gribben was assigned to the School of Rations, then on 16 December 1919 to the School of 1(S)ARD, an aircraft repair depot assignment. Gribben, now a Captain (Flying), was transferred to the Unemployed List with effect from 24 January 1920.[8]

On 4 May 1920 he was granted a short service commission as Flight Lieutenant (A), retaining his last substantive rank. However, on 10 August 1920, Gribben's short service commission was cancelled. The Supplement to *The London Gazette* of 22 February 1921 confirmed that Gribben relinquished his commission in the Royal Ulster Rifles with effect from 1 April 1920. He retained his rank of Captain.[9] However, the medal index card generated in respect of Gribben indicates that he also saw service as a Lieutenant in the 1st Yorkshire and Lancashire Regiment prior to joining the 5th Royal Irish Rifles.

Gribben flew over forty different types of machines, including numerous experimental types, over the course of his career.[10] The Royal Aircraft Establishment at Farnborough may in the modern era be associated with the Hawker Harrier or the Concorde, but in Gribben's time it was the former Balloon Factory. The 'factory' element had been dropped by 1918, when research was the establishment's focus. Gribben's legacy to aviation may well be his exceptional work as a test pilot rather than his military achievements as an ace.

On 10 December 1927, a Capt. E. Gribben and Mrs. E. Gribben sailed from Liverpool on the SS *Alca*, a Yeoward Line cruise ship which was to visit Lisbon,

Madeira, and the Canary Islands. The use of the rank 'Captain' in his details suggests that he was still a reservist of some description. Their address is recorded as being '39 Courtfield Gardens, London SW5'.

On 14 March 1930 the War Office announced that Captain Edward Gribben MC, 18th London Regiment, late 5th Battalion Royal Ulster Rifles (Special Reserve), was confirmed as Captain with effect from 15 March 1930. Gribben is recorded as having been in the Supplementary Reserve of Officers.[11]

Gribben was promoted from Captain to Lieutenant-Colonel with effect from 1 November 1934, at this stage with the 18th London Rifles.[12] The Army Sport Control Board of the War Office published the volume *Games and Sports in the Army*, in which—in the 1934 edition—Gribben features as a boxing umpire, with the caption 'Capt. E. Gribben MC, 18th London Regt, Duke of York's HQ, Chelsea'. It's interesting to note that Gribben's transfer from the Royal Ulster Rifles to a London Regiment was to one with a very strong Irish connection—the 18th were the London Irish Rifles Battalion of the London Regiment.

Gribben travelled on the *Queen Mary*—the Cunard White Star liner—from Southampton to New York on 22 July 1936. Although was put down as an 'executive', he travelled 'tourist' class. His wife Margaretta was also recorded as travelling with him. They gave their address as 91 Cromwell Road, London, and their nationality as Northern Irish. Tracing this couple from the electoral registers for the Borough of Kensington and Chelsea reveals a Captain Edward Gribben and a Margaretta Elenor Blanche Gribben as residents of 39 Courtfield Gardens in the Redcliffe Ward. They lived there in 1927, 1928, 1929, 1930, and 1933, sharing the first and second floors of a four-storey over-basement house with several others.

One difficulty in tracing Gribben's military career in both world wars is the large number of Edward Gribbens with whom he might be confused. The RAF Muster Roll for 1918 records E. J. Gribben under the service number 40124, while in the Second World War, a Captain Edward Gribben MC (74853) was gazetted on 20 October 1939 in respect of an appointment as Flight Lieutenant with effect from 1 September 1939, with seniority backdated to 1 November 1938. That particular Edward Gribben was also gazetted on 16 December 1941. And there was another Edward Gribben, an Edward James Gribben (35838), who ultimately went on to reach the rank of Wing Commander in the RAF, an OBE being gazetted on 1 January 1945 in respect of the New Year Honours list. Similarly, an Edward Seaton Gribben died on 18 April 1965 at the RAF Hospital in Uxbridge; however, his widow was 'Bessie Gribben'.

It is likely that Gribben served under the service number 74853 in the Second World War (the second possibility of the above), and he tended to use 'E. C. Gribben', the middle initial representing his mother's maiden name. Gribben's wife, Margretta Eleanor Blanche Gribben of 'The Chateau, Cushendall, Co. Antrim', died on 8 February 1965. Her estate was valued at £56,699. Probate was granted to the Northern Bank, which suggests that Edward pre-deceased her.

11

HAZELL,
Tom Falcon
(43 aerial victories)

Born: 7 August 1892, Co. Galway
Died: 4 September 1946
Awards: Military Cross, Distinguished Service Order, Distinguished Flying Cross and Bar

Major Tom Falcon 'Bill' Hazell was one of Ireland's foremost aces. His aerial exploits have given him a special place in British military aviation history: Hazell was not only one of the premier 'balloon-busters'—a skill which required considerable skill and courage against such well defended targets—but he also achieved remarkable success against enemy aircraft. Hazell served as a highly successful ace with No. 1 Squadron, later becoming the highest-scoring pilot with No. 24 Squadron.

His father Thomas was from Co. Galway, but his mother Cecile was English. Thomas Senior was a 'land agent and magistrate.' Hazell had two sisters, Frances and April, and two brothers, Cecil and Arthur. The family lived with a governess and four other servants. Falcon was not living with the family according to the Irish census of 1911, but another sister, Phyllis, had since been born. Their complement of servants included a chauffeur, a parlour maid, a housemaid, and a cook/domestic servant. The same census also put down Tom's mother as being from Somerset. She was actually the daughter of an English naval officer, Captain Cecil Buckley, who won the VC for a series of raids against enemy coastal installations on the Sea of Azov, Crimea. (Tom's wartime balloon-busting aerial raids would appear to have had a maritime precedent in the family.)

Tom is recorded in the UK census of 1911 as resident at Manor House, Tonbridge, Kent; Cecil, his brother, was also a boarder there. Tonbridge was a reasonably prestigious public school, with close links to the Worshipful Company of Skinners, one of London's oldest livery companies and one with many links to the Ulster Plantation.

Hazell's pre-war career has a number of gaps but it is generally accepted that he attended the University of London in 1911 prior to joining the South Irish Horse in September 1914. However, Hazell's medal card records him as having been a

Lieutenant in the Royal Inniskilling Fusiliers and a Captain in the RAF, with no mention of any previous service.[1] He was commissioned as a 2nd Lieutenant with the 7th Battalion of the Royal Iniskilling Fusiliers on 27 September 1914, and promoted to Lieutenant with effect from 4 June 1915.

Hazell transferred into the RFC in the spring of 1916. He served with No. 5 RS in Warwickshire from 12 April to 28 April 1916 while undergoing flight training. Hazell survived a bad crash in June, but obtained his wings on 6 June 1916. On 28 June Temporary Lieutenant Hazell, Royal Inniskilling Fusiliers, was to be transferred to the General List, as a Flying Officer in the RFC.[2] On 19 December 1916 Hazell was posted to No. 1 Squadron in France. He briefly served with another Irishman, Edward Dawson Atkinson, but the latter took command of 'A' Flight upon the death of Capt. J. M. E. Shepherd. Hazell served with 'B' Flight.

On the morning of 4 March 1917 Hazell became detached from the rest of 'B' Flight due to engine trouble at 15,000 feet, east of Ypres. He managed to glide back to Ballieul and make a successful dead-stick landing. The other members of his Flight—Major C. J. Quentin Brand and Lieutenant V. C. A. Bush—managed to bring down a Roland two-seater in Hazell's absence. Later that afternoon, however, Hazell achieved his first aerial victory, sending a German down out of control near Westhoek when flying a Nieuport (A6604). His next decisive aerial victory did not come until 24 April 1917. In a Nieuport (A6738) Hazell was leading 2nd Lieutenant L. M. Mansbridge in a two-man line patrol when they caught an Albatros two-seater near Armentières. Hazell got underneath the Albatros's blind spot and fired thirty rounds. The German machine began emitting smoke from the fuselage as it lurched downwards into a steep dive. According to some accounts the observer drew a pistol and leaned over the side, firing at Hazell, but he was more than likely already dead, his body slumped over the side—bits of the disintegrating fuselage or exploding ammunition could have given the impression of him fighting back. His victims were probably Leutnant Henrich Klose and Unteroffizier Otto Haberland of FA(A)227. On 9 May 1917 Hazell sent another Albatros two-seater down, but on this occasion it was 'out of control' rather than in flames. On 24 May Hazell had a mishap flying Nieuport B1632, when he experienced engine failure at 6,000 feet after take-off. Hazell hit telephone wires and overturned in the course of effecting an emergency landing, but he only suffered minor injuries.

Hazell was promoted from Flying Officer to Temporary Captain, with effect from 25 May 1917. On 27 May a young Dubliner, 2nd Lieutenant John Anthony O'Sullivan, was killed when his Nieuport (A6670) plunged to earth during a practice flight. No. 1 Squadron were suffering a steady stream of losses—injuries and fatalities—from crashes as much as combat incidents. Perhaps it was a combination of poor training, pilot error, pilot fatigue, and the overstretching of maintenance crews and material resources; at any rate, there was a casualty almost on a daily basis throughout June, July, and August 1917, which cannot be blamed on the Flight Commanders like Hazell.

In June 1917 Hazell really made an impact, obtaining six victories that month alone, all in Nieuport B1649, having taken command of 'A' Flight upon Atkinson's return to Home Establishment. One interesting encounter came on 4 June 1917, when Hazell claimed the destruction of an Albatros DIII near Hollebeke. The enemy aircraft lost a wing after being hit with half a drum. On that day the German ace Paul Strähle, of Jasta 18, recorded the loss of his colleague Offizierstellvertreter Matthias Denecke. Strähle states that three Nieuports attacked their five-man formation out of the sun, and that Denecke's aircraft broke up in the air when hit. Strähle had brought down Nieuport A6678 of No. 1 Squadron on 25 May, the pilot Lieutenant. J. R. Anthony dying of his wounds, and kept its rudder as another of his trophies—his favourite, supposedly. On 26 May Strähle brought down another Nieuport, B1685 of No. 1 Squadron, with the pilot—2nd Lieutenant R. R. MacIntosh—surviving as a PoW. Neither Strähle nor Hazell would have been aware of this private war between the two squadrons, however.

Other sources record Hazell's decisive aerial victory on 4 June as occurring as part of a larger fracas in which ten Sopwith Triplanes of No. 1 (Naval) Squadron, some S.E.5as from No. 56 Squadron, and a SPAD from No. 19 Squadron engaged a formation of twenty German aircraft. This aerial combat resulted in four claims for Hazell, but none were considered decisive: in extensive encounters of this nature, there was often little time to shoot accurately before becoming a target oneself, and the danger of collision was quite high if 'target fixation' took over. Hazell was succeeding in aerial combat, but the number of confirmed victories was still slow to build.

The most noteworthy of Hazell's aerial victories of that month came on 8 June 1917, when he got into a dogfight with a formation led by Hermann Göring. Hazell led a dawn patrol of four Nieuports at 05.25 a.m., which at 06.40 encountered Göring's formation of five Albatros Scouts from Jasta 27. Hazell attacked an Albatros with a broad white band painted around its black fuselage behind the cockpit and his fire hit the enemy scout, which turned over before going down in a vertical dive. However, during the fighting Jasta 27 were joined by elements of Jasta 8. Two Nieuports were shot down: 2nd Lieutenant R. S. L. Boote by Oberleutnant Voigt of Jasta 8, and 2nd Lieutenant Frank Dalloway Slee by Göring himself. Both Boote and Slee survived to be taken prisoner. A third Nieuport, flown by 2nd Lieutenant Eric Gordon Nuding, was badly shot up. He crashed behind the British lines, the plane wrecked.

Göring's account of taking down Slee may be ridiculously embellished, but little more than most pilots' memoirs, even when they were aware of the potential for alternative accounts to emerge.

A mad series of turns begins ... loops, turns, zooms, sideslips—we try every trick and stunt. We often ... look certain to collide. The Englishman is a brilliant, skilled and dashing flier. I slip down in a turn; my opponent promptly sees his chance and hammers away at me furiously with both his guns ... Once more I pull my machine straight up and fire at the Englishman ... Again he joins battle furiously ... I hurl myself at him with one last desperate effort ... He goes down, turning over and over; his engine stops—shot to pieces. He catches his machine when close above the ground and attempts to make a landing, but fails and crashes. He is thrown out of the machine ... A telephone message from the Front reported the capture of my opponent, an experienced scout pilot who had shot down five German machines.[3]

The sad reality was that Göring's victory over Slee was over a rookie Australian pilot who had only joined No. 1 Squadron from flying school just four days previously. Similarly, Boote had only been with the squadron less than a week. There's sometimes a lingering accusation that Hazell was reckless with his own life and that of the men under him, but this does not accord with the facts: on 7 June 1917 the Allies blew Messines Ridge and the Third Battle of Ypres commenced. Aerial activity levels were extremely high, and the attrition rate correspondingly so. On 21 June a Dublin teenager, 2nd Lieutenant Thomas Malcolmson McFerran, was killed when his Nieuport (B3495) was shot down in a combat involving four enemy aircraft.

In July 1917 Hazell continued to lead the offensive patrols, often two-Flight arrangements, with twelve aircraft, such was the scale of the air war at this stage. On 12 July Hazell scored three aerial victories, but lost another rookie pilot, 2nd Lieutenant R. E. Money-Kyrle, who suffered a broken shin bone in a crash-landing after being shot up in a dogfight initiated by Hazell, in which Money-Kyrle got his sole aerial victory of the war.

On 26 July 1917 Hazell's Military Cross citation was gazetted:

Temp. Lt Thomas Falcon Hazell, Gen. List and RFC

For conspicuous gallantry and devotion to duty. On several occasions he displayed marked courage and determination in attacking and destroying hostile aircraft.[4]

On 10 August Hazell led A Flight on escort duties for eight F.E.2ds of No. 20 Squadron, which were on a photographic mission. The 'Fees' all returned safely, with 108 photographs taken in all, but two of the escorting Nieuports were lost. Hazell and another pilot claimed one Albatros each, but the attrition rate for the squadron, let alone the Flight, was just too high. Those lost were Captain A. B. Jarvis and 2nd Lieutenant J. F. Henderson. Obviously Hazell was the Captain/Flight Commander, and 'Captain Jarvis' held that rank from his Army days. Jarvis was killed and Henderson taken PoW. Although 'who got who' is uncertain, Captain Colin Brown of No. 13 (Naval) Squadron attributes the death of Leutnant Hubner of Jasta 4 to Hazell on 12 August 1917. The high rate of kills and losses that accompany Hazell do not reflect badly on him, but should rather be seen as a consequence of the duties assigned to the squadron: on 12 August the much-praised and highly-regarded Fullard lost two of his Flight (McLaren killed, Read taken PoW) to Göring's Jasta 27. The Germans dropped a message bag a few days later, with letters from Henderson and Read to confirm that they were alive and well. The Third Battle of Ypres was underway, so offensive patrols to frustrate enemy observation, together with escort duties for reconnaissance and photographic missions, were essential. Thousands of lives could be spared by accurate information, and thousands of casualties inflicted by well-ranged artillery; the loss of a dozen scout pilots in the course of supporting these and other operations may not have weighed as heavily on the minds of those planning the missions.

Over the course of July and August 1917, Hazell had eleven confirmed aerial victories. On 24 August he was posted to Home Establishment. While he had served with No. 1 Squadron, Hazell had twenty confirmed aerial victories, one of five pilots to manage this feat with the squadron—remarkable, but equally a reflection of that period of the war in which casualties were appallingly high. What is surprising is that he was not awarded a bar to his Military Cross.

Hazell became an instructor with the Central Flying School, serving in that capacity for nearly ten months. His promotion from Lieutenant (Temporary Captain) to Major (Flying) upon appointment as Instructor was gazetted on 16 August 1918. However, by this stage, Hazell had returned to action with No. 24 Squadron. It's often thought of as quite 'Irish' on account of the early aces, such as Byrne and Cowan, but the highest-scoring Irish aces with the squadron were McElroy and Hazell in 1918. The American ace, Bill Lambert, recalls Hazell arriving on 28 June, and that 'Hazell was an outstanding air-fighter but very reckless. He seemed not to worry about danger.' On 4 July 1918 he scored a victory over a Fokker D.VII, sending it down out of control near Cerisy. Over the course of July 1918 he was to obtain five further aerial victories when flying the SE.5a (E1388), four of which were against well-defended balloon targets. However, the recklessness needed to attack these targets was matched by an equally onerous responsibility for executing ground attack missions effectively. Interestingly, the American ace Lambert was quite prepared to follow Hazell into almost any situation, but baulked at the prospect of shooting horses as part of a ground strafing operation. Still, he had plenty of admiration and respect for Hazell's determination.

Hazell mentioned a balloon he had seen in the same spot for the past few days and said 'Tomorrow I'm going to try for that one.' Knowing Hazell, I mentally bet two to one on his getting it ... About 12.30 Hazell's six S.E.5s roared away over the tops of the trees. He had been talking during lunch of going after balloons as soon as they had delivered all their bombs. Once he had made up his mind to do something neither 'hell nor high water' could stop him. The word 'fear' was not in his vocabulary. He seemed to bear a charmed life and any number of times had returned with his aeroplane full of holes.[5]

On 8 August 1918, according to RAF Communiqué No. 19 of 1918, Hazell opportunistically engaged in a ground attack, firing at guns and limbers which were on the road to Rosieres. Several units broke away into the fields and got bogged down. The S.E.5a was not armoured for ground attack operations, and any successful attacks on ground targets usually brought it into the effective range of small arms fire from ground forces. However, Hazell was to achieve an outstanding eleven aerial victories in that month alone. He also had a spectacular escape. In Illingworth's history of the squadron, Hazell's survival is recorded in an incident against Jasta 4 on 22 August 1918:

> Hazell again put up a marvelous show when sent out to keep balloons down, and deliberately shot one down under the very noses of its escort of seven Fokkers, which afterwards came down and riddled his machine with holes—petrol tank first shot—then his propeller and two longerons, in spite of which he fought his way back with eyes full of petrol, and landed in the aerodrome within thirty minutes of starting off.[6]

The great German ace, Leutnant Ernst Udet, in his autobiography *Mein Fliegerleben* (published in English as *Ace of the Black Cross*), describes the encounter in which he claimed Hazell as his sixtieth victory.

> An excited voice on the telephone: 'Two balloons have just been shot down here. The enemy squadron is still circling over our position.'
>
> We take off at once, the entire fourth Staffel with all available machines. We head towards Braie at three thousand metres altitude. Below us the chain of German balloons, obliquely above us the English Flight, consisting of five S.E.5s ... Suddenly, one of them darts past me down towards the balloons. I push down and go after him. It is their leader. The narrow streamer flaps in front of me. I push down, down, down. The wind screams in my cables. I must catch him, stop him from getting to the balloons.
>
> Too late! The shadow of his aircraft glides across the taut skin of the balloon like a fish through shallow water. A pin-point of blue flame quickly spreads over the whole ill-fated balloon. At the next moment a fountain of fire shoots up where, just a moment ago, the golden yellow bag had floated with a silken glow ... In a very tight turn, the Englishman goes almost straight down. The troops at the balloon cable winch scatter, but the S.E.5 has already flattened out and sweeps westward, hugging the ground. He is down so low that the machine and its shadow merge into one. But now I am on his tail and a wild chase begins, hardly three metres above ground. We hop telegraph poles and dodge trees. A mighty jump, the church steeple of Marécourt, but I hang on to him. I'm not about to let go.
>
> We fly parallel with the main road leading to Arras. Flanked by high trees ... He flies to the right of the trees, I to the left. Every time there is a gap in the trees I fire.

Alongside the road, on a meadow, German infantry is camped. Although I am on his neck, he fires at them. This is his undoing.

At that moment I jump the treetops—hardly ten metres separate us—and fire. A tremor runs through his machine; it wavers, tumbles into a spin, hits the ground, bounces up again like a stone rebounding from the water, and disappears in a mighty hop behind a small birch grove. A dust cloud rises.[7]

Udet then describes an indecisive encounter with the other three S.E.5s intent on vengeance. However, despite the dramatic ending Udet thought he had seen, Hazell managed to nurse home his crippled aircraft (B8422). It was struck off the squadron strength, beyond repair.

Hazell finished the war with a remarkable forty-three aerial victories to his name. He was No. 24 Squadron's highest-scoring pilot. Although the victory standards vary from Air force to Air Force, Hazell's overall score would be the joint 21st highest score of the war if one were to regard all victory claims equally. The citation for Hazell's bar to the DFC was gazetted on 2 November 1918:

Lieut. (T./Capt.) Thomas Falcon Hazell, MC, DFC

This officer has accounted for twenty-seven enemy machines and four kite balloons. On the 8th August he shot down two machines out of control, and destroyed a third in the air. In these combats he was so heavily engaged that all his instruments were wrecked, and only one strand of his elevator control cable was intact. Relentless in attack, Capt. Hazell displays disregard of personal danger in a marked degree. (The award of the DFC to this officer is also announced in this Gazette. MC gazetted 26th July 1918.)[8]

As may be noted, Hazell's achievements were outstripping the rate at which military honours were being awarded. Confusingly, his DFC citation was also gazetted in the same issue:

Lieut. (T./Capt.) Tom Falcon Hazell, MC

This officer is conspicuous for his bravery and skill, having destroyed twenty enemy machines and four kite balloons. On one occasion, while attacking troops on the ground, he observed seven enemy scouts above him; he at once engaged them, shooting down one out of control. Some days later he, with another pilot, attacked a kite balloon, driving it down in flames; they then attacked a second balloon, driving it down in a deflated condition. (The award of a bar to the DFC is also announced in this Gazette; MC gazetted 26th July 1918.)[9]

On 5 November 1918 the Air Ministry announced that Hazell had been promoted to Acting Major, with effect from 22 October 1918. He was appointed to the command of No. 203 Squadron, the former No. 3 (Naval) Squadron of the great Irish naval ace Francis Dominic Casey. (Naval squadrons and aces are far beyond the scope of this book.) Hazell's appointment was to replace the hugely respected Raymond Collishaw, and Hazell was the first non-Canadian to command the squadron. According to Leonard 'Tich' Rochford, Hazell gave some of his best and most experienced pilots an opportunity to return to Home Establishment.

> Shortly after assuming command Hazell, who I suspect, had been looking at squadron personnel records, commented on the rather long time I had been with them and suggested that I might like a spell on Home Establishment. This was the last thing I wanted as not only were our tails well up and victory in sight but I was enjoying my flying as much as ever. When I explained this to him Hazell said 'All right, Tich, but just let me know whenever you feel you've had enough.'[10]

These actions date to October 1918 and seem to contradict the idea of any lingering recklessness or extravagance with men's lives.

Hazell's military honours were still only catching up with his astonishing kill rate. The award of the DSO was gazetted on 9 February 1919, which clearly makes reference to his September 1918 exploits with No. 24 Squadron.

Capt. (A./Maj.) Tom Falcon Hazell, MC, DFC1 (FRANCE)

> A brilliant fighter, distinguished for his bold determination and rare courage, he has accounted for twenty-nine enemy machines, twenty being destroyed and nine driven down out of control; he has also destroyed ten balloons. On 4th September he rendered exceptionally valuable service in leading his Flight to attack hostile balloons that were making a certain road impassable.
>
> Within an hour three of these balloons were destroyed, Major Hazell accounting for two. (MC gazetted 26th July, 1917; DFC gazetted 2nd November 1918, Bar to DFC same date.) [11]

Hazell's brother Cecil resigned his commission as Captain in the Royal Marines on 25 April 1919. Hazell's career, at this stage, was also on a slight downward trajectory, as he lost rank in the post-war era, for he relinquished the rank of Acting Major with effect from 2 April 1919. Nevertheless, by 1 August 1919 he had been promoted to Captain (Aeroplane).[12]

The RAF Pageant at Hendon became a major event during the interwar years, but Hazell was one of the billed highlights for the inaugural event in July 1920—he engaged in the destruction of a balloon, his wartime party piece.

On 30 June 1922 Hazell was among those promoted from Flight Lieutenant to Squadron Leader in the Air Ministry's bi-annual promotion list. Hazell commanded No. 45 Squadron at RAF Hinaidi, Iraq. Basil Embry, later Air Chief

Marshal, served there from October 1922, during which time the squadron was undergoing transition, from 'the Flying Camels' engaged in troop transportation, mail services, and some ground support operations, to a bomber unit. The two Flight Commanders under Hazell were Ralph Cochrane and Robert Saundby, the latter a First World War ace like Hazell. (These Flight Commanders were to become Air Chief Marshal the Hon. Sir Ralph Cochrane GBE, KCB, AFC, and Air Marshal Sir Robert Saundby KCB, KBE, MC, DFC, AFC.) Hazell's squadron had recently received the Vickers Vernon, a twin-engined troop transporter. However, by November 1922 Arthur 'Bomber' Harris took command. One gets the impression that Embry approved of the change of leadership.

> Harris took over command from Hazell and at once made himself felt. With that driving force and ruthless will to get things done which are characteristic of him … he transformed the unit from an ordinary squadron capable only of transport work into a highly efficient fighting unit, with a bombing capability second to no other squadron in the RAF at that time … He also tightened up discipline, which had become a little lax in the carefree existence of life in an undeveloped country.[13]

However, a confusing sequence of Air Ministry notices indicate that Squadron Leader Hazell was transferred from No. 55 (Iraq Command) to command No. 45 Squadron (Iraq Command) with effect from 1 November 1922, but by 21 November 1922 had reverted to command of No. 55 Squadron. There was some difference between the squadrons: No. 55 Squadron was involved in what could euphemistically be described as 'air policing' operations, although most of the tribes subjected to military aerial bombardment from D.H.9As would dispute any definition that bore even the slightest resemblance to policing or patrolling. It's unclear whether Hazell's command of either squadron was for any appreciable length of time.

On 15 March 1923 it was announced that Major Hazell's arranged marriage to a Miss Riddick would not be taking place. It's unclear whether Hazell would otherwise have been left with a spare ring at the altar or whether he called it off. However, in other respects Hazell was becoming 'non-effective', as he was transferred from No. 55 Squadron to RAF Depot (non-effective pool) on 22 July 1923 on transfer to Home Establishment. He need not have feared for No. 55 Squadron: by November 1923 it was under the command of the former Royal Dublin Fusilier, Squadron Leader Edward Roux Littledale Corballis.

Hazell was assigned to No. 111(F) Squadron, Duxford, to command with effect from 1 December 1923.[14] This was an old airfield that had been used by No. 8 Squadron during the war and No. 2 Flying Training School until April 1923, when No. 19 Squadron was re-formed there. However, the No. 111 Squadron ORB states that in October 1923 it was reformed under its original number as a fighter squadron for Home Defence duties, with headquarters and one Flight at Duxford, and on 1 April 1924 the establishment was increased by an additional Flight and equipped with Sopwith Snipes. A third Flight was formed on 1 January 1925, and the squadron equipped with Siddeley Siskins (Jaguar Engine Mark III, 375 hp). The squadron was commanded by Hazell from 1 December 1923 to 8 February 1925, and on his posting overseas was temporarily commanded by Flight Lieutenant H. W. Woollett until Squadron Leader G. W. Roberts assumed command on 2 March 1925.[15] (In addition to being at Duxford as a Home Defence Squadron, from April 1925 onwards it became involved in the training of pupils as a pilots, i.e. a Flying Training School role of sorts, but by late 1925 the first Siskin III fitted with the Jaguar Mk.IV supercharged engine arrived from the contractors. The squadron therefore became the first true high-altitude RAF squadron.)

Unfortunately for Hazell, his next posting was to command another bomber squadron. He was appointed to No. 60 Squadron on 27 March 1925. For those with an interest in the First World War, the squadron number will forever be associated with fighters; but, by 1925, the new No. 60 Squadron was flying the D.H.9A. On 4 April 1925 Hazell crashed a D.H.9A (H52) on landing at Sorarogha, North-West Frontier, India. He survived but the aircraft was a 'Category W' wreck. It appears to have been an unlucky aircraft, having been previously crashed by No. 60 Squadron and No. 27 Squadron prior to that. Both of these squadrons had rotated a Flight at particular locations, so it's possible that some of the more difficult aircraft were left *in situ* and taken on the books of the relevant squadron in the course of each reorganisation.

Hazell continued his migration around the airfields and depots. On 11 June 1927 he was posted to RAF Depot, Uxbridge. This was the HQ for the Air Defence of Great Britain (ADGB) due to its proximity to London, but Hazell was not involved in this aspect of Uxbridge. Hazell was placed on the retired list at his own request, which was gazetted on 19 July 1927.

We cannot know whether Hazell continued to reside in the UK for any appreciable length of time following his retirement. In the Second World War, he served from February 1944 onwards as Company Commander of 'D' Company, Pattingham Home Guard, which formed part of the 24th Staffordshire (Tettenhall) Battalion. He died at Newport, Co. Mayo, on 4 September 1946.

12

HEGARTY,
Herbert George
(8 aerial victories)

Born: 31 October 1887, Co. Galway
Died: 14 December 1953
Awards: Military Cross, Mentioned in Despatches

Hegarty's parents were Dr John Adam Hegarty of Clonbur, Go. Galway, and Blanche du Moulin Dockeray, from Dublin. Blanche's father was John William Dockeray, a prominent Church of Ireland clergyman, and had at one stage served as Rector of Cong in the Diocese of Tuam.

The Irish census of 1901 records Herbert's parents and one of his sisters (Pauline Ruth) as resident in Clonbur, Co. Galway, with three servants. In this census Hegarty is recorded as being a student at Portora Royal School, Enniskillen, Co. Fermanagh. He uses 'George' and not 'Herbert' as his first name in the census return. Portora had many famous past pupils, such as Oscar Wilde and Samuel Beckett, and alumni of aviation-related interest, such as Desmond Arthur, the pre-war aviation pioneer—and supposed 'Ghost of Montrose'. Hegarty was one of several to serve with the RFC, joined by Donegal man 2nd Lieutenant Herbert Augustus Johnston.

The Irish census of 1911 records Hegarty's parents as still being resident in Clonbur with two servants, and that they had four children. Herbert George's siblings, besides Pauline Ruth, were brother Cecil and sister Mary Emily Catherine Moira. This sister married General Sir Edward Pellew Quinan—the brother of Barrington 'Punch' Quinan, a Calcutta-born Irishman who was killed in the First World War serving with the RFC. Mary ultimately became Lady Quinan. As may be noted in the 1911 census return, neither Herbert George nor his brother Cecil are present in Ireland. By this stage Cecil had moved to Canada and Herbert George had emigrated from Ireland to Hong Kong. He worked with the Hong Kong & Shanghai Banking Corporation (HSBC) from 1911 until his enlistment.

Herbert George's brother Cecil was the first to enlist: Lance-Corporal Cecil John Hegarty (regimental number 24259) was assigned to the 13th Battalion, 3rd Infantry Brigade.[1] Looking at an actual scan of the Attestation Paper for Cecil, it would appear that he had previous military experience in the Irish Yeomanry. He enlisted on 22 September 1914, and was ultimately to rise to the rank of Captain.

Hegarty's uncle (Blanche's brother), Cecil Eustace Dockeray, was killed on 29 April 1916 in the Easter Rising. British soldiers shot Dockeray and William John Rice, who were both night clerks at the Arthur Guinness brewery. They were killed in separate incidents, together with two Canadian officers, a Lieutenant Worswick and a Lieutenant Lucas of the 2nd King Edward's Horse. The Guinness Brewery had made great efforts to encourage its staff to enlist in support of the British war effort and—following the usual token court martial hearing and exoneration of the British soldiers who'd done the shooting—Guinness made the point of issuing a statement to refute any suggestion that the murdered men had been in any way associated with Sinn Féin, an uncharacteristic act of defiance on the company's part.

Like his brother, Hegarty had quite some pre-war military training prior to enlistment. He was a member of the Scouts Company of the Hong Kong Volunteer Corps. Lieutenant-Colonel A. Chapman, Commander of the HKV Corps, provided a detailed breakdown of Hegarty's pre-war service in the ranks. Hegarty joined as a private on 23 October 1911, and was promoted to Lance Corporal on 24 October 1912, Corporal on 7 January 1914, Sergeant on 25 August 1914, and Sergeant Major on 12 February 1916. He was commissioned as a 2nd Lieutenant on 11 May 1916, as mentioned in the *London and China Telegraph* of 17 July.

Hegarty returned to Europe to enlist, but via a curious route. On 3 or 4 April 1917 Herbert G. Hegarty arrived at Victoria, British Columbia, from Hong Kong on the SS *Empress of Russia*. It would not appear that Hegarty had travelled from Hong Kong to Canada to enlist, but if he had and was rejected on the grounds of health or suitability, I cannot locate a corresponding file in respect of Hegarty on the database of Attestation Papers and Enlistment Forms of the Canadian Expeditionary Force.

The passenger lists of the SS *St Paul* show that Hegarty travelled First Class from New York to Liverpool in April 1917, arriving in Liverpool on the 30th. His occupation is put down as 'banker's assistant' and his country of last permanent residence China, although his address is given as 'Poliska, Clonbur, Co. Galway'. In all likelihood Hegarty, by then thirty years of age, had the intention of enlisting in Canada with persons known to him or his brother, but continued to the UK to do so instead.

Hegarty's Air Ministry service records state that his date of birth was 31 October 1887 and that his permanent home address was Poliska House, too (and which is still in existence).[2] Hegarty's next-of-kin is recorded as Mrs E. J. Hegarty of 'Lampeter, Mount Hermon, Woking, Surrey'. His records state that in civilian life Hegarty was a banker with the Hong Kong & Shanghai Banking Corporation (HSBC) from 1909 to 1917. Confusingly, his work address is given as 9 Gracechurch St, the bank's HQ in the City of London. However, Hegarty may have originally been based in the bank's London operations in 1909, prior to his move to Hong

Kong in 1911. Hegarty's War Office service records include positive mention from Lieutenant-Colonel Chapman, who wrote:

> This officer has an excellent record for keenness and efficiency in all the ranks in which he has served. His personality and manner leave nothing to be desired.[3]

Lieutenant-Colonel Chapman had issued a certificate—dated 8 March 1917—to grant leave for the duration of the war from the Hong Kong Volunteer Corps. An illegible note from another Chinese-based officer—dated 9 March—stated, 'in my opinion, 2nd Lieutenant Hegarty will make a very good officer.' The local bank manager in the Primrose Hill branch also provided a character reference. Hegarty's application for a commission stated that while on leave he would be drawing £400 per annum from the bank, so he had some private means available.

Regardless of how Herbert George Hegarty reached the RFC, he passed his medical examination on 31 May 1917, and was promoted to Temporary 2nd Lieutenant with effect from 8 June 1917.[4] Hegarty reported to the School of Military Aeronautics on 8 June. He began his training with No. 5 TS on 14 July 1917, and transferred to No. 28 TS on 13 September, being appointed Flying Officer with effect from 8 September. On 15 September Hegarty was transferred to the 2 Aerial School of Aeronautics, subsequently being posted to the Central Flying School's 'A' Squadron on 16 October.

On 28 November 1917 Hegarty finally got to a frontline squadron, No. 60 Squadron, which by this stage was flying S.E.5s. It was one of the elite units of the RFC and by the end of the war had achieved over 300 aerial victories. The two pilots most associated with it are the Victoria Cross winners Albert Ball and Billy Bishop. However, it also boasted four Irish aces—Hegarty, Molesworth, Sydney Pope, and Alfred William Saunders—and numerous Irishmen among its early commanding officers. However, by the time of Hegarty's arrival in the squadron in November 1917 both Molesworth and Pope had moved on. On 18 November 1917 Pope was brought down near St Julien, and he returned to Home Establishment on account of his wounds.

Hegarty's impact was not immediate: he did not achieve his first victory until 28 January 1918, when he sent an Albatros D.V down out of control near Kortemarck. Hegarty was to steadily increase his score over the following months, with two aerial victories in February, one of which went down in flames. On 16 February Hegarty's S.E.5a (B523) came down with engine failure, but both he and the aircraft were saved. On 26 March 1918 Hegarty crashed S.E.5a (B523) just outside the aerodrome, due to engine failure upon return from offensive patrol. He survived without injury but was quite shaken. Just days later, on 30 March, Hegarty destroyed another Albatros D.V, this time in a different S.E.5a (C5381) from the jinxed B523. RFC Communiqué No. 133 of 1918—one of its final communiqués prior to amalgamation into the RAF—records Hegarty's victory of 30 March 1918, in which he crashed an enemy aircraft near the village of Theux after chasing it down to 500 feet.[5]

Hegarty had no qualms over getting in close with the S.E.5a, something that was considered tactically hazardous and not the best use of the aircraft's superior climb and dive performance. RAF Communiqué No. 7 of 1918 record's Hegarty's victory of 14 May 1918, one of two credited to him that month.

> 2Lt H. G., Hegarty, 60 Sqn, observed an EA two-seater flying west at a low height. Lt Hegarty attacked the EA and fired 300 rounds at a range of 100 yards, closing until he almost collided with the EA. The EA side-slipped to the ground and attempted to land on a small hill with trenches on the crest, ran into the trenches and half turned over.[6]

There's a suggestion that Hegarty shared in the destruction of an LVG on 21 May 1918, but although Captain Belgrave appears to refer to the involvement of Hegarty and a Lieutenant Duncan, neither were credited with a share of the kill. Hegarty's period of service with the squadron had a significant overlap with Dubliner Alfred William Saunders's. Neither appear to be mentioned in the same sentence in any of the memoirs of those who flew with No. 60 Squadron, for instance those of the New Zealander Captain A. J. L. Scott; and yet, Saunders took command of 'A' Flight in July 1918, so he and Hegarty were necessarily overlapping in combat missions. There's a widely-published photograph of Hegarty and Saunders arm-in-arm in front of the Albatros D.Va (5734/17, which became RAF G159) that Lieutenant W. J. A. Duncan had captured. (Duncan is balanced precariously on the machine and on Saunders's shoulder, so perhaps Saunders's arm around Hegarty is a gesture of physical support, too, rather than affection.) Hegarty's final victories are generally recorded as having occurred on 30 June and 1 July 1918. On these two consecutive days he flew an S.E.5a (D5992), destroying an Albatros D.V near Rainecourt and a Halberstadt C near Bray.

However, Hegarty's service record claims that he was transferred to No. 99 Squadron on 20 June 1918 to be Temporary Captain. *The London Gazette* of 5 July 1918 refers to Hegarty's appointment as Temporary Captain with effect from 13 June 1918. It would therefore appear that Hegarty remained with and fought for No. 60 Squadron regardless of any notional appointment date elsewhere when promoted. Hegarty was transferred from No. 60 Squadron to Home Establishment on 16 July 1918.

> Captain Hegarty left for HE on 16 July and the same day, in Hegarty's former aircraft, his replacement, Captain Dell-Clarke, took off and crashed five minutes later while doing low-level aerobatics over the aerodrome and was killed.[7]

Hegarty was awarded the Military Cross; its citation was gazetted on 18 September 1918:

T./2nd Lt Herbert George Hegarty, RAF

For conspicuous gallantry and devotion to duty on offensive patrols. During recent operations he destroyed four enemy machines and drove down two. He is a bold and fearless pilot, and has done splendid work.[18]

Hegarty's service record also makes reference to 'Major-General J. M. Salmond, RAF Communiqué No. 9' in respect of the Military Cross. This suggests that the award may have been based on the combat report the latter submitted to the Air Ministry for the period 27 May to 2 June 1918.

Hegarty was assigned to No. 4 School of Aerial Fighting, at Freiston in Lincolnshire, serving there from 8 August 1918 to 6 February 1919 when he was released to Oswestry in Shropshire for dispersal. On 28 March 1919 the Air Ministry announced that Hegarty had been placed on the Unemployed List with effect from 6 February 1919.

In the immediate interwar period Hegarty's Irish family were to become reasonably well known in the horticultural world. A pink variety of the Kaffir Lily (Schizostylis coccinea) is named 'Mrs Hegarty', after his mother Blanche. Her stock of Schizostylis at Poleska, Clonbur, came from Lord Mountmorres of Ebor Hall, Clonbur. (This chap was assassinated on 25 September 1880 near Rusheen, probably not for evicting tenants—which he regularly did—but for his role as a magistrate. Herbert's father, Dr John Hegarty, had to attend the scene, finding six gunshot wounds on the body.) Blanche Hegarty's lily was exhibited in London and won an Award of Merit in 1921. The Hegartys are believed to have made a tidy sum from the lily.

An examination of passenger records indicates that on 1 April 1919 Hegarty travelled on the SS *Tamba Maru* from Birkenhead, destined for Yokohama, Japan. He travelled alone, First Class, and recorded as a permanent resident of China. Although there's a passing reference to Hegarty in the *Singapore Free Press and Mercantile Advertiser* of 26 June 1920, he did not remain permanently the Far East: on 14 September 1923 Hegarty travelled on the *Caledonia* from London to Hong Kong. On this occasion he took his wife Eleanor and their two children, Eleanor (aged three) and Patrick (aged one); the family travelled First Class. His occupation was still a 'banker' and their former address in the UK was 'Lampeter, Mount Hermon, Woking, Surrey.' It would appear that a nurse, Ms Lily Lunn, accompanied them.

It's unclear how long Hegarty served with HSBC in Hong Kong. He died on 14 December 1953 a resident of Allens, Beercrocombe, Taunton (in Somerset). In recent years his service and gallantry medals have been auctioned on more than one occasion, most recently selling for £5,000 from Spink of London in November 2012. (The auction catalogue contains an interesting photograph of Hegarty with a delegation of pilots from the Imperial Japanese Navy.) They are now available once more, from the London Medal Company. The auction house have, on this occasion, included details of almost twenty aerial combats in which Hegarty was engaged.

HERON,
Oscar Aloysius Patrick
(13 aerial victories)

Born: 17 September 1896, Co. Armagh
Died: 5 August 1933, Dublin
Awards: Distinguished Flying Cross, Croix de Guerre (Belgium)
Commemorated: Glasnevin Cemetery, Dublin

Captain Oscar Heron was the eldest son of Charles and Annie Heron (née McKenna). The Irish census of 1901 records the family as resident at English Street Lower in Armagh Town. Oscar was the eldest of three sons. His parents were both primary school teachers. The family also had a domestic servant. By 1911 the family had moved to Banbrook Hill, in the north of Armagh City, in a house adjacent to the local school. Oscar's grandfather, Jeremiah McKenna, was resident with them at the time, a widowed pensioner originally from Limerick City. Oscar's father Charles was from Co. Tyrone, while his mother Annie was from Co. Kildare. The family had three domestic servants present, one of whom, Anne Doody, was aged sixty and from Co. Kildare, which would suggest that she had been formerly on the staff of Jeremiah McKenna. Oscar's father, Charles, was the Principal of St Patrick's National School, Banbrook Hill.

Oscar Heron was appointed Temporary 2nd Lieutenant (on probation) with effect from 13 December 1917.[1] Heron would appear to have trained as a pilot without any period spent as an observer. Shortly after the formation of the RAF on 1 April 1918, Heron was assigned to No. 70 Squadron. He did not have the most auspicious start with the squadron. On 20 May he experienced a bad landing in a Sopwith Camel (D6568) after losing his way during a practice flight. He came down on No. 205 Squadron's airfield. On 11 June Heron crashed Camel D1804, a venerable old machine that had served with two other squadrons; he was injured, but not seriously.

On 30 June 1918 Heron scored his first aerial victories in Sopwith Camel D6492, sending down an Albatros D.V out of control and destroying another in flames. His combat report indicates that Heron was flying 'DOP', the 'deep offensive patrol' so bitterly hated by many pilots, not least among them Air Vice-Marshal Arthur Gould Lee MC. Flying in hostile territory to bring on an enemy attack left the initiative and advantage to the Germans: they could chose to engage or simply leave the RAF pilots to fly aimlessly until engine trouble or weather conditions changed in favour of a German attack. And if a German pilot suffered injury or his aircraft any damage he could immediately attempt a landing, whereas the RAF pilots would likely to be taken prisoner, or killed in the descent from the ground fire brought to bear on a stricken aircraft. The DOP in the First World War was not the equivalent of the Rodeo fighter sweeps of the Second World War, for in the latter conflict there was air-to-air and air-to-ground communication capability, whereas in the former the pilots had to rely on signal flares and waggling wings.

Heron's report shows the superior manoeuvrability of the Camel in dogfights, and the extent to which pilot training had improved over the course of the war, such that a young and inexperienced pilot like himself would still have good positional awareness.

While on a DOP with 15 Camels at about 15,000 feet, I saw 9 E.A. below me and at about 12,000 feet. I dived down on the tail of one and fired about 200 rounds into him at a range of 25 feet. He zoomed, stalled, fell on his back and spun down to about 1,000 feet obviously out of control, and seemingly with his engine on. I could not see him right down as a second E.A. above me attacked me. He shot off my windscreen. I side-slipped, zoomed, did two half rolls, and got on his tail, and fired about 300 rounds and saw him dive in flames. Three E.A.—apparently Fokker biplanes—then attacked me from above. I did vertical banks and half rolled, firing at every opportunity. They drove me down to 2,000 feet. I then dived westwards.

Heron's commanding officer noted that Lieutenant Roland McPhee in Camel 8108 had confirmed one of Heron's two kills as going down in flames. McPhee actually engaged an Albatros that had attempted to get on Heron's tail when he was closing for the kill on the second Albatros, but did not get a decisive burst of fire at it. Another Albatros went down smoking, but this was accredited to Captain John Todd, their Flight Commander.

On 15 August Heron's Camel (D6492) stalled on landing. Once again he survived without serious injury. On 19 August Heron, Captain Walter McFarlane Carlaw, and Lieutenant Wilson manned a three-Camel offensive patrol over Dickebusch Lake at a height of 15,000 feet, when they observed five Fokker biplanes diving on a patrol of S.E.5s. No. 74 Squadron was to confirm No. 70 Squadron's effectiveness: Carlaw attacked one, which crashed between Warneton and Comines, while Wilson's victim fell just east of Messines. Heron's victim was not a clean kill. Initially he fired 150 rounds at 100 yards' range, which sent the enemy aircraft into a glide—presumably its engine was damaged, or the fuel tank punctured, and so the pilot had to switch off the engine. Heron followed it down eastward, firing a further burst from just 50 yards. The Fokker DVII then began to dive steeply, but Heron followed it down to 5,000 feet, firing continuously until it crashed between Houthem and Hollebeke.

On 28 September 1918 Captain Carlaw and Heron were on a low-flying patrol and bombing mission when they became involved in a series of engagements. Northeast of Passchendaele, Heron was flying in Camel D6696 at just 1,200 feet when he encountered three Fokker DVIIs, which dived on him. He made a climbing turn to evade them and got onto one's tail. The Fokker's fuselage was painted black, with a black and white chessboard check pattern on the rudder. Heron fired 100 rounds at close range and it went into a fatal spin. When a French SPAD came to Heron's assistance, the two remaining Fokkers climbed away into cloud cover. Heron's account was verified by a 2nd Lieutenant Copp, who saw the German aircraft crash.

Two days later, on 1 October, Heron was flying a low-line patrol near Ardoye in Camel E7201 when he spotted an L.V.G. two-seater, which had a dark blue fuselage, speckled wings, and a rudder painted with black and white stripes. Heron dived past him, did a climbing turn, and dived under the two-seater, firing in short bursts into the underside of the fuselage. The German went down in a series of stalls, then lurched into a dive and spin, hitting the ground in a vertical dive. Most likely the pilot was dead or dying, and the altitude would have been too low for the observer to make a successful parachute descent, if indeed he was still alive and sufficiently uninjured to attempt escape, that is. This was to be Heron's only aerial victory against a German two-seater: all his other kills came against the excellent Fokker DVII fighter. Over the course of October 1918 Heron was credited with nine aerial victories, the joint highest score of any RAF or USAS pilot on the Western Front that month. The other nine-kill ace of the month was Captain Camille Henri Raoul Lagesse, who flew S.E.5as with No. 29 Squadron. In fact, the final months of the war were invigorated by the success of the S.E.5a; its top pilots were the Canadian 'Dozy' Claxton in June, Irishman G. E. H. McElroy in July, South African A. W. Beauchamp-Proctor in August, and balloon-busting Englishman Sidney Highwood in September. However, Heron's success in a Camel-equipped squadron does make him stand out.

Heron also shared the capture of a Fokker D.VII on 9 October 1918. RAF Communiqué No. 28 of 1918 refers to Heron taking on fifteen Fokker biplanes, destroying two, and saving another Camel pilot's life.[2] RAF Communiqué No. 29 of 1918, which covered the period from 14 to 20 October 1918, records Heron's award of the DFC, although this was not announced generally at the time. Heron's achieved his final aerial victory on 28 October, in a large-scale engagement in which six Fokkers were claimed by Heron's Flight. The next day, the Air Ministry announced that Heron had been promoted to Temporary Captain while employed in an acting capacity as Captain (Aeroplane). Heron's DFC citation was gazetted on 8 February 1919:

2nd Lt (Acting Capt.) Oscar Alois Patrick Heron (France)

An officer conspicuous for his skill and daring in aerial combats. He has accounted for eight enemy aeroplanes. On 28 September he attacked, single-handed, three Fokkers; one of these he shot down. On another occasion he, in company with five other machines, engaged six Fokkers, all six being destroyed, 2nd Lieutenant Heron accounting for two.[3]

On 21 April 1919 Heron experienced a hard landing in Sopwith Snipe E8198, losing part of the undercarriage. No. 70 Squadron only received their Snipes at the end of February, but by April had suffered almost a dozen serious incidents.

The conferral of the Belgian *Croix de Guerre* on Heron was gazetted in July 1919.[4] His rank was then described as '2nd Lieutenant, Acting Captain', so he was serving at two grades above his home rank, which was typical for temporary Flight commanders. In August Heron was graded as Captain for purposes of pay and allowances from 1 May 1919 while employed as Captain (Aeroplane). However, Heron was transferred to the Unemployed List with effect from 10 August 1919.[5] However, a subsequent notice in October 1919 indicates that he was appointed Flying Officer from Pilot Officer.[6] It would appear that he was posted to India on a short service commission.

In March 1921 Heron got married in Bangalore, yet strangely enough, his service location is given as RAF Ambala—over 1,300 miles away. The ecclesiastical returns for the British India office show the marriage to have taken place on St Patrick's Day (17 March), at St Patrick's Cathedral, Bangalore. Heron's wife, Jose Jonlaz, was four years older than him. On 21 June Heron arrived at Liverpool on the *City of Poona,* an Ellerman Line steamship, returning from Bombay via Karachi.

Curiously, Heron's service record is largely empty.[7] Heron transferred to Reserve Class 'C' on 7 November 1922, and relinquished his commission with effect from 7 November 1926. However, it is not inconceivable that Heron joined the *Cabhlach Eitleacht Éireann* shortly after it was reconstituted as the Irish Air Corps. Heron's promotion to the rank of Captain may well have taken place in the context of the unstable and fluid situation in the new Irish flying service: allegedly Captain John Arnott (Acting Second-in-Command of Flying) was frog-marched to the dock at gunpoint when it was discovered that he had been a member of the 'Black and Tans'.

By this stage Heron's native County Armagh had—through the provisions of the Government of Ireland Act 1920 of December that year—been absorbed into Northern Ireland. No partition of Ireland was ever going to be completely successful, but the arrangement chosen was not reflective of the wishes of the local population in a considerable area of what was being incorporated into the new Northern Ireland. Churchill's reference to the 'dreary steeples' of Fermanagh and Tyrone underplay the deadly nature of British political misjudgment in refusing to allow for an adequate political settlement. The local government elections of January 1920 and 12 June 1920 had seen Nationalist majorities elected in several of the principal local authorities (Counties Fermanagh and Tyrone, and the Londonderry Corporation) that were to become part of Northern Ireland, and many Nationalists had hoped that they would give rise to the realisation of the right to self-determination. (In any event, these councils were suspended for seeking allegiance with the Republic of Ireland.) However, large Unionist minorities existed in Co. Fermanagh and Co. Tyrone. Similarly, Nationalist majorities existed in southern areas of Co. Armagh and Co. Down. Several sub-county local authorities (urban and rural district councils) declared allegiance to *Dáil Éireann*, including Newry and Downpatrick in Co. Down. By the time the Anglo-Irish Treaty came into effect in 1922, the thirty-two-county Republic of Ireland (*Poblacht na hÉireann*) had the allegiance of elected representatives from within Northern Ireland and the Treaty-created Irish Free State (*Saor Stat Éireann*), which was to supersede the Southern Ireland entity of the 1920 partition. One other matter of note in the emerging situation was that the Irish White Cross facilitated tens of thousands of Catholics who had been burned out or otherwise displaced from Northern Ireland. Although the numbers were not large in terms of the overall population or in the context of other comparable European conflicts in the 1920s, many Northern Nationalists saw it as a political admission that Northern Ireland was unwilling or unable to protect its Catholic communities. Heron was one of a small minority of northern Catholics who re-located to the Irish Free State rather than return to Northern Ireland after the First World War. This was, nevertheless, emphatically a freely chosen rather than a forced migration. His brother Charles was to become a Superintendent in *An Garda Síochána*, the Irish Free State police.

Heron joined the Irish Air Corps at an important juncture: the Army Mutiny of 1924 would appear to have been used as a pretext to purge the Irish Air Corps of some of its ex-RAF personnel (William Jasper McSweeney, J. J. Flynn, W. D. Hardy, to name but a few). But Heron did not suffer any particular difficulties though he did have to re-train from being a single-seat fighter pilot to mastering big buses such as the D.H.9 bomber, which the Irish Air Corps acquired several of, for use in a range of reconnaissance and combat roles.

The D.H.9s supplied to the Irish Air Corps were used extensively in the Irish Civil War, when the Irish Free State defeated the forces of the so-called Republic of Ireland and so confirmed its supreme territorial jurisdiction over Southern Ireland. The first two D.H.9s (ex-RAF serials H5797 and H5830) arrived at Baldonnel on 1 January 1923, but D.IV of 'B' Flight, No. 1 Squadron, Irish Air Corps (ex-H5823) crashed just days later, killing Lieutenant R. T. Nevin. Initially there were six D.H.9s in service, with two further aircraft being delivered to replace losses. Heron was involved in a significant milestone in Irish aviation history when on 20 February 1926, two D.H.9s and three Bristol F2.bs undertook the Irish Air Corps' first 'search and rescue' mission. They were deployed in the search for a missing trawler. However, on the return journey Heron's D.H.9 (Irish Air Corps D.V, RAF ex-H5823) suffered engine failure. They crashed near Oughterard, Co. Galway. Both Heron and his observer, Sergeant J. Maher, were unhurt but the aircraft was a write-off.

In October 1929 Heron had a short paper published in the Irish military journal *An t-Oglach*.[8] He argued that in the immediate post-war years the overhang of military surplus had retarded the development of many aspects of civil aviation in Europe, an opinion running counter to the generally held view of the enormous progress made through the adaptation of military aircraft to civil use.

There were large stocks of military machines on hand at the end of the war ... the line of least effort ... was taken, viz. the making of alterations to the existing military machines to convert them to civil use. This habit of modifying existing aircraft in details in preference to striking out on new lines has persisted to the present day in the British construction of aircraft for civil purposes.

A comparison of the exhibits at the British Aero shows of 1920 and 1929 demonstrates very effectively the remarkably slight development that has taken place in the intervening nine years in the design of civil aircraft.

Heron's view was that the aircraft industries in France and Great Britain were heavily dependant on military orders and that this set their priorities in the commissioning of designs and improvement of performance. Furthermore, the relatively small size of these countries and their existing civil infrastructure held against civil aviation. In contrast, Heron viewed the USA on account of its vast size and distance from any potential enemy as allowing for the priorisation of civil aviation. From Ireland's perspective, Heron argued that any civil aviation scheme would need to give due attention to flying clubs, to encourage the technical schools to teach aeronautical engineering skills and trades, and so forth: one gets the impression that Heron was laying down a practical shopping list of achievable demands that would grow the capacity for the dual development of civil and military aviation in Ireland.

Irish Army GHQ had intended to send Captain Heron and Lieutenant A. Russell on an RAF flying instructors' course at the Central Flying School, RAF Wittering, in February 1932.[9] However, Russell was replaced by Lieutenant D. J. McKeown. Then, in early January 1932, it was decided to send only one officer, and Lieutenant W. Keane was selected for the course, which lasted from 2 February to 16 April 1932. Any number of reasons could have applied for the decision not to send Heron; he was ex-RAF, and the Irish Army was making a point of stamping out that culture in favour of a Nationalist mindset for their Air Corps. Similarly, Russell and McKeown were graduates of the 1922–23 wings course. In any event, Keane, a cadet from the 1926–1928 class—who therefore had neither an RAF nor an IRA background—was to perform well at RAF Wittering and became a highly respected instructor in the Irish Air Corps.

Heron was killed on 5 August 1933. He was flying a two-seater Vickers Vespa, with Private Robert Tobin as his crew. They were engaged in a mock dogfight with three Avro Cadets as part of the inaugural Dublin Air Pageant, when Heron failed to successfully pull the aircraft out of a spin. He died in the crash, while Private Robert Tobin died of wounds the following day. They crashed in view of Heron's wife and a crowd of 12,000 at the Phoenix Park. Three days previously, Lieutenant J. P. Twohig was killed in a crash while rehearsing for the air pageant, and Heron had been one of his pall-bearers. Heron left a wife but no family.

14

HUSTON,
Victor Henry
(6 aerial victories)

Born: 13 October 1890, Belfast
Died: 10 April 1941
Awards: Military Cross, Order of Merit (Chile)
Commemorated: St George's Chapel, Westminster Abbey, London

Major Victor Huston was the son of William Wentworth Huston and Elizabeth Victoria Huston (née Simpson). He was one of nine children, and had five sisters and three brothers. The Irish census of 1901 records the family as resident at Waterloo Gardens in the Duncairn Ward of Belfast. Huston's father was originally from Armagh, and his mother from Co. Kildare. The family would appear to have moved around quite a lot: his sisters, Eileen and Dorothy, and his brother, Claud, were born in South Africa, whereas Victor and the others were born in Belfast.[1]

Victor H. Huston sailed on the SS *Lake Manitoba* from Belfast to St John's, Newfoundland, Canada, on 31 March 1910, although it would appear his age was misrecorded as twenty-four instead of twenty. The British Columbia marriage registrations record Huston marrying Sarah Ballie on 11 November 1912. Her parents were Scottish, not Canadian.

Huston joined the Canadian Expeditionary Force (Canadian Army Service Corps) in Vancouver as a corporal (service number 36122) and served with the Divisional Supply Column (Motorized Transport).[2] His Attestation Paper lists his occupation as 'motor engineer' and his previous military service as with the 11th Hussars. He sported a dragon tattoo on his right arm, and had a scar over his left eye and several on the back of his neck. One of his brothers, Private Claud Wentworth Huston, enlisted in Canada on 23 September 1914, but his service number is 18648, and he was assigned to the 9th Battalion, so it would appear that the brothers enlisted in different locations.

Huston arrived in France in 1915. The next-of-kin address for Mrs. Sarah Florence Huston at 90 Castellain Road, Maida Vale, suggests a wartime move to London. Huston was appointed a Temporary 2nd Lieutenant in the Canadian Army Service

Corps with effect from 13 September 1915.[3] Victor's other brother, Corporal Gerald Marcus Huston, was killed on 7 December 1915 while serving with the 7 Signal Company, Royal Engineers; Gerald had been awarded the Distinguished Conduct Medal (DCM) in 1915. One of their sisters, Dorothy, was to serve with the Voluntary Aid Detachment (VAD) as a nurse from 4 February 1918 to 19 October 1919. The fourth of the Huston brothers, Donald, joined the RAF towards the end of the war. (His date of birth was 17 July 1900, so it can be assumed that his enlistment was at the earliest opportunity.) Donald was still stationed at the Cadet Training Wing when the war ended.

Victor Huston did not serve long with the Canadian Army Service Corps; he transferred to the RFC, being assigned to the No. 2 School of Aeronautics on 22 July 1916.[4] Huston transferred from Bournemouth to No. 27 RS, and was then posted to Gosport, on 6 September 1916. Huston was appointed a Flying Officer in December 1916, and posted to No. 18 Squadron from then onwards.[5]

Huston scored his first aerial victory on 15 February 1917, when flying F.E.2b A5445, destroying a German two-seater over Grevillers. On 17 March 1917 (St Patrick's Day), Huston flew F.E.2b 4990 with a Lieutenant E. Ford as his observer on escort to a photography mission, and was forced to land near Thiepval, with their engine and radiator shot through. They fared better than the other photography escort, as Lieutenants Parkinson and Taylor in F.E.2b 4896 crashed after their ailerons and controls were shot away, with Taylor hospitalised for wounds received in the crash.

On 5 April 1917, when flying F.E.2b 4969 with the Irish ace Giles Blennerhasset as his observer, Huston sent down two German Albatros D.II fighters over Inchy. Of the 'Combats in the Air' reports for the squadron, a report on 24 April 1917 indicates that an F.E.2b (4998) piloted by Huston, with a Lieutenant E. A. Ford as his observer, was on photographic duties at 10,000 feet between Baralle and Bourlon when it encountered a number of German aircraft of various types. Huston reported the following:

> Fired one double drum at an Albatros Scout at about 250 yards while he was circling from our left front towards our rear. The tracers appeared to strike the machine, which went down in a vertical nose-dive over Dury.
>
> Fired about 60 rounds with back gun at another Albatros Scout who was diving on the formation from the side. Range about 300 yards. He dived between Baralle and Villers Gagnicourt. A few minutes later a machine was seen on the ground near this point, and a plate was exposed of the place.[6]

And yet, only one aerial victory was attributed to Huston and Ford for the engagement. In February, April and May 1917 Huston was to achieve six aerial victories in all. This was an excellent outcome considering that No. 18 Squadron was not a 'scout' squadron *per se* and that at the outset of Huston's time with the squadron the adverse weather conditions in January 1917 would have limited the opportunities for photographic reconnaissance.

Huston was awarded the Military Cross, which was gazetted on 18 June 1917:

Lt Victor Henry Huston, ASC and RFC

For conspicuous gallantry and devotion to duty He has rendered valuable service when on photographic reconnaissance. He has always shown the greatest skill and courage in leading attacks on hostile machines, and thus enabling valuable photographs to be secured behind the lines.[7]

Huston is one of only a handful of pilots or observers to become an ace with No. 18 Squadron, which was a multifunctional unit during its early years before converting to D.H.4 bombers.

Huston returned to Home Establishment on 7 July 1917, and was assigned to Hendon Aircraft Acceptance Park on 15 August. He was injured on 15 September. There are a number of Medical Boards examinations recorded on his service record, which on 17 October initially certified him as 'unfit for general service, 2 months,' but granted three weeks leave. A further examination on 17 November stated that Huston was again unfit for service for two months, and permitted to undertake light duty but no flying. Huston was then posted to Norwich Aircraft Acceptance Park on 7 December for home service, but no flying duties were permitted. A medical board examination on 10 January 1918 continued to prohibit flying.

However, this did not prevent Huston from being promoted to the office of Temporary Captain, which was gazetted on 7 January 1918, with the appointment dated to 5 August 1917.[8] On 7 March 1918 an assessment permitted limited dual flying duties, but a subsequent assessment stated 'no flying until ordered by next MB.' On 20 March 1918 Huston was appointed Captain, graded as Flight Commander.[9] This was described as a 'special appointment.' However, a medical board assessment of 4 May 1918 stated that Huston was declared 'unfit for general service, 4 weeks,' but was fit for home service flying duties.

Huston was loaned to the Chilean government on 20 September 1918 on 'special duties' for one year. His role was to instruct and assist the Chilean Air Force, for Britain had supplied fourteen seaplanes and fifty aeroplanes to Chile. Huston reported for duty with the Chilean authorities in late October 1918, and various publications there show a photograph of Huston in the company of Lieutenant Armando Cortínez on the 28th, in which Huston appears to be aided by a walking stick rather than carrying an officer's staff. Cortínez has a cigarette in one hand and is helping Huston with the other.

According to Chilean sources, within weeks of arrival, Huston made the first formal proposal to merge the naval and military air arms into an independent Air Force.[10] Colonel Pedro P. Dartnell largely accepted the proposals, but there were still inter-service rivalries and petty empires to overthrow in the course of the unification of aviation services into an independent branch of the Army and Navy. Still, Huston's efforts in training pilots on the new machines meant his voice carried weight when it came to institutional reform.

The Chilean Minister of War announced on 12 December 1918 that a Lieutenant Godoy, of the Military School of Aviation, had that day flown from Santiago to Mendoza in Argentina using a Bristol. It took one-and-a-half hours to fly over the Cordilleras of the Andes, and in so doing establishing a height record. The announcement stated,

> The Minister of War takes this opportunity of congratulating the British Government upon the excellence of this British aeroplane, and feels that the result of the Flight does the greatest honour to the instruction given to Chilean airmen by the British Major Huston.[11]

Huston's instruction duties had indeed borne early fruit: a further telegram confirmed that Lieutenant Godoy flew from Espejo to Mendoza, a distance of 247 miles, in one hour and twenty-eight minutes, maintaining an average height of 20,000 feet.

By January 1919 the first batch of aircraft had reached Valparaiso.[12] These were to form the nucleus of the Chilean air service. Major Huston was to act as chief instructor of the new force, while an Engineer-Lieutenant Solano was to be in charge of the technical side for the Naval section. (The combination of seaplanes and aeroplanes must have given rise to quite a number of logistical headaches.)

On 17 March 1919, St Patrick's Day, the new Chilean Air Force came into existence, with Colonel Pedro Dartnell Encina at its head. However, Huston's work was not finished: on 3 July 1919 he took a Chilean seaplane on its first flight, in a Sopwith Baby Clerget 130-hp engine (No. 2103), in the Bay of Talcahuano. Taking into account local sensitivities, Huston made sure that a Captain Diego Aracena Aguilar also had the honour of making that flight that day.

Huston received the Chilean Order of Merit. However, I have been unable to identify any record of the award being conferred on Huston or any permission granted by the King to facilitate him accepting the honour. (Usually permission to accept foreign military decoration would be published in *The London Gazette*.)

Huston ceased secondment to the RAF with effect from 30 September 1919.[13] Huston returned to Army duty and relinquished his temporary RAF commission with effect from 30 September 1919, which was gazetted on 23 January 1920. His name was incorrectly spelled 'Houston', but a corrected notice was issued in *The London Gazette* of 20 February 1920.[14]

However, these official movements to his Army-*versus*-RAF home grade designations did not affect Huston's service in Chile, where he set a South American altitude record of 7,076 metres on 26 November 1919. Huston flew an S.E.5a.

On 14 December 1920 Huston departed from Valparaiso, Chile, to Liverpool on the SS *Oropesa*. In the passenger lists his profession is still recorded as 'adviser to Chile Govt' and his address as the Chilean Legation in London. Huston's relationship with South America did not end here: on 1 April 1921, Huston was among the 178 passengers on the SS *Andes*, which sailed from Southampton to Buenos Aires. His address is recorded as 32 Westbourne Terrace, London, and his intended final destination Chile.

Huston had been succeeded by a Major Scott, who continued the British-Chilean bilateral cooperation programme, which gave rise to Chilean National Directive No. 6 of August 1925, establishing a *Dirección General de Aeronáutica* under Lieutenant-Colonel Mariano Navarrete.

Victor's youngest sister, Victoria, was to serve in the Women's Auxiliary Air Force (WAAF) in the Second World War and is commemorated on the Glenavy War Memorial as 'LAC V. K. Huston', but records her service branch as 'WRAF', which had been dissolved in 1920. The reference to 'LAC' suggests that Victoria served after 1940, as the rank of Leading Aircraftwoman did not exist in the early stages of the WAAF's existence.

Huston was killed in an air raid on Coventry on 10 April 1941. The Commonwealth War Graves Commission records his address as 66 Dorset House, Gloucester Place, London NW1. He died at Gulson Road Hospital in Warwickshire. Huston's Military Cross and Chilean Order of Merit are recorded, but his age is erroneously put down as forty-five, when in fact he was fifty-one. His wife, Florence, died on 2 February 1948 in British Columbia.

15

KELLY,
Edward Caulfield
(5 aerial victories)

Born: 1896, Galway
Died: 1 July 1942, New Guinea
Commemorated: St George's Chapel, Westminster Abbey, London

Edward Caulfied Kelly was born in Ballinasloe, Co. Galway, to Edward J. and Margaret Kelly. Edward was the eldest of three sons, and their parents ran a hotel on Dunlo Street with his grandmother. Kelly's father and grandmother were from Co. Roscommon, while his mother was from Co. Wicklow.

According to his Air Ministry service record Kelly had been a student at Trinity College Dublin from June 1913 to December 1914.[1] However, he does not appear on the University of Dublin Roll of Honour. There is a somewhat lengthy explanation for this appearing in his Air Ministry records, but it lies in his original application to obtain a commission and not in his RAF career. In July 1915 Kelly sought to join the colours. He was living in Dublin at the time, with an address at the Belvedere Hotel. Kelly sought a commission in either the Royal Dublin Fusiliers 'or any Irish regiment'. His character reference was attested by Rev. J. J. Madden, St Joseph's College, Ballinasloe, and his education by the Director of Skerry's College. Kelly also passed a medical examination on 12 July 1915.

Kelly aimed high. On 14 July 1915 he wrote to Harold John 'Jack' Tennant MP, Under-Secretary of State for War. Tennant was brother-in-law to Prime Minister H. H. Asquith, though not close. Kelly heard nothing further and so on 27 July 1915 he wrote from the family hotel in Ballinasloe to the War Office. Kelly helpfully pointed out that his recommendation had been signed by Colonel Henry Kennard, who served as Officer Commanding of troops in Dublin, was related to the former ADC to the Lord-Lieutenant of Ireland, and would in 1916 help organise the suppression of the Easter Rising in Dublin.

In a minor bureaucratic mix-up Kelly was not actually issued with the standard letter to inform him that his commission would be gazetted—and that he should purchase his officer's uniform and so forth—but H. J. Tennant's parliamentary secretary had been informed that Edward C. Kelly was one of those listed, and so had written to Kelly to that effect. (The individual listed was in fact an Edward Charles Kelly.) But on 6 August 1915 the Director of Military Training at the War Office issued the originally-intended correspondence to Kelly, a PFO, telling him to enlist in the ranks.

> I am directed to inform you it is regretted that there is no prospect of a vacancy occurring to which you could be suitably appointed. I am however to suggest that if you were to enlist, and if after an adequate period of training you were recommended by your Commanding Officer as to being in every respect suitable for appointment to a temporary commission, as further application on your behalf would receive consideration.[2]

Having expected to go in the front door rather than the servants' entrance, so to speak, Kelly would not let the matter rest. He had already purchased his uniform and equipment, too. And so he corresponded with T. J. Hanna at Westminster and with John Redmond MP, leader of the Irish Parliamentary Party. But Redmond had expended great political capital in throwing his weight behind the war effort in the hope of having 'Home Rule' granted to Ireland, and these sorts of incidents were not helpful. Furthermore, Tennant's office then had to issue an awkward clarifying letter, telling Kelly to either enlist or to join the local OTC, i.e. the Inns of Court or the University of Dublin Trinity College OTC. Kelly wrote to John Redmond MP to say that his father wouldn't consent to him joining the OTC and that in recent months over 85 per cent of appointments had been given to men with no military training. Redmond raised the matter with Tennant once again. Hanna's correspondence with Tennant indicates that Redmond personally considered 'this case ... under all the circumstances ... a very hard one.' The background material on file then took a slightly comic turn. One official wrote,

> I think in the light of what has occurred that you should try to fit this man in somehow. You can hardly tell him to go and enlist after he has been informed that he will be gazetted to a commission and has ordered his uniform.

Another official, however, spoke for many when he pronounced that 'this young man appears to be a young publican and not the type who should be put forward as an officer.' Nevertheless, H. J. Tennant MP and John Redmond MP had an understanding that the matter would be resolved.

After some creative reviews of the paperwork, on 23 September 1915 a memo to file stated that Captain Rendell spoke to Colonel Dooher, concluding, 'This candidate to be accepted.' The mysterious Trinity College studies and Officer Training Corps addition to his background arise in this context. On 28 September 1915 Kelly was assigned to the 6th Battalion of the Leinster Regiment, obtaining a commission as a 2nd Lieutenant, attached to the Royal Dublin Fusiliers. His appointment was duly gazetted on 5 October. He was told to report to the school of instruction in Dublin on 9 October 1915.

Kelly's initial training was with the 4th (Special Reserve) Battalion of the Leinsters, which was based at the Curragh Camp in Co. Kildare. In November 1915 Kelly inquired about the possibility of a transfer to the Royal Artillery, which was rejected. Kelly's infantry service history is complex, for although he was with the 6th Leinsters, which were part of 10 (Irish) Division, he was then attached to the 7th Royal Irish Rifles, which were part of 16 (Irish) Division. Consequently, although he was wounded in July 1916 and ultimately invalided from the Front suffering from injuries and 'shell shock', I've been unable to identify the incident in either of the battalion War Diaries. Kelly was sufficiently well to be moved from the field hospital to Boulogne in August 1916 and from there he was returned to England on the HMHS *Cambria*. The Medical Board returns show that he was hospitalised at the 4th London General Hospital, on Denmark Hill, but that he was later granted leave until the next medical examination in late October 1916.

However, something more immediate was worrying Kelly in September 1916, while at home with the 3rd Reserve Battalion of the Leinster Regiment in Cork. Kelly required urgent dental treatment. Accordingly he wrote to the RAMC in Dublin, requesting that his damaged teeth be removed at King George V Hospital in Dublin and that he be fitted for dentures. But although a wounded officer could be granted an artificial appliance or denture, in Kelly's case the teeth were decayed before any damage was sustained on active service. The application was rejected. Kelly moved to a London address in early October 1916. Over the course of October, November, and December 1916 the medical boards made findings of 'severe' disability, which would suggest that the diagnosis of 'shell shock' was one needing regular review.

In November 1916 Kelly applied to transfer to the RFC as an observer. The groundwork he laid down for this application meant it fared better than his near-disastrous bid for an Army commission. In November 1916 Major R. G. T. Currey of 3rd Battalion, Leinster Regiment, gave a reference to state that Kelly was 'well grounded in map reading, use of compass and elementary sketching.' Kelly himself stated that he had a thorough knowledge of internal combustion engines and mechanical engineering, a fair knowledge of Morse code, and a good knowledge of amateur photography.

Kelly subsequently transferred to the RFC in early 1917, reporting to Reading on 12 March 1917. By 5 April Kelly was with No. 45 Squadron as an observer. This squadron was to undergo a number of incarnations: a two-seater unit on the Western Front, a single-seater scout squadron in Italy, and finally a single-seater squadron on the Western Front. At the time Kelly joined it was equipped with a variety of Sopwith 1½ Strutter two-seater combat aircraft and a handful of Nieuport two-seaters. On 26 April he survived his first crash, when the Nieuport two-seater (A6732) piloted by Lieutenant J. H. Forbes crashed after take-off. Forbes had already damaged another Nieuport (A6736) just days earlier, so Kelly was not with the luckiest of pilots.

On 9 May 1917 Kelly scored his first aerial victory, flying as the observer in a Sopwith 1½ Strutter (A8225) piloted by 2nd Lieutenant William Wright. They destroyed an Albatros D.III north-west of Seclin together with another aircraft from No. 45 Squadron. On 12 May Wright and Kelly crashed on the aerodrome, wrecking their Sopwith 1½ Strutter (A8225). In the month of May 1917 Kelly was to achieve five aerial victories, four of which were with Wright and one with a Lieutenant Geoffrey Cock. Two of his victims went down in flames. Kelly's last victory came on 28 May 1917, destroying an Albatros D.V in flames over Comines. Kelly was wounded in the engagements that day. Kelly describes the crash and its consequences:

> I was wounded over Lille on May 28th by machine gun bullets and the machine was so badly shot about that control was almost impossible. It crashed heavily on landing and I was thrown out on my left shoulder. The scapula of this shoulder does not appear to have gone back to its normal place, with the result that my back is partially deformed.

Kelly was hospitalised on 29 May and was transferred back to Home Establishment on 30 May 1917. It had been an extremely short career at the European frontline but quite a distinguished one. Official developments were slow to catch up with Kelly's situation. On 11 June 1917 *The London Gazette* reported Kelly's promotion to Flying Officer (Observer) with effect from 21 May 1917 and seniority backdated to 7 April 1917.

On 7 August 1917 a medical board examination at the Prince of Wales Hospital in Marylebone held that Kelly was unfit for general service for a three month period. The gunshot wounds were to his left thigh and buttock. Kelly also had injuries to the left scapular, which arose from the crash rather than enemy fire. Further treatment at a convalescent hospital was recommended. Kelly was sent to Escrick Park in York. From there Kelly wrote to the Director of Air Organisation, enquiring as to whether he would still receive flying pay from the date he'd crashed in France. Writing from hospital Kelly also made enquiries about a wound gratuity, indicating that he had been wounded twice before the crash and had not applied for or received any recompense.

Presumably to keep him on the pay books and notional strength of the RFC, on 11 October 1917 Kelly was assigned to HQ ETB, from which they assigned him to No. 3 TS on 15 October 1917 at Shoreham. On 30 November 1917 Captain W. H. Anderson, RAMC, attached to No. 3 TS, certified Kelly as having recovered from his wounds and that he could go forward for pilot training. However, he found Kelly to be somewhat weak-chested and recommended a TS in Egypt or the South of France.

On 4 January 1918 Kelly was ordered to attend the Air Board Office, for transfer to Egypt for pilot instruction. In February 1918 HQ in the Middle East enquired as to when Kelly had been certified fit for duty and so were given the riddle of deciding how to reconcile the various communiqué and *London Gazette* references to 'Caulfield-Kelly', 'E. C. Kelly', and so forth. In March 1918 Captain I. M. Matheson, CO of No. 21 TS at Ismailia, wrote to explain to HQ 32nd Wing that the various names all related to the same person.

On 27 July 1918 Kelly was assigned to 38 Training Wing, No. 58 TS. He was promoted to Temporary 2nd Lieutenant, Leinster Regiment, with effect from 29 May 1918, and assigned to No. 144 Squadron on 4 August 1918.[3] This squadron had been formed on 20 March 1918 and had only been assigned to the RAF's Palestine Brigade on 14 August 1918, equipped with D.H.9 bombers. The aerial bombardment of the Turkish forces throughout September 1918 was decisive in the success of the Arab Northern Army under Sherif Feisal and Colonel T. E. Lawrence, and No. 144 Squadron largely annihilated sections of the Turkish Eighth and Seventh Armies. However, Kelly ended up in hospital again and on 20 September 1918 was returned to Base Depot, Middle East.

On 31 October 1918 Kelly was assigned to HQ Training Brigade. It would appear that over the course of the winter Kelly worked at a succession of training facilities. On 17 January 1919 Kelly's promotion was amended to state that he had been promoted from Lieutenant (Observer) to Lieutenant (Aeroplane) with effect from 29 May 1918.[4] On 6 February 1919 he was assigned to No. 60 TDS, from which he ended up with No. 30 TS on 1 July 1919, which was at this stage training in the D.H.9. Eventually, on 14 August 1919, No. 30 TS returned to RAF Northolt, Uxbridge. Kelly was granted a short-service commission, as Flying Officer, in September 1919.[5] On 17 February 1920 *The London Gazette* reported that Kelly had resigned his commission on the grounds of ill health.[6]

Kelly applied for a position in the Colonial Office in January 1920, with the Colonial Office writing to the Army Council on 30 January 1920 to seek a full report. Kelly was being considered for appointment to the position of an office holder rather than a clerical entry grade; details were sought of Kelly's experience and capacity as an officer—his powers of leadership, tact in dealing with subordinates, capacity for work, and so forth. Any aptitude or experience of his in administrative, legal, policing, or financial duties was also being scrutinised. Kelly had most likely aimed high, for a position in the Treasury, Audit, or Customs Services.

However, because of the confusion arising from variations on his name, the War Office return to the Colonial Office was somewhat inaccurate. For instance, on 4 February 1920 in an internal memo one official requested that it be stated whether Kelly had any decorations, honours, rewards, or mentions, wounds, or service overseas. From a series of different officials' glances at Kelly's service with the Leinster Regiment they deduced that he had not been wounded and had not been ordered overseas. Consequently, on 26 April 1920 the War Office wrote to the

Colonial Office to say they'd no reports on him, but that the Colonial Office should contact the Air Ministry. The confirmation of Kelly's service delayed his admission to the Colonial Office. However, Kelly did not remain idle. On 19 March 1920 Kelly travelled on the P&O SS *Nankin* from London to Bombay. He travelled First Class, his occupation listed as 'Broker's Assistant'. His ultimate destination was recorded as the Federated Malay States.

It is not clear when Kelly was appointed an agricultural inspector based in Kavieng, New Ireland, or when he came to live in Papua New Guinea. He was taken prisoner by the Japanese forces in 1942, and killed on 1 July 1942 in the South China Sea, off the Philippines, in the sinking of the SS *Montevideo Maru*, which claimed the lives of 1,053 Australian troops and civilian internees. On 22 June 1942 an American submarine, the USS *Sturgeon*, had tracked the vessel, believing it to be carrying cargo, and launched four torpedoes, eventually claiming her. It remains Australia's worst maritime disaster. Also killed were an Alfred Ernest Dickenson Banks from Dublin and a Walter James Ryan from Tullow, Co. Carlow. Among the notable casualties was the Rev. Syd Beazley, uncle of the Australian Labour Party leader Kim Beazley. Tom Vernon Garrett, the grandfather of Peter Garrett, the lead singer in Midnight Oil, was also killed (as referenced by Garrett in the song 'In the Valley').

Kelly's death is sometimes the subject of confusion, as there was an Edward Kelly, serving with the Merchant Navy, son of an Edward and Margaret Ellen Kelly, who was killed on the SS *Akeld* on 9 March 1940, i.e. matching parental names and a maritime death.

16

KIRK,
Walter Alister
(7 aerial victories)

Born: 6 August 1887, Belfast
Died: 7 June 1961
Awards: Distinguished Flying Cross

Walter Alister Kirk was born in Belfast to Robert and Jessie Henry Kirk, and was their eldest surviving child. In 1901 the family lived in Breda, Co. Down. He had three brothers (John Wilson, Stanley McClure, Thomas Morgan) and one sister (Jessie Eileen). The family also had two servants. Kirk's father was a tile and metal merchant. In the 1911 census return the family were still resident at Breda, with two different servants, but by this stage Walter had become a motor engineer, his brother John an assistant in their father's business, and their brother Stanley a medical student.

On 11 October 1913 Kirk embarked on the SS *Sussex*, a Federal Line steamship bound for Sydney from Liverpool. By this time he was an engineer, and he travelled First Class. Kirk lived in Sydney but embarked from Brisbane on 24 September 1914, on HMTS *Star of England*, a troopship with the capacity of 499 men and 476 horses. He enlisted on 24 August 1914 as a private (Service No. 61) and served with the 2nd Light Horse Regiment, Machine Gun Section.

Kirk rose to the rank of Sergeant with the Machine Gun Section of the 2nd Light Horse, was demoted back down to the rank of Private, then commissioned as an officer on 18 December 1916. In July 1917 he transferred to the flying services and by October 1917 was posted to the Australian Flying Corps as an observer.[1] The Australian Flying Corps had a small number of Irishmen in its ranks, but the greatest Irish contribution lay with those of Irish ancestry. Famous Australians of Irish parentage included the Kingston McCloughry brothers. Of course, while those of Irish ancestry—such as Edward Patrick Kenny, G. F. Malley, P. J. 'Ginty' McGinnis (the co-founder of Qantas airlines), and Frank Ryan Smith—were to feature in the Australian Flying Corps squadrons, others—such as H. J. 'Jimmy' Larkin, Arthur O'Hara Wood, and Alexander Augustus 'Jerry' Pentland—were absorbed into the

RFC and RNAS. Pentland flew SPADs in Cairnes's No. 19 Squadron and Dolphins in Callaghan's No. 87 Squadron, but had little overlap with either man. (The Pentlands of Blackhall were a prominent Anglo-Irish family. Jerry's father was the surgeon Alexander Pentland, who only emigrated from Ireland in the 1880s, and served as a major in the Australian Army Medical Corps during the war.) Jerry actually spent time in Ireland recuperating from typhoid fever. Apart from the air aces, prominent Irish-Australians were to be decorated for a hugely diverse range of gallant actions—Frank McNamara won the Victoria Cross for landing beside a stricken colleague and successfully evacuating him under fire.

No. 1 Squadron, Australian Flying Corps, constituted No. 67 Squadron, RFC. However, the numbering for the Australian squadrons of the RFC was slightly out of sequence due to the manner in which they were deployed. No. 67 (Australian) Squadron RFC was assigned to service with the British Expeditionary Force in Egypt and Palestine. No. 2 Squadron (No. 68 RFC) and No. 4 Squadron (No. 71 RFC) of the Australian Flying Corps were sent from Australia directly to England, where they performed their training in RFC depots. No. 3 Squadron of the Australian Flying Corps (originally No. 2 and No. 69 RFC) was formed in September 1916 in Egypt. Its personnel were drawn from No. 1 Squadron and from the Australian Light Horse in that theatre. Eventually, Nos. 2, 3, and 4 Squadrons were to be assigned to the Western Front. Kirk is remarkable in that he obtained all his aerial victories in the Middle East.

There is sometimes confusion as to Kirk's service history on account of a 'Private Walter Kirk' (RNAS F20338, RAF 220338) also appearing on various Air Ministry returns.

On 19 January 1918 Kirk undertook a special reconnaissance mission as observer to Lieutenant Mills of No. 111 Squadron, RFC. He recorded,

The towns between the Seil el Kerahi (a stream running into the southern end of the Dead Sea) and Kerak are well built, and surrounded by much ploughed land. Kerak appears to be situated in a position of great natural strength. There are several well-built three-storied yellow houses in the town, and a good reservoir with water. The Plateau of Moab is an open tableland, with many cattle grazing and much plough.

The road running east to the station at El Kutrani is in good condition, and the northern road also appears excellent. Large flocks and many Bedouin shelters seen on the Seil el Buksase (running through Kerak to the Dead Sea). From the mouth of this stream northward the cliffs run straight into the sea, and the only apparent landing-places are the mouths of the wadys, where there are small beaches. One or two small boats were seen at the mouths of most of these streams along the eastern coast.[2]

Several bombing raids were organised on foot of the reconnaissance missions of this nature. On 23 February, in a Bristol F2.b (F1247) piloted by Lieutenant

C. C. Cameron (another former Light Horse), Kirk undertook two separate photographic reconnaissance missions. On 19 March, as observer to Cameron, he had an indecisive engagement with a German aircraft on its way home from a bombing raid on Damieh. On 24 March, as observer to Lieutenant A. R. Brown, Kirk discovered a large troop train at Leban, bound for Amman. They strafed it, and upon it halting fired over 700 rounds into the fleeing troops.

On 27 March, in a Bristol F2.b, Lieutenant Headlam and Kirk had a decisive aerial engagement, which led to Kirk's first two kills. It must be noted that when one uses the phrase 'forced to land' in the context of the Middle Eastern theatre, it still counts as a decisive aerial victory. Unlike the Western Front, where there was the possibility of shelter in a trench or shell-hole, in the Middle East a grounded enemy was invariably strafed until immolated.

Headlam and Kirk, reconnoitring Amman in the early morning of March 27th, met two A.E.G. two-seaters at 5,000 feet and drove them both to ground; one of them (Headlam records) flew around in dazed circles at 1,000 feet, then landed, and Kirk fired into it on the ground. Several men came to help the pilot, but were driven off by the Australians' fire. 'Tracer' bullets were manifestly hitting the crippled two-seater, and 'neither pilot nor observer were seen to leave the machine.'[3]

On 22 May Kirk was an observer in a Bristol F2.b (B1299) flown by Ross MacPherson Smith, who like Kirk had seen service in the Australian Light Horse. They were on dawn patrol with another Bristol F2.b, flown by Irish-Australian ace Edward Patrick Kenny, with W. J. A. Weir as his observer. They attacked two Albatros D.Vs over Nablus, at 11,000 feet, and unusually for the 'Brisfit' did so like a conventional two-seater, i.e. relying solely on the guns of the observers Kirk and Weir. Both Albatrosses went down out of control and one decisive claim was attributed to each Bristol F2.b. They began to attack when they came out of a climbing turn, according to Smith;

I got right under his tail and Kirk put in a full double drum at 50 yards' range, a puff of smoke came out of the enemy aircraft and he started to glide. I then dived onto his tail and fired 40 rounds with front gun at close range.[4]

At this stage the Australian Flying Corps were expected to not only conduct bombing raids and reconnaissance missions, but also mapping and photographic duties. On 8 June Smith and Kirk made the first Allied reconnaissance of Haifa and the adjacent coastline, returning with photographs of the port. On 11 June Smith and Kirk, in Bristol F2.b (B1299), accompanied by Bristol F2.b (B1226) of Lieutenants Stooke and Kreig, forced a Rumpler to land near Tul Keram and destroyed it on the ground. On dawn patrol on 19 June, Smith and Kirk forced another Rumpler to land, destroying it on the ground near Jericho.

Smith kept underneath the enemy's tail, allowing Kirk a line of fire while denying the German observer the same. The high-speed turns pinned the four men to their seats and blurred their vision, making accurate shooting difficult. Nevertheless, one of Kirk's bursts managed to knock the German observer down in his cockpit. The enemy pilot, apparently losing his nerve, then attempted to dive away. Smith seized the opportunity and latched onto his tail, firing a devastating burst at close range. The enemy aircraft went into a spiral dive, with Smith in hot pursuit ... Smith circled the hapless machine while Kirk fired 300 rounds into it.[5]

On 21 June Ross Smith and Kirk, accompanied by Paul and Weir, were returning from a flight up the Lubban–Nablus road on reconnaissance when they identified a suitable target and took the opportunity to attack—a train with infantry entraining at Burkan, just north of Samaria. Ross Smith described the carnage:

We descended to 1,000 feet and machine-gunned train and troops in station. Panic ensued, and troops ran everywhere. Train started north, and we flew alongside it firing at close range with apparently good result. Both machines concentrated fire on locomotive and varnished coach with white roof. We then turned south and attacked Messudie station from 1,000 feet, causing panic amongst troops. We flew along road to en Nakurah station, firing at motor-transport and other targets on the road. We attacked the MT park, a large camp, and the station at en Nakurah, from 1,000 feet. Troops ran from tents and dumps seeking cover in all directions, apparently very demoralised. One two-horse limber bolted, last seen going south. Considerable machine gun and rifle fire experienced at all railway stations.[6]

Lieutenants Paul and Weir inflicted similar casualties. From the beginning of July to the Turkish armistice on 31 October 1918, it is generally agreed that No. 1 Squadron completed 2,862 hours' flying. This involved 157 strategic and 77 photography reconnaissances; 604 square miles of enemy territory photographed; 150 bomb raids; 21 tons of bombs dropped; 241,000 rounds of machine gun ammunition fired, either in aerial combat or against troops on the ground; 17 German machines destroyed in combat, and 53 others driven down.

On 1 July Ross Smith and Kirk strafed the camp and aerodrome at El Kutrani. By this stage the Ottoman forces were desperate, being both unable to move munitions or personnel safely via railway and mercilessly strafed when they attempted to move them by camel trains. On 9 July Smith and Kirk, with Paul and Weir, flew as far as Jenin to photograph the camps and aerodrome. This descended into the usual one-sided strafing massacre, but with the unusual development of finding enemy aircraft and crews to strafe, an occurrence that repeated itself days later.

The two Bristol Fighters descended to 2,000 feet and circled the aerodrome, Ross Smith taking photographs ... the escorting machine blazing off ammunition into the hangars. Then a motor-car appeared at the aerodrome … and, as though obeying some order, five enemy scouts were suddenly wheeled out with engines running. Kirk fired 100 rounds into them impartially. The motor-car rushed out to them; orders were apparently countermanded; the engines of the machines were stopped. The Australians remained over the place for twenty minutes, waiting for the Germans to rise, and shooting off a short burst at every man who showed himself. Two days later the same four airmen repeated the performance near Nablus. The Balata aerodrome was small and sparsely populated; consequently, after firing only a few hundred rounds at its hangars, 'we flew round in circles', reported Ross Smith, 'attacking, in turn, transport parked at Balata, and horse-lines and small camps on the east side of Nablus. About fifty men were in the courtyard of barracks at Nablus shooting at us. Kirk fired 100 rounds at them, and they all ran inside. Troops in this vicinity appeared panic-stricken, and ran in all directions.' The two Bristols then flew home along the Lubban road, stampeding horse-teams and men on motor-lorries, and throwing traffic on the road into the utmost confusion.[7]

On 21 July Ross Smith and Kirk got to destroy two more Albatros D.Vs. They were on dawn patrol at 11,000 over Wadi el Auja when the engagement took place. At only 50 feet from the ground Smith got the decisive burst from the front gun. The second was shot down near a little wadi near the Nablus road. Kirk photographed the remains of both aircraft and they resumed the patrol.

One observer with the squadron, Leslie William Sutherland, in his memoirs *Aces and Kings*, described Ernest 'Pard' Mustard and Kirk as 'fanatics', who 'set out to know every bit of the gun by its Christian name.' They obsessed over ammunition and prepared their drums meticulously to avoid sand and dust causing any faults that would jam the weaponry.[8] That he needed to know how everything worked probably reflected more on Kirk's engineering and mechanical mindset prior to the war, however. The memoirs of pilots and observers are often littered with references to gun stoppages (e.g. 'no. 1', 'no. 3'), whether in the breech, on the belt, or in a bent cartridge. One of the few tools actually permitted in the cockpit was a hammer! Kirk and Mustard were not unreasonably versed in how to strip down a gun in mid-flight. No. 1 Squadron of the Australian Flying Corps continued operations through November 1918, monitoring the armistice, but by that final month, six of their twenty aircraft were struck off charge.

Kirk's DFC citation was gazetted on 8 February 1919. Given the inseparability of Smith and Kirk, it was a joint citation.

Capt. Ross Macpherson Smith, MC (Australian LH and Australian FC) (EGYPT)
Lt Walker Alister Kirk (Australian FC) (EGYPT)

During the months of June and July these officers accounted for two enemy machines, and they have been conspicuous for gallantry and initiative in attacking ground targets, frequently at very low altitudes. The keenness and fine example set by these officers cannot be over-estimated. (Capt. R. M. Smith's MC gazetted 11th May 1917; Bar to MC 26th March 1918. The awards of first and second Bars to the DF Cross are also announced in this Gazette.)[9]

Kirk was discharged on 25 February 1919. Despite only having lived in Australia for a few months of his life, Kirk opted to return there, where he was to live and work as an engineer. He died in June 1961.

17

MANNOCK,
Edward 'Mick'
(61-65 aerial victories)

Born: various dates in 1887, 1888, and 1889 in Aldershot, Hampshire; Brighton, Sussex; Ballincollig, Co. Cork; Dundalk, Co. Louth
Died: 26 July 1918
Awards: Victoria Cross, Military Cross and Bar, Distinguished Service Order with Two Bars
Commemorated: Arras Flying Services Memorial, France; Wellingborough War Memorial, Northamptonshire; War Memorial, St Mary the Virgin, Wellingborough, Northamptonshire; Mannock Memorial Plaque, Canterbury Cathedral

Major Edward Corringham 'Mick' Mannock has been the subject of dozens of books and hundreds of articles, yet many aspects of his life remain the subject of controversy. Neither his place of birth, date of birth, nor even the location of his death, can be agreed on.

It is indisputable that his mother was Julia Sullivan, from Ballincollig, Co. Cork. Julia's parents were Mick and Honora Sullivan, whose families had worked at the gunpowder mill in Ballincollig, and on the Colthurst family estate at Ardrum, Inniscarra, Co. Cork (not at the Bowen-Colthurst's Blarney Castle estate, as is sometimes stated).

Mannock's father, Edward Mannock Senior (aka Corringham), is an enigma. Apparently born in 1858, probably in England, he repeatedly lies about his birthplace on official documents, with claims as far apart as Dublin and Grimsby. He enlisted with the 2nd Dragoon Guards—the Royal Scots Greys—in April 1879 and so had a number of years' service by the time he was stationed in Ballincollig. Edward Senior converted to Catholicism to marry Julia Sullivan and they were married at Saint Mary and John's Church, Ballincollig, on 4 February 1883. He served in Egypt from September 1884 to July 1885 and received claps for the Nile and Abu Klea actions (the failed attempt to reach Khartoum and relieve General Gordon's besieged holdouts there). In 1886 Mannock's older brother, Patrick John

Corringham, was born, probably at Aldershot, Hampshire—once again, a garrison town. Yet there is a question mark over the legitimacy of this brother's birth, given that Edward Senior was posted in Egypt until mid-1885. The latter's service with the 2nd Dragoon Guards was not one of stable progress: he was reduced to Corporal from Lance Sergeant in October 1887. In May 1890 Edward Senior was convicted of absence and gambling, demoted to the rank of private, and forced to forfeit his good conduct badges.

According to the UK census of 1891, the family was living at 76 Spencer Road, St Pancras, London, under the false surname of 'Corringham'. Edward Senior makes a number of other false claims: to have been born at St Pancras, to be 'of independent means' when he was merely living on the lump sum he had received upon being discharged from the cavalry. Curiously, Edward Senior's brother, John Patrick 'Jack' Mannock, the professional billiards player, alternates his birthplace between Dublin and London in the census returns too. Clearly, several of the Mannocks liked to adjust their birthplaces between Ireland and England as the circumstances suited. It's not inconceivable that there were gambling debts or proceeds at stake. Mick Mannock stands out, however, in that throughout his adult life, in his aviator's certificate and on his passport application, he consistently recorded his birthplace as Ballincollig, Co. Cork.

On 1 June 1892 Mannock's father re-enlisted and presented at the 5th Dragoon (Princess Charlotte of Wales's) Guards barracks at Aldershot. Mannock claimed to have been from Dalkey, Co. Dublin. On this second set of his service papers (3777), Edward Senior had passed a medical examination in Bradford on 31 May 1892 and for his next of kin address used that of his sister Christine in Bradford. He was promoted from Private to Lance Corporal on 11 November that year, and to Corporal on 6 September 1893. He served in India from September 1893 to June 1894, with a further three years on Home Establishment garrisons from June 1894 to September 1897. However, in June 1895 it was discovered that Mannock Senior had previously served with the 2nd Dragoons. By 30 May 1897 he had risen to the rank of Lance Sergeant, but on 22 July was arrested and tried for theft. He was convicted, demoted to rank of Private, and imprisoned until September 1897. Upon discharge from prison Mannock was posted again to India, and served there from September 1897 to October 1899, after which he served in South Africa during the Boer War.

Mannock's early youth was spent in Highgate, following his father's discharge from the 2nd Dragoons. Mannock's biographers generally have it that Edward Senior was a violent drunk, and that it was this adversity that Mannock had to overcome in his childhood years. His father's various movements had a profound impact on Mannock's life, too: when the 5th Dragoon Guards were initially posted to India, the family moved there. They lived at Meerut, north of Delhi. Some of Mannock's detractors referred to his cod-Irish accent, but in reality he lived with his Irish mother while his father was stationed at various overseas postings; his

1. An officer demonstrates the precarious position the observer had to take to man the rearward-firing gun in a F.E.2d. (*IWM, Q69650*)

2. Joseph Cruess Callaghan in
Royal Munster Fusiliers uniform.
Note the shamrock underneath the
cap badge. (*Royal Aero Club*)

3. Giles Noble Blennerhassett.
(*Private collection*)

4. D.H.2 'pusher'. (*IWM, Q67534*)

Above left: 5. Sidney Edward Cowan. (*Royal Aero Club*)

Above right: 6. Patrick Anthony Langan Byrne. (*Royal Aero Club*)

7. Nieuport 17 scout. (*IWM, Q45379*)

8. William Earle Molesworth (top left) as a Sandhurst cadet in 1913. (*RMA, Sandhurst*)

9. Edward 'Mick' Mannock. (*Royal Aero Club*)

10. Edward Dawson Atkinson. (*Royal Aero Club*)

11. Robert Gregory portrait by Charles Haslewood Shannon. (*Dublin City Gallery, The Hugh Lane*)

12. Sopwith Camel. (*IWM, Q67556*)

13. Oscar Heron (seated centre) with the Irish Air Corps. (*Irish Military Archives*)

14. S.E.5As of No. 1 Squadron with Mannock's No. 85 Squadron in the foreground, July 1918. (*IWM, Q12063*)

15. George Edward Henry McElroy. (*RMA, Sandhurst*)

16. Conn Standish O'Grady in the Second World War. (*IWM, O'Grady Collection*)

17. Sopwith 1½ Strutter. (*IWM, Q67507*)

18. An officer from Walter Alister Kirk's No. 1 Squadron, Australian Flying Corps, explains the Bristol's armament to local Arab fighters. (*IWM, Q58702*)

19. D.H.4. (*IWM, Q80861*)

20. Bristol F.2b of McCormack and Tyrrell's No. 22 Squadron. (*IWM, Q11997*)

21. Victor Henry Huston (centre) with Lieutenants Armando Cortínez and Dagoberto Godoy, the first two pilots to cross the Cordillera de los Andes. (*Museo Nacional Aeronautico*)

22. Alfred William Saunders. (*Royal Aero Club*)

23. Henry George Crowe. (*Royal Aero Club*)

24. David Mary Tidmarsh. (*Royal Aero Club*)

sisters and brother were born in England, Ireland, and Scotland, but he was reared in India and would have been the product of all these influences. While Mannock's father was posted to South Africa during the Second Boer War and opted to stay there—transferring into the 7th (Princess Royal's) Dragoon Guards (aka the 'Black Horse') for the remainder of the war rather than return to India—Mannock in effect grew up with his Irish mother in India, educated by Jesuits. He spent nearly a decade of his life there.

Mannock contracted a seriously debilitating amoebic infection during that time. In Ira Jones's biography and MacLanachan's *Fighter Pilot*, his condition was dramatised into the myth of 'the ace with one eye' and a congenital defect from which he never recovered. Later biographers, such as James Dudgeon, Frederick Oughton, and Vernon Smyth, were writing in the era of living legends such as Douglas Bader—who flew after losing his legs—and so the pre-war melodramatics of Jones or MacLanachan lost their remarkability. Adrian Smyth dispenses with the myth altogether.

Mannock's early life in India would have been coloured by the appalling disparity of wealth and power there, and this experience is often cited as the basis upon which his socialist beliefs were formed. However, there were many other influences on his belief system, not least the return to the UK in his early teens in 1902, whereupon he was exposed to the realities of poverty in England (they were living at the Cavalry Depot in Canterbury). Mannock's father was invalided from the 7th Dragoons on 13 March 1902, and deserted them shortly after his return from the Boer War. He then entered into a bigamous marriage with a Lydia Charlotte Wood on 10 July 1904. (Appallingly, Edward Senior also had the first child of that relationship named Edward).

Mannock's eldest sister, Jess, married a soldier, Edward Charles Ainge, in September 1905. Ainge had served in India with the East Kent Regiment (the Buffs). The rest of the family moved to Jones Cottages, Canterbury, in September 1906. His sister Nora was allowed to attend the local St Thomas's RC school, but the two boys had to work to support the family. Mannock worked in a greengrocer's and a barber's; his brother Pat became a clerk in the National Telephone Company, and he joined him there in 1908.

Mannock had trained with the (Anglican) Church Lads' Brigade, mainly due to the influence of Cuthbert Gardner, a local solicitor who kept Mannock engaged in local debating societies. A family friend, Fred Rawson, encouraged Mannock to join the volunteer Territorial Force, which he did; as well as get him outdoors, it gave him an outlet for his sense of initiative, teamwork, and organisational skills.

In 1911 Mannock transferred from the ledger clerk position to that of linesman for the National Telephone Company. They posted him to Wellingborough, Northamptonshire. In 1911 he was living at 64 Melton Road, Wellingborough, which was the house of Albert Walter Joyce. Both Mick and Joyce were recorded as being telephone inspectors in the census that year.

During his time with Wellingborough's Post Office Engineering Department, Mannock was regarded as a socialist, and was known as 'Pat' or 'Paddy'.[1] He played cricket and football in Wellingborough with the local Wesleyan congregations, which undermines the 'ace with one eye' myth. Mannock continued to worship as a Catholic, and is recorded on the 1914–1918 'Roll of Honour' on St Mary the Virgin church on Knox Road, Wellingborough. Labour was locally proactive here, and contested the December 1910 election against the sitting Liberal MP in East Northamptonshire. Mannock became good friends with the local Indendent Labour Party organiser, A. E. 'Jim' Eyles. He moved into the spare room of the Eyles family home at 183 Mill Road. All of Mannock's many biographers agree on the Eyles' impact on Mannock, both in terms of providing a family environment to him and a political soundboard through which he developed his beliefs. Mick participated in the local YMCA mock parliament. He then sat as MP for Waterford in honour of John Redmond, the leader of the Irish Parliamentary Party. Mannock's engaged performance as the local Labour party secretary was considered a key factor in Walter R. Smith's breakthrough for Labour in Wellingborough in the general election of 1918.

In February 1914 Mick moved to Turkey, to exploit the opportunities for an experienced rigger in the cable-laying operations at the *Société Anonyme Ottomane des Téléphones*. He initially worked as a supervisor of linesmen and was subsequently promoted to an administration role. With the outbreak of war in August 1914 Mannock was unlucky in the general 'keep calm and carry on' position of the Foreign Office, who expected a short war and wanted to keep Turkey neutral for as long as possible, a position which was contradicted by the hawkish military elements in the Admiralty, which had sought to seize two new battleships awaiting delivery to the Ottoman Navy. However, the net result was that British citizens were not evacuated upon the outbreak of war. Following a British declaration of war on 5 November 1914, Mannock was interned with a large number of British and French nationals. During the months of Turkish custody the internees suffered appalling conditions. Mannock's release was secured on 1 April 1915. He was suffering from dysentery and malaria, but was able to pass an Army medical less than two months later. It is likely that subsequent lurid accounts of his PoW experiences were coloured by stories of captivity in the aftermath of the *Second* World War, namely at the hands of the Japanese, and in fact drew little from the realities of Mannock's imprisonment decades before.

Regardless of the degree of maltreatment at the hands of the Turks, Mannock developed a deep hatred of the enemy. Its intensity has been the subject of much speculation, but it would appear to be genuine and not some dramatic device invented by biographers. But his patriotism must not be confused with bloodlust: Mannock's initial service was with the Home Counties Field Ambulance—hardly the most aggressive outfit.

Private Mannock, under the service number 8153, enlisted in May 1915, distinguished by a 'slight scar over left eyebrow'. In his full medical examination on

22 and 25 May 1915 at Ashford, Kent, the keenness of his vision is recorded as 6/6 in each eye. His next of kin address was 10 Bruce Street, Belfast, so presumably by this stage his mother was resident with his sister Jessie back in Ireland. His brother Pat had got married on 1 June 1915 to Dorothy Beatrice Stone, and there is regular correspondence between Mannock and the married couple from this time onwards.

At Halton Park Mannock combined his anti-German views with that of being a socialist orator. However, the RAMC was not the place for Mannock; although promoted to private to Lance Corporal, to Corporal, to Sergeant, to Staff Sergeant over a short few weeks in May and June 1915, Mick nevertheless sought appointment as an officer cadet in the Royal Engineers.

In this application for a commission Mannock's date of birth is recorded as 21 May 1888, which is closer to the Dundalk date of birth in his father's service papers than it is to the 24 May 1887 date used in Mick's later RFC papers. The 24 May date was of course Queen Victoria's birthday and the date from which 'Empire Day' would have been calculated. Mick passed another medical examination, on 22 November 1915, with 6/6 vision in each eye.

His transfer to the Royal Engineers Signal Section took Mannock to Bedfordshire in March 1916. He was promoted to Temporary 2nd Lieutenant by June 1916 but his time with the Royal Engineers was not a happy one: he was nearly twenty-nine or perhaps thirty years of age—quite a bit older than the intake of young cadets—and he was still politically vocal. The Easter Rising in 1916 would have occurred at that time. Although none of Mannock's biographers have identified any correspondence between Mick and Jim Eyles on the Irish situation from this period, it is likely that he faced some unease over the use of British field artillery in the narrow civilian-populated inner city streets of Dublin. Mannock opposed violent confrontation, but would probably have still been the subject of anti-Irish prejudice.

Mannock applied for a transfer to the RFC in June 1916. This umpteenth medical yet again records equal scores for both the left and right eyes.[2] It would appear that Mannock had been motivated to transfer after a chance encounter with an old workmate from Northampton, Eric Tompkins, who was based at the Central Flying School. Mick's younger sister got married in Belfast to a John McIntosh in early 1917, but Mick does not appear to have travelled to attend.

Mannock was posted to No. 10 TS, which was based at Joyce Green at Dartford Creek. It was here that he first encountered James McCudden, who had been sent there to instruct students on how to survive a spin. Mannock took on board what was said but upon putting a D.H.2 into a spin at well below the danger level of 2,000 feet and recovering, he was lucky to survive, landing just inches from a shed containing explosives. McCudden, son of an Irishman from Co. Carlow, is very generous in his description of Mannock's reckless act:

The pupils here during the period of which I write were very good. One I particularly remember named Mannock. One day he came to me and said that I was the cause of saving his life. I had only just previously given him instructions on what to do if he unfortunately got into a 'spin'. He had just had his first spin and remembered my advice, which I think at the time was to put all controls central and offer up a very short and quick prayer.[3]

At the time of writing his memoir McCudden was already very familiar with Mannock. McCudden seeks to further unravel the RFC's policy of not praising individual pilots by adding the following:

Mannock was a typical example of the impetuous young Irishman, and I always thought he was of the type to do or die. He now holds the DSO and MC and a bar, and at the time of writing has accounted for over two score of German machines.

At Joyce Green Mannock began to keep a diary. One of the earliest inscriptions on its facing pages is by the Irish poet Paul Charles Stacpoole O'Longan in March 1917. That month, Mannock was posted to Clarmarais.

There are few personal thoughts entered in his diary for this period, but in April he records leaving a show early in disgust. There is also passing reference to a Jeannette, a local French teenager who worked in the mess, but the relationship would appear to have been platonic. Mannock was posted to No. 40 Squadron on 6 April and by the 8th had broken an axle on landing, having lost his leader in the foggy conditions. Already this may have prompted whispers of cowardice and that Mannock had deserted from his formation. He was quite unpopular in the early weeks there, partially because of his outspokenness: Mannock had a lot of life experiences, some very good technical and mechanical knowledge, and a strong desire to get involved. This would not have sat well with a culture of deference, in which new pilots would have been expected to hold their tongue. Another factor may have been that someone from Mannock's socio-economic and cultural background would have been expected to 'know one's place' when in the company of gentlemen officers. However, this was 'Bloody April', during which the RFC was being slaughtered in the effort to ensure the offensive at Arras could be maintained, and Mannock's outspokenness would have been problematic.

On 9 April 1917 Mannock's Nieuport (B1502) overturned in high winds after landing. In his diary he consoles himself with the fact that a more senior officer did the same thing later that day. On the 19th, Mannock's Nieuport (B1540) was catastrophically damaged, with the lower right-hand place breaking off at 1,500 feet. In his diary of 20 April he records that on the previous day he had survived a serious mechanical failure when up on gun practice. This seems to have led him to anxiously undertake his own gunsighting and double-check the flight-worthiness of an aircraft, which would have alienated the riggers and armourers. It also fed into the rumours that he was an idle boaster who had lost his nerve.

Mannock struck up an unusual friendship with Desmond Herlouin de Burgh, a Unionist from Co. Monaghan and a member of the Anglo-Irish gentry. De Burgh later rose to the rank of Air Commodore, responsible for radar and OBOE developments on RAF pathfinders. By April 1917 de Burgh had accounted for at least two German aircraft and would have been a central enough character in the life of the squadron. Typically, both men argued passionately on every subject, but it at least helped Mannock into some social engagement with the other members of the squadron. De Burgh is quoted as having said,

> We had two things in common ... we were both Irishmen, and we both dearly loved an argument. ... Many was the time when we would argue fiercely on some highly controversial subject such as politics, socialism or religion—he usually won the argument, though heavens knows what his views really were. As a curious contrast to the warfare of the tongue, Mannock was very keen on boxing, and as I had done a good deal, we often used to blow off steam by having a 'set to' in the mess ... I think, on the whole, that I used to get more than I gave, as he had the height on me, and a slightly longer reach; but I had him at footwork.[4]

The sight of two Irishmen arguing and then boxing may not have been the most dignified way to become known in the squadron. However, de Burgh had at least perceived that, for all Mannock's public views on politics and religion, he was still enigmatic on a personal level and few got to know the real man. Another observation of de Burgh was that, alongside his hatred of the Germans, there was another issue which used to rattle him: 'society' women.

> [This] caused us all no small amount of amusement—it was only necessary to leave a copy of one of the weekly papers open showing 'The beautiful Lady ... who is organising a charity concert in aid of ... etc.' for Mannock to go off the deep end for about half an hour.[5]

Not that Mannock had any particular dislike of women. Rather, this was more a manifestation of his distaste for *noblesse oblige*, in which the supposed burden of duty on the rich and powerful also justified their privilege. It was also an expression of his disgust for high society occasions in which a vacuous hostess would regard a pilot as a social prop to better decorate a function, in much the same way that a previous generation had relied on the occasional cavalry officer or naval captain as human wallpaper to fill out an important event.

De Burgh also indicates that experienced pilots of the squadron, such as himself, who'd fought hard and well with F.E.8 'pushers', might react badly to having their experience set at naught by upstarts, such as Mannock, who'd trained on tractor biplanes.

Mannock was one of the, to us, new school who was used to tractors, and had been taught such things as rolls and half rolls—all of which were more or less strange to us. There was no doubt about it that the new pilots coming out to us about this time had been taught far more than we had about handling an aeroplane.[6]

On 22 April 1917 Mannock wrote,

Now I can understand what a tremendous strain to the nervous system active service flying is…. When it is considered that seven out of ten forced landings are practically 'write offs', and 50 per cent are cases where the pilot is injured, one can quite understand the strain of the whole business.

Mannock's early days with No. 40 Squadron were increasingly fraught. Externally, he had to cope with the pressure of being perceived as a coward; then, there was the overwhelming weight of expectation he had placed on himself to succeed. He was badly shot up on 7 May 1917, and Captain Keen reported on his return that he believed Mannock had been shot down. Mannock was badly shaken upon his return, to find Keen deflecting blame by implying that Mannock had deserted his formation. However, later that day, in an attack on German observation balloons, of the six aircraft they lost Captain Nixon and four of the other survivors crashed, either behind British lines or on the aerodrome. Only Mannock made it home, but he was again badly shot up. He had, however, scored his first aerial victory, destroying a balloon.

On 9 May 1917 Mannock was part of a three-man patrol to engage a German aircraft. In the encounter Mannock was bounced by three other enemy aircraft and suffered engine failure.

I thought it was all up. We were 16,000 feet up at the time. I turned almost vertically on my tail—nose-dived and spun down towards our own lines, zig-zagging for all I was worth with machine guns crackling away behind me like mad. The engine picked up when I was about 3,000 feet over Arras and the Huns for some reason or other had left me. I immediately ran into another Hun … but hadn't the pluck to face him. I turned away and landed here with my knees shaking and my nerves all torn to bits. I feel a bit better now, but all my courage seems to have gone after that experience this morning.[7]

Mannock was probably also suffering from oxygen-deprivation-induced fatigue as a consequence of high-altitude flying, with ocular strain and earache also being likely side-effects. He told the Eyles family that 'I always feel tired and sleepy, and I can lie down and sleep anywhere or at any time.'[8]

Mannock missed out on several combats due to being sent on various other duties, such as retrieving aircraft from Omer. It was clear that Major Tilney was aware of the extent to which Mannock was under strain but also was not in a position to rotate frontline staff from the squadron to Home Establishment unless they were at breaking point. However, hostility to Mannock was lessening as the months passed and he was earning respect as he continued to stay alive. On 16 May 1917 he went to Omer for rest and recuperation with Captain Gregory and some other lieutenants. It was a short respite, as on 19 May 1917 he had a forced landing.

At least Mannock's No. 40 Squadron had upgraded from the F.E.8 to the Nieuport: his friend, the gloomy teenage Irish poet O'Longan, ended up in No. 41 Squadron, which was still attempting to persevere with the F.E.8. O'Longan didn't last for long; he was killed on 1 June 1917 by the German ace Oberleutnant Hans Bethge of Jasta 30. O'Longan's rudder (A4887) joined the 'trophy wall' decorating the roof of the hangar that housed Bethge's Pfalz Scout.

On 2 June 1917 Mannock wrote,

> Our Captain Gregory—just gone back to HE [Home Establishment]—has been awarded the 'Legion de Honneur' [*sic*] for especially good service. He deserved it!

The facing pages of Mannock's diary bear inscriptions from various pilots. Gregory's entry of 'Don't let your wires sing!' is dated 27 May 1917 and may actually have been written in by Mannock himself, as the subsequent note below records that Gregory was killed in an air accident in February 1918. On balance it would appear that there was no hostility between Mannock and Gregory, who was quite similar in profile to de Burgh and other Anglo-Irish landlords with whom Mannock got on well.

On 7 June 1917 Mannock wrote, 'I brought my first dead certain Hun down this morning.' Mannock's description of the kill does not accord with the bloodthirsty monster he is generally imagined to be. His victim was probably Vizefeldwebel Eberlein of Jasta 33, who was wounded but survived.

The 'Combats in the Air' reports for No. 40 Squadron record that on 9 June 1917 Mannock shot up two German aircraft, expending a whole drum of ammunition. Mannock nevertheless stated that a third German went down after being attacked by Lieutenant Bond. However, Bond gave no reciprocal verification of Mannock's efforts. Bond's wife refers to Mannock as 'Kelly' in the publication of her husband's letters. Bond bears no malice to Mannock; 'though his judgment is not always good he is absolutely without fear and does his job thoroughly.'[9]

Mannock was to swing between exultation and despair. On 14 June he shot down two Germans and claimed, 'I felt like the victor in a cock-fight!' but within days had received an eye injury and wrote, 'Feeling nervy and ill during the last week. Afraid I am breaking up.' His demeanour would change accordingly. One kill described by Mannock does show that he still had plenty of human empathy:

Luckily my first few shots killed the pilot and wounded the observer ... I gathered a few souvenirs, although the infantry had first pick. The machine was completely smashed, and rather interesting also was the little black and tan terrier—dead—in the observer's seat. I felt exactly like a murderer. The journey to the trenches was rather nauseating—dead men's legs sticking through the sides with putties and boots still on—bits of bones and skulls with the hair peeling off, and tons of equipment and clothing lying about. This sort of thing, together with the graveyard stench and the dead and mangled body of the pilot (a NCO) combined to upset me for a few days.[10]

The dead NCO was Vizefeldwwebel Reubelt, and the observer Lieutnant H. Bottcher. Their DFW aircraft was from Schlasta 12.

Mannock got to take leave in June 1917. Visiting his family was a difficult experience: his mother was drinking more heavily and was back in England, having briefly lived in Belfast with Jessie, whose marriage was disintegrating. Mannock gave his mother money but went on to stay with the Eyles family. As Smith records,

> The Eyles family had never seen him so totally immersed in any one subject, nor so enthusiastic. Pat could be found standing on the table, playing out untried methods of attack, with Jim putting on a brave face—or keeping a straight face—as he pottered around the kitchen waiting to be shot down. Mannock acknowledged that age was not on his side, but felt sure he could compensate [by] working out fresh tactics ... ('You watch me bowl them over when I return!).[11]

If Mannock was still facing bouts of nausea before he flew, he was becoming increasingly confident in the air. Some have equated to an actor's trepidation before going on stage or an artist before a performance; but Mannock was certainly not a drama queen—his actions claimed lives. The killing did not dehumanise him at this stage; if anything his increasing proficiency and confidence led to him being more magnanimous with the enemy. On 20 July 1917 Mannock wrote,

> Ran into three of the finest Hun pilots I ever wish to meet. Had quite an exciting and enjoyable ten minutes' scrap. Those Huns were artists. Do what I could I couldn't get a line on them, and it was six against three. Eventually they flew off, apparently none the worse for the encounter. I shall always maintain an unsullied admiration for those Huns. The aircraft battery people reported the battle as one of the most splendid exhibitions of tactics they had ever seen. We did nothing but swear.[12]

There are several accounts of indecisive combat engagements in which Mannock was not awarded a kill, e.g. the squadron's 'Combats in the Air' report for 27 July states that Mannock was part of an offensive patrol that attacked seven Albatros Scouts near Lens. Mannock, who flew a Nieuport (B3554), stated that his Aldis

Sight malfunctioned and so his aim was inaccurate. It does highlight the problem with Mannock's self-maintenance regime on the gunsight and mounting: it was no longer good enough, notwithstanding the previous reassurance it had afforded him. On 19 August Mannock wrote in his diary,

> Had a splendid fight with a single-seater Albatros Scout last week on our side of the lines and got him down. This proved to be Lieutenant von Bartrap, Iron Cross.... He came over for one of our balloons—near Neuville-St-Vaast—and I cut him off going back. He didn't get the balloon either. The scrap took place at 2,000 feet up, well within view of the whole Front. And the cheers! It took me five minutes to get him to go down, and I had to shoot him before he would land. I was very pleased that I did not kill him ... had a great ovation from everyone. Even Generals congratulated me. He didn't hit me once.[13]

The next day Mannock overshot the runway and collided with a haystack when arriving at the Advance Landing Ground from Bruay. His Nieuport (B3554) wasn't damaged, but it was a useful reminder of fallibility. His diary at this time also makes reference to the elusive 'purple man', which most aviation historians would identify as the great German ace Werner Voss. Mannock enthused, 'he's a marvel ... he manoeuvred so cleverly.' Once again it must be taken that, for all the outward Hun-hating bluster, Mannock was still capable of respecting his enemies. His comments echo those of his friend McCudden, who after the engagement that resulted in Voss's death praised his skill and bravery.

On 5 September 1917 Mannock wrote in his diary of several encounters the previous day, during which he had sent down a German aircraft in flames.

> I got in about 50 rounds in short bursts while on the turn, and he went down in flames, pieces of wing and tail etc. dropping away from the wreck. It was a horrible sight and made me feel sick.... Prior to that at 9.40 a.m. I had a beautiful running fight with another two-seater at 17,000 feet from Bruay to east of Lens. This one got away notwithstanding the fact that I fired nearly 300 rounds at close range. I saw the observer's head and arm lying over the side of the machine—he was dead apparently—but the pilot seemed to be alright. He deserved to get away really as he must have been a brave Hun.[14]

The foregoing would suggest that although Mannock publicly bragged of getting a 'flamerino', there was more to him than the anti-German bravado he displayed. He also seemed to have respect for his surviving victims. These two Germans lost may have been either from FAA 240, Vizefeldwebel Eddelbuttel (wounded) and Leutnant Kuhn, or from FAA 235, Vizefeldwebel G. Frischkorn and Leutnant F. Frech (both killed). A balloon observer, Lieutenant G. Pilgrim, saw a German Halberstadt drop a container near British lines a few days later. The message read,

The 4th Sept I lost my friend Fritz Frech. He fell between Vimy and Lieven. His respectable and unlucky parents beg you to give any news of his fate. Is he dead? At what place found he his last rest? Please throw several letters that we may find one. Thank before, His friend, K. L.

It took several months for this to reach Mannock, but he did write to the parents in Konigsberg. The Germans regularly dropped canisters to notify the RFC of the fate of British casualties over German lines, and there was a corresponding obligation to let the Germans know of the fate of casualties if requested.

Mannock was awarded the Military Cross, which was gazetted on 17 September 1917:

T./2nd Lt Edward Mannock, RE and RFC

For conspicuous gallantry and devotion to duty. In the course of many combats he has driven off a large number of enemy machines, and has forced down three balloons, showing a very fine offensive spirit and great fearlessness in attacking the enemy at close range and low altitudes under heavy fire from the ground.[15]

Interestingly, although Mannock's medal citation mentioned three balloons, only the record of one aerial victory against balloons survives for the period in question. It's therefore no surprise that Mannock's final tally of aerial victories remains the subject of so much debate.

On 27 September Mannock intervened to save the life of the German ace Leutnant Waldhausen (the 'Eagle of Lens'), who had been shot down by the South African Lieutenant Tudhope of No. 40 Squadron, and/or Major Charles Booker and Herbert Thompson of No. 8 (Naval) Squadron. Waldhausen had shot at a parachuting kite balloon observer, and the troops on the ground wanted to execute Waldhausen.

Mannock ceased keeping his diary in September 1917. Most likely it was due to the sheer pressure of operations: he could not record every thought on the dozens of men he was sending to their deaths—he had scored six victories in September 1917 alone.

Mannock was awarded a bar to his Military Cross, which was gazetted on 18 October 1917. He was unhappy with the transition from the Nieuport to the S.E.5a. The problem appeared to be with the engine reliability as much as the armament. On 23 November his S.E.5 (B4884) suffered engine failure and he had a forced landing near Dainville. In MacLanachan's memoirs this is dramatised into a situation in which Mannock was left crouching in a rat-infested, corpse-strewn trench, screaming to be rescued. Apparently General 'Boom' Trenchard was visiting the squadron a week later, arriving when Mannock was returning from a combat flight in which the gun had jammed. Apparently not recognising Trenchard's rank, he launched into a lengthy tirade when asked about the performance of the squadron's new mounts, while Major Tilney tried to made placatory noises and interjections to shut him up. The S.E.5a was equipped with Gogu Constantinescu's synchronisation gear to allow a machine gun fire through the arc of the propeller, but it was a novel sonic gear, unlike the mechanical gears that German aircraft had used for years. Consequently this Vickers gun on the S.E.5a had a much slower rate of fire than the traditional Lewis gun on a sliding-rail ('Foster') mounting on the top of the Nieuport's wings, and was also more prone to jamming. However, despite Mannock's rant, a few days later Trenchard sent a gunnery officer from HQ over to the squadron for further feedback on the specific difficulties being encountered.

By this stage the future ace George McElroy, had been with the squadron a number of weeks but had crashed several aircraft and Mick had to argue for McElroy to be given another chance. McElroy eventually got his first victory in December 1917 but drew criticism rather than praise from Mannock for losing the Flight other targets, but Mannock and McElroy were to become good friends.

Mannock was given extended leave on 6 January 1918, being returned to Home Establishment. The number of aerial victories attributed to Mannock during his time with No. 40 Squadron varies between seventeen and twenty-two, depending on whether the balloon kills are attributed, and on whether we are to take at face value the aerial victories Mannock believed he had accrued by that stage as referenced in his diary entries.

Mannock was reassigned from HQ Training Brigade to No. 74 Squadron on 11 February 1918. Mannock drew heavily on personal experience when teaching at the squadron while it was based at Hertfordshire. He would not necessarily have been a good instructor but his mantra—'always above; seldom on the same level; never underneath'—was drummed into pupils' minds. Ira 'Taffy' Jones served with No. 74 Squadron, and it is his biography of Mannock that helped build the legend of this unit as the 'Tiger Squadron', with over 200 victories in the few months of the war that it was mobilised (April to November 1918). However, overall the squadron's record would stand as broadly comparable to other S.E.5a-equipped squadrons, with a like-for-like combat role. One remarkable aspect, however, was their excellent kill:loss ratio, as they were to lose less than forty pilots in the corresponding period.

Mannock's mental deterioration continued nonetheless. His fears of being shot down in flames had been recounted to many, and it was known that Mannock claimed he would shoot himself if his aircraft caught fire, but by 1918 death had become an obsession. It did not affect his ability to kill, as on 12 April 1918 he scored two victories. He succeeded in having one of these attributed to his entire 'A' Flight, however, going to some length in his combat report to involve everyone in the action:

Each pilot in rotation engaged the hostile machine at close range. I followed the machine down for a few thousand feet and noted that it appeared out of control.

It … eventually crashed NE of Bois de Phalempin, E of Carvin. The whole Flight should share in the credit for this HA.

What is evident is that the magnanimity with which he had thus far treated opponents was diminishing. After Manfred von Richthofen's death on 21 April 1918, a member of the squadron proposed a toast to the Red Baron, but Mannock walked out in disgust.[16]

Mannock sent a German down in flames on both 23 April and 29 April. According to Mannock's combat report in respect of the first kill, the aircraft had a black body, white-tipped tail, and silver- and black-chequered top planes. Mannock's fire triggered an explosion in the cockpit, and the aircraft fell vertically in flames—it was not a case of strafing a stricken opponent, though there is a common misconception that Mannock kept firing until his opponents went down in flames. In the kill of 29 April, Mannock had been on line patrol in S.E.5a (D278) when he encountered a

… strange type single-seater. Very long fuselage, swept back wing tip, very pronounced mackerel shaped tale.

It may well have been a Fokker D.VI, of which less than fifty saw service on the Western Front.

The contrast between the respectfully sensitive Mannock of No. 40 Squadron and the increasingly morose, Hun-hating wreck that was emerging at No. 74 Squadron is stark. In one incident he strafed a German two-seater they had forced down, killing the pilot and observer. This conduct was in itself not particularly exceptional, but Mannock's vehemence in his defence of his actions afterwards was. The death of his protégé Henry Dolan on 12 May sent Mannock into a rage. Mannock was still very much a professional pilot, however, and any additional 'vengeance' flights would have been counterbalanced by his sense of responsibility and loyalty to his other charges: he was not reckless with their lives or his own. Prior to Dolan's death on 12 May, Young's 'B' Flight had also lost Stuart-Smith, Bright, and Skeddon, while 'C' Flight had lost Begbie. Mannock had trained the majority of these men at London Colney in Hertfordshire, so their deaths would have weighed heavily on him.

On 12 May, in S.E.5a (C1112) on evening patrol near Wulverghem, Mannock attacked a large formation of enemy aircraft and destroyed two Albatros D.Vs and a Pfalz DIII;

Fired at rear machine at close range and at right angles. EA side-slipped under me and collided with another Albatros which was banking below. Both fell to pieces. Engaged another Pfalz from behind and fired almost a drum from Lewis and same number from Vickers. Machine went down vertically and I was able to observe it dive into the ground.

The combat report provides a useful example of the attack from right angles. Mannock had perfected the 'deflection shot', in which one estimates the angle and speed of both aircraft and hits the opponent as it passes through the intended position. Flying like this required steady nerves and so it must be assumed that Mannock was still mentally stable. Much is made of one incident in which he pranced around the mess, celebrating some 'flamerinoes' with a 'sizzle, sizzle, wonk' dance, but this should be understood in the context of trying to raise morale among new recruits, including a nervous seventeen-year-old South African pilot, 'Swazi' Howe, who Mannock was to assist with his first kill later that week. Mannock wasn't quite the psychopath he is often portrayed to be, but he was certainly on the way to a mental breakdown.

Mannock achieved twenty victories in May 1918, of which at least six went down in flames. In one fight on 21 May he scored another triple-victory, destroying all three opponents near Hollebeke. However, one of the more unusual encounters occurred on 17 May. Mannock in his regular S.E.5a (D278) saw a number of Camels being circled by Albatrosses. Mannock gave the signal to attack and destroyed one Albatros. He was immediately engaged by the other enemy aircraft from above and behind, was forced to spin away, and was chased to the British lines. Mannock noted bitterly, 'as far as I could see the Camels took no part in the engagement.' Caldwell was to supplement the combat report with a note to state that the Camels of No. 210 Squadron confirmed Mannock's destruction of an Albatros. Despite the merger of the RFC and RNAS into the RAF, the old naval squadrons still performed to their own agenda. In this case No. 210 Squadron was the once-formidable No. 10 (Naval) Squadron, of Collishaw's famous 'Black Flight', but there was much internal dissension in the final months of the war and it's likely that they would not have responded well to an ex-RFC finger-clicking at them.

On 18 May Mannock toyed with a yellow and black Halberstadt two-seater when perfecting his deflection shot, sending it down in flames. The kill was witnessed by William Cairnes, the Irish ace, who was to go down in flames within a fortnight of that combat. Ludendorff's northern offensive in the spring of 1918 had put the RAF under tremendous pressure, losing 1,000 aircraft in five weeks. Mannock would have been acutely aware of the attrition rate, and the expendability of the men at his disposal, but he and 'Grid' Caldwell were lavished with praise for keeping squadron morale high. The Canadian ace 'Clem' Clements recalled:

> We developed into a family really, Grid and Mick saw to that, an efficient, happy team … On the rare occasions that gloom did settle in the mess, Mick was just the man to handle it. He didn't give a hoot how he did it, as long as the men ended up happy and morale was maintained. He was always the life and soul of the party, although this never interfered with our respect for his authority.[17]

On 6 June Mannock sought to have the entire patrol credited for the destruction of a Pfalz over the Houthoulst Forest. On 9 June he had Lieutenants Kiddie and Clements jointly credited with another of his aerial victories, as the Albatros 'was engaged almost simultaneously' by these patrol members. It is occasions such as these that can give rise to the misconception that Mannock 'gave away' dozens of kills. He was still credited with an aerial victory in these circumstances: there were no 'decimal aces' at that time, i.e. a shared kill would increment each pilot's score by one but would only increase the squadron's total by one.

In a letter dated 16 June, Mannock wrote to his sister Jess admitting,

> Things are getting a bit intense just lately and I don't quite know how long my nerves will last out … These times are so horrible that occasionally I feel that life is not worth hanging on to myself.[18]

In June 1918 Mannock was to obtain a total of at least eleven victories—including another triple victory—before being promoted to take command of No. 85 Squadron. Yet he was in no fit mental state to be placed in a greater position of responsibility; his sense of duty and loyalty to the men were being misdirected at a time when he needed to be taken off frontline duties. When Mannock returned to the Eyles family, on leave prior to the appointment, he was no longer able to control the shaking and twitching in his hands. In the Eyles' kitchen at Mill Road he broke down completely:

> His face, when he lifted it, was a terrible sight. Saliva and tears were running down his face; he couldn't stop it. His collar and shirt-front were soaked through. He smiled weakly at me when he saw me watching and tried to make light of it; he would not talk about it at all. I felt helpless not being able to do anything. He was ashamed to let me see him in this condition but could not help it, however hard he tried.[19]

Apparently Mannock got to succeed the great Canadian ace 'Billy' Bishop as head of No. 85 Squadron on the grounds that the pilots thought James McCudden, Bishop's originally intended successor, was too common. McCudden was killed in a flying accident on 9 July 1918. Whatever the reasons behind Mannock getting the nod, this was an elite squadron—Bishop had got to select the best from among hundreds of applicants—with which Mannock's efforts at perfecting formation flying and combat tactics would be better rewarded than when he was simply keeping inexperienced pilots alive in No. 74 Squadron.

'Taffy' Jones's biography of Mannock adds plenty of real and imagined conversations with Mannock that can neither be confirmed nor refuted into the mix. One story is that Mannock claimed to Jones that he had reached Bishop's score of seventy-two. This is a recurring problem with the Mannock legend: among his many, many admirers there's a tendency for them to denigrate the achievements of others, rather than just celebrate Mannock's proven successes. Bishop was disliked by many;

his 'lone wolf' tactics naturally gave way to that of team players like McCudden and Mannock. Unfortunately, Jones's ventriloquism of Mannock for young readers of the 1930s almost reaches parody—'Taffy, when you see that tiny spark come out of my SE, it will kindle a torch to guide the future air defenders of the Empire along the path of duty.' Jones also ticks the box in the requirement for a counterbalancing humanising element: he gives Mannock a sweetheart, an Irish nurse called Sister Flanagan, to whom he intended to propose once the war was over.

However, one well-recounted incident occurred on 20 July 1918. At a farewell luncheon for his friend Gwilym Hugh 'Noisy' Lewis (author of *Wings over the Somme*), Mannock and McElroy remonstrated with one another over flying too low and following victims too far down to verify their victories. Many decades later, Lewis gave an oral interview in which he repeats a version of the account first-hand. Lewis also gives a very positive account of his experiences with Mannock, describing him as the finest patrol leader they ever had.

On 26 July 1918, in his third week in charge of No. 85 Squadron, Mannock took a rookie New Zealand pilot, Donald Inglis, out on a mission to get his first kill. Mannock riddled a German two-seater, killing the observer/gunner and allowing Inglis to finish it off. However, they had followed the aircraft too far down, and were within range of machine gun and rifle fire from the German trenches. Both Mannock and Inglis were hit by ground fire. Inglis managed to crash-land on the Allied side of the lines but saw Mannock, in S.E.5a E1285, go down in flames between Colonne and Lestrem.

There has been much speculation as to the exact location where Mannock was buried and whether he did shoot or jump before the crippled aircraft caught fire. It is possible that he was killed by ground fire and/or that his body fell or was thrown clear from the wreckage. The personal effects returned by the Germans indicate that the body may have been singed but was not burned. In February 1921 the Imperial War Graves Commission noted that German records indicated that Mannock 'is believed to be buried 300 metres North-West of Pierre au Beure on the road to Paucut or Pacant.'[20] Too many attempts have been made to hang elaborate stories on this scant piece of information.

On 3 August 1918 Mannock's sister-in-law, Dorothy, wrote to the Air Ministry, enclosing a letter of condolence that his brother had received from a clergyman, Rev. Bernard W. Keymer, on 28 July 1918. Corporal Patrick John Mannock was at the time serving with the Tank Corps (service number 306922) on the Western Front—a less than ideal situation in which to hear of Mannock's death, but Rev. Keymer had meant well. He was padre with No. 40 Squadron and had only dined with Mannock a week previously.

Lieutenant W. E. W. Cushing of No. 85 Squadron wrote on 26 July to Pat along similar lines, but praising his skill, bravery, patience in teaching others, and his leadership. That such a diverse range of people corresponded with the family suggest widespread respect for Mannock, and their writing to his brother

Pat implies that they were aware of the dysfunctional nature of his family circumstances back home.

A second bar to his DSO had been in the course of approval, and its citation was gazetted on 3 August 1918:

Lt (T./Capt.) Edward Mannock, DSO, MC (formerly Royal Engineers)

This officer has now accounted for 48 enemy machines. His success is due to wonderful shooting and a determination to get to close quarters; to attain this he displays most skilful leadership and unfailing courage. These characteristics were markedly shown on a recent occasion when he attacked six hostile scouts, three of which he brought down. Later on the same day he attacked a two-seater, which crashed into a tree. (The announcement of award of Distinguished Service Order, and First Bar thereto, will be published in a later *Gazette*).[21]

On 16 September 1918 the citation for Mannock's DSO and for the first bar were both gazetted:

T./2nd Lt (T./Capt.) Edward Mannock, MC, RE, attd RAF

For conspicuous gallantry and devotion to duty during recent operations. In seven days, while leading patrols and in general engagements, he destroyed seven enemy machines, bringing his total in all to thirty. His leadership, dash and courage were of the highest order.

T./2nd Lt (T./Capt.) Edward Mannock, DSO, RE, and RAF

For conspicuous gallantry and devotion to duty. In company with one other scout this officer attacked eight enemy aeroplanes, shooting down one in flames. The next day, when leading his Flight, he engaged eight enemy aeroplanes, destroying three himself. The same week he led his patrol against six enemy aeroplanes, shooting down the rear machine, which broke in pieces in the air. The following day he shot down an Albatross two-seater in flames, but later, meeting five scouts, had great difficulty in getting back, his machine being much shot about, but he destroyed one. Two days later, he shot down another two-seater in flames. Eight machines in five days—a fine feat of marksmanship and determination to get to close quarters. As a patrol leader he is unequalled. (DSO gazetted in this *Gazette*.)[22]

However, it was imperative that some recognition would be given for Mannock's sustained efforts at going beyond the call of duty over a prolonged period of time. A campaign began to have Mannock awarded a posthumous Victoria Cross. Ronald

McNeill (later Baron Cushendun), was the local MP for Canterbury, and was strongly supportive of the campaign; ironically, he was a staunch Ulster Unionist who would have bitterly opposed Mannock's views on Home Rule for Ireland. (Irish Unionists had represented Canterbury previously, for instance Major Francis Bennett-Goldney until he was killed while serving with the RASC. Bennett-Goldney was a suspect in the theft of the Irish Crown Jewels in 1907.)

The Casualties Branch wrote to Julia to report Mannock as missing, believed killed. In the following months there were exchanges of correspondence on various matters; his mother wrote to the Air Ministry on 27 February 1919 to thank them for forwarding medals and diplomas posthumously conferred by the Royal Aero Club and the American club. Julia Mannock's address at this point in time was '15 Witton Rd, Sixways, Aston, Birmingham'. Although it is believed that Mick's older sister Jessie had also moved from Belfast to England and was working in a munitions factory, it is unclear whether she was looking after their mother in Birmingham, who is often described as succumbing to alcoholism at this time. In May 1919 Mick's younger sister wrote to the Air Ministry asking whether Mick's death had been officially confirmed. Nora (Helena 'Lena') gave her address as 'Mrs. L. McIntosh, 14 Rockview Street, Belfast', so it would appear that she had remained in Belfast but her mother had moved in the opposite direction.

In July 1919 Winston Churchill obtained Royal Assent for the award of the VC to Mannock. The award is what is termed a 'periodic' award, i.e. it is not for a specific instance of bravery but for outstanding courage over a particular period. Mannock's Victoria Cross citation was gazetted on 18 July 1919:

His Majesty the KING has been graciously pleased to approve of the award of the Victoria Cross to the late Captain (Acting Major) Edward Mannock, DSO, MC, 85th Squadron RAF, in recognition of bravery of the first order in Aerial Combat:

On the 17th June 1918, he attacked a Halberstadt machine near Armentières and destroyed it from a height of 8,000 feet.

On the 7th July 1918, near Doulieu, he attacked and destroyed one Fokker (red-bodied) machine, which went vertically into the ground from a height of 1,500 feet. Shortly afterwards he ascended 1,000 feet and attacked another Fokker biplane, firing 60 rounds into it, which produced an immediate spin, resulting, it is believed, in a crash.

On the 14th July 1918, near Merville, he attacked and crashed a Fokker from 7,000 feet, and brought a two-seater down damaged.

On the 19th July 1918, near Merville, he fired 80 rounds into an Albatross two-seater, which went to the ground in flames.

On the 20th July 1918, East of La Bassée, he attacked and crashed an enemy two-seater from a height of 10,000 feet.

About an hour afterwards he attacked at 8,000 feet a Fokker biplane near

Steenwercke and drove it down out of control, emitting smoke.

On the 22nd July 1918, near Armentières, he destroyed an enemy triplane from a height of 10,000 feet.

Major Mannock was awarded the undermentioned distinctions for his previous combats in the air in France and Flanders:

Military Cross. Gazetted 17th September 1917.
Bar to Military Cross. Gazetted 18th October 1917.
Distinguished Service Order. Gazetted 16th September 1918.
Bar to Distinguished Service Order (1st). Gazetted 16th September 1918.
Bar to Distinguished Service Order (2nd). Gazetted 3rd August 1918.

This highly distinguished officer, during the whole of his career in the RAF, was an outstanding example of fearless courage, remarkable skill, devotion to duty and self-sacrifice, which has never been surpassed.

The total number of machines definitely accounted for by Major Mannock up to the date of his death in France (26th July, 1918) is fifty—the total specified in the Gazette of 3rd August 1918, was incorrectly given as forty-eight, instead of forty-one.[23]

It is unclear why they revised downwards Mannock's tally, as the higher figure accurately matches squadron records. However, in July 1919 the Army of the Rhine and the Air Ministry exchanged correspondence in reference to a subsequent total of seven enemy aircraft destroyed and four brought down out of control, these figures being supplied for consideration in the course of deciding the award of the Victoria Cross. Overall, Mannock accounted for at least sixty-one enemy aircraft, a figure at which the aviation historian Norman Franks arrives from a detailed traversal of surviving combat reports, squadron operational record books, and war diaries at Wing and Brigade level.[25] Franks also offers a likely explanation for some of the additional eighteen claims attributed to Mannock by other sources or which are mentioned in his diaries. However, Franks offers no explanation for discounting one of the two aerial victories mentioned in the VC medal citation as having occurred on 20 July 1918.

However, regardless of whether Mannock reached sixty-one, -five, or seventy victories, he remains one of the RAF's highest-ever scoring aces, and Ireland's greatest fighter pilot ever. In all likelihood, Mannock was the greatest RAF pilot of all time, but it is not just through the narrow logic of his kill score that he should be judged. Rather, his combat career must be considered as a whole—no-one inspired such devotion as a Flight Commander, and he was *the* master tactician, who enhanced the capability of those with whom he flew. For a socially awkward and introverted man, he excelled at motivating and keeping up morale among his colleagues. He acted with total disregard for his own personal health and wellbeing, and went far beyond even the highest call of duty.

Mannock's legend would not be complete without another appearance by his pantomime villain father. Some accounts claim that Edward Senior turned up for the medal ceremony, made off with the VC, and that it had to be retrieved from a pawnbrokers by the other family members. This is most likely a by-product of various film scripts. Mannock's service records indicate that the Casualties Branch and the Air Ministry inter-departmental correspondence in April 1919 records his next-of-kin as his mother, at '96 Ettington Road, Aston, Birmingham'. On 7 May 1919 a formal letter was issued to Julia Mannock at that address to state that the Air Council had concluded that Major Mannock died on or since 26 July 1918. However, in September 1919 the Air Ministry and Army Council exchanged correspondence over an application for the posthumous decorations of Mannock. It contained the alarming phrase, 'It will be seen that Mr E. Mannock, 29 Siebert Rd, Westcombe Park, Blackheath, SC, is father and next of kin to the deceased officer,' and enclosed a letter dated 23 August 1919 from Mannock's father which made the following remarks:

> Would you be good enough to inform me what steps are necessary for me—the above deceased officer's father—to claim his Victoria Cross and other decorations?

Note that he cleverly avoided a claim to being his next of kin and so could not be prosecuted for making false representations. Mannock's father had also corresponded with the RAF Records Section on 19 August 1919, i.e. after the potential posthumous medal goldmine had become known from the gazetted citations. He writes in the manner of a next of kin, without actually claiming to be one:

> The above named officer was my son and I am approaching you in the hope that you will be able to supply me with the following information concerning him.
> (1) Has the fact of his death been established or officially presumed.
> (2) Was a will or testamentary writing left by him or known to be in existence?

The Air Council duly took the bait and wrote to Mannock's father on 23 August that, regrettably, his death had been accepted and there was no record of a will executed by Mannock. Regardless of what exactly transpired next, the VC remained in the family for many years, retained by Pat and Dorothy in a bank vault in Edinburgh.

Mannock remains one of the most successful yet enigmatic and misunderstood fighter aces of the war. Although many pilots' memoirs are full of praise for him, it is uncertain what his post-war legacy would have been had he survived. Jones could imagine Mannock as a future Prime Minister, but in reality Mannock would probably not have survived in the shark pool of parliamentary politics, not least the catastrophic Ramsay MacDonald coalitions of the 1920s and 1930s. De Burgh had similar but more down-to-earth views of Mannock's potential involvement in politics and public affairs:

> Had he lived, he would have made a marvellous politician; he had all the Celtic fire to move multitudes. And what a leader of a lost cause!
>
> But I don't think that present-day politics would have seen much of him. He was nothing if not sincere, and nothing if not a clean fighter. And where would such find a place in Party Politics?
>
> It is a personal regret of mine that I only knew Mannock for such a short time, and that when I was the 'old hand' and he the new. I could so obviously learn far more from him than he ever could from me—but I never had that privilege.
>
> There are very few one meets in the course of one's life who can be labelled as outstanding personalities, but he was one of them.[25]

Mannock would more likely have joined the mass ranks of unemployed demobilised soldiers rather than enter politics, perhaps returning to fight the Germans over Spain in the 1930s. He would have been unable to prevent the slaughter at Guernica or to slow the march of fascism in the 1930s, but he would have made an impact and perhaps inspired people in a way unimagined by Jones in his worship of the 'King of the Airfighters'.

18

McCLINTOCK,
Ronald St Clair
(5 aerial victories)

Born: 13 July 1892, Co. Carlow
Died: 22 June 1922
Awards: Military Cross

Major Ronald St Clair McClintock was born at Rathvinden, Leighlinbridge, Co. Carlow. He was the youngest son of Susan Heywood McClintock (née Heywood-Collins), from Glasgow, and Arthur George Florence McClintock, JP for Carlow, Down, Kildare, King's County (Offaly), and Wicklow, born in Dublin.

In 1901, Ronald was living with his brother Stanley and their parents at Leighlinbridge, together with four servants. By 1911, Ronald was living with his older brother John in Mahonstown, Co. Meath, while his parents were still resident at Leighlinbridge with Ronald's brothers, Robin and Edward, and his sister, Jane.

Several of Ronald's brothers also served in the British Army: Lieutenant John Heywood Jocelyn McClintock in the 18th Hussars; Lieutenant-Colonel Edward Stanley McClintock in the Royal Artillery; and Lieutenant-Colonel Arthur George McClintock of the 8th Hussars, who was awarded the DSO in 1917.[1]

According to the records of the Irish Petty Sessions Registers, on 3 April 1914 McClintock was charged with the willful prevention of free passage of persons on a public road. The offence took place on 26 February, but it's unclear whether this landowner's son was manning the barricades of some protest or if it was simply a local altercation. He was convicted and ordered to pay a fine of 5s, with a further 1s 6d in legal costs.

Ronald's war medal records state that he enlisted as a Private in the Ceylon Planters' Rifle Corps (No. 2167) before obtaining a commission as a 2nd Lieutenant in the West Lancashire Brigade of the Royal Field Artillery.[2] McClintock enlisted on 17 November 1914, obtained his commission with the RAF in December 1914 and served in Egypt before transferring to the RFC. McClintock was promoted from 2nd Lieutenant to Temporary Lieutenant with effect from 5 July 1915.[3]

In December 1915 McClintock joined No. 2 Squadron as an observer. There are several air combat reports relating to McClintock's time with the squadron, but the priority for No. 2 Squadron at the time was to arrange artillery, direct counter-battery fire, and undertake aerial photography rather than to engage in aerial combat, i.e. if attacked, pilots were expected to disengage and return safely.

On 13 February 1916, Captain P. Babington and Lieutenant McClintock were on artillery registration duties in a B.E.2c (2801) over Arras when they observed several German aircraft. Their response was to attack them:

> We got under a double fuselaged machine slightly to the right flank and engaged him at about 200 yards. He turned away and we engaged an Albatros on our tail and fired two drums at him and he turned also. Then a Nieuport looked suspicious and proceeded to chase us in spite of showing circles by banking.
>
> By this time the hostile machine had ... returned to their side of the line. It was impossible to fit directly underneath either machine as the French 'A' [anti-aircraft fire] were very accurate and would not cease firing.[4]

The combat report is intriguing insofar as the skies were relatively empty of aircraft in comparison to the later war years: banking to show one's markings would invite fire in the event that the machine was hostile. A better approach would have been to change direction and observe the response. It was 5 p.m. on a February evening, and with the sun setting in the West their B.E.2c would have cast a silhouette from many angles. By this stage in the war the roundel (cockade) was in use by French, British, and Russian forces (later the Italians would adopt the latter's version). 'Showing the circle' did not prevent ground fire from infantry either, who generally presumed every aircraft overhead was hostile, or in some cases took the approach of the over-cautious sentry and fired if the aircraft couldn't respond to the password or challenge to halt.

On 24 February Babington and McClintock were once again on artillery patrol in B.E.2c (2801) when they fought an indecisive aerial combat. They were on artillery patrol from Loos to Béthune and back to Hulluch when they encountered an Albatros—

> We ... manoeuvred to get under him. Both guns were used all the time; following the hostile machine to a point just east of Béthune where a quantity of paper or tinsel was dispatched and the machine headed towards Hulluch. We pursued until we had finished all the six drums of ammunition and the hostile machine had crossed the line. Several tracer bullets were seen to hit the machine, which apparently did not reply to our fire, owing to our position probably.

There's no clear reason why tinsel would be dropped for air-to-ground communication. By this stage of the war both sides had signal lamps and flares, and were even testing klaxon horns. The Germans may have been attempting to drop material that would be visible on the ground and thus help range their own artillery, and tinsel would disperse over a wide area. I've been unable to find a matching German source for what was being attempted, but the German offensive on Verdun had begun that week, so the Albatros may have been experimenting on a variety of air-to-ground techniques over an area that would not cause confusion to their own troop movements.

On 29 February—a leap year—Babington and McClintock were in their regular B.E.2c (2801) on a photography and artillery patrol when they had what they must have thought a decisive aerial combat with one of two Albatrosses over Loos.

> We ... noticed two Type 'A' hostile machines coming over the line east of Loos ... After several shots had been exchanged the hostile machines made off in the direction of Béthune, one a considerable way in front of the other. We gave chase, firing intermittently and when half-way to Béthune were joined by two other 2.cs ... when just SE of the Foret [de Nieppe] one hostile machine was hit and immediately went down in a very steep nose dive, but apparently under control. We continued to chase the other machine to Havingbrouk just south of Cassel and back over the line at Armentières. As we had expended all our ammunition and were short of oil and petrol we landed at No. 1 aerodrome at Bailleul and afterwards proceeded home.

This was classified as 'driven down' rather than 'driven down damaged' or 'out of control' and so was not regarded as a decisive aerial combat. Had the enemy aircraft been sufficiently damaged to have to force-land and been observed to do so, they would have been awarded the aerial victory.

On 13 March McClintock the B.E.2c (2081, possibly a mis-recording of 2801), piloted by Lieutenant W. G. B. Williams, was on artillery registration duties at 7,500 feet over Wingles when it encountered an enemy two-seater:

> While doing target with the 73rd Brigade a hostile machine was seen to be approaching from over Vermelles. It was immediately engaged from our front mounting, it being about 100 feet above us. Owing to the fact that the hostile machine kept on making S turns in order to fire at us, we were able to keep pace with it. This machine was followed to just North-West of Hantay. From a distance of about 50 yards several bursts were seen to enter the enemy's fuselage, and after firing three drums the machine ceased firing and was seen to dive steeply out of sight towards the earth. Pilot thinks that engine failure caused by a hit was the reason for descent.

McClintock and Williams signed the report, countersigned by Major C. F. Murphy, CO of No. 2 Squadron. However, there's a hand-written note in the margin: 'do not claim.' This suggests that at Wing or Brigade level the claim was disallowed, or perhaps awarded to another unit, who would have encountered a damaged German two-seater in a rapid descent.

On 28 March McClintock had a close encounter, which was mentioned in RFC Communiqué No. 32, of March 1916:

> 2nd Lt Williams and Lt McClintock, 2 Sqn, took some photographs urgently required by the 1st Corps. They had to fly at 3,000 feet owing to the gale. One of the elevator controls was shot away and the machine was riddled with bullets.[5]

On 1 April Williams and McClintock were on patrol in their regular B.E.2c (2614) when, perhaps unwisely, they attempted to attack a hostile kite balloon near Méricourt. They were immediately attacked by an L.V.G. The enemy aircraft was hit with over one and a half drums of ammunition and it 'dived to earth over Sallaumines.' However, Williams and McClintock did not claim it as a 'forced-to-land,' for they did not believe it to be out of control when descending. A hand-written note on the combat report indicates that it was regarded as 'driven down'.

On 3 April Williams and McClintock were on a mission in B.E.2c 2614 at 8,500 feet over Annay, photographing the German third line of defences, when they encountered two enemy aircraft—an Albatros and an L.V.G., but 'much faster and with far greater climbing powers.' They needed the help of their Bristol Scout escort to escape, for 'our machine was hit in several places, on the fuselage, rudder and tail.' McClintock made it through the encounter without injury.

McClintock was promoted from Flying Officer (Observer) to Temporary Lieutenant with effect from 4 April 1916. McClintock transferred from No. 2 Squadron for pilot training. On 26 October his engagement to Mary Gordon (Milly) Laird was announced. On 20 December 1916 they were married at the Church of the Holy Trinity, Kensington Gore. They were to have two children.

McClintock was promoted to Temporary Captain in the Army with effect from 17 January 1917, with the 3rd West Lancashire Brigade, RFA. McClintock was promoted from Flying Officer to Flight Commander with effect from 1 January 1917. On 28 June 1917 the War Office announced that McClintock, a (Temporary) 2nd Lieutenant, would retain the temporary rank of Captain, RFC, and remain seconded.[6] This was always something of an administrative balancing act, of allowing an officer act to several ranks above his home grade while not losing the tenuous relationship between responsibility and promotion. However, the RFC was a branch of the Army, therefore a temporary rank in the RFC would not preclude the possibility of the officer obtaining that rank in the Army if he were to return there from the RFC or, post-April 1918, the RAF.

In July 1917 McClintock transferred to No. 64 Squadron as Flight Commander. In March 1918 No. 64 Squadron was re-organised after being re-equipped with the SE.5a, and flew ground attack operations in addition to the scout/fighter squadron duties. McClintock scored his first confirmed aerial victory on 18 March 1918. Over the course of March he achieved three further aerial victories. His final victory with the squadron came on 2 April, which entailed the destruction of an Albatros D.V over Fricourt. RAF Communiqué No. 1 of 1918 reports the encounter:

> Capt. RSC McClintock, while leading a patrol of 64 Sqn, observed seven EA Scouts against which he led his patrol; he engaged one EA, diving at it and firing about 100 rounds at 40 yards range. The EA went into a flat spin and fell completely out of control and was observed to crash.[7]

However, McClintock was not the only Irish ace to serve with No. 64 Squadron: Edward Dawson Atkinson also scored many of his victories with the squadron.

In late April 1918 McClintock became Flight Commander of No. 3 Squadron. This squadron had its origins in the Air Battalion of the Royal Engineers. (The great ace James McCudden served with the squadron as a mechanic, having originally served with the Royal Engineers.) McClintock was promoted to Temporary Major while employed as Major (Flying), with effect from 20 April 1918.[8] Those with an Army background often raised an eyebrow at seeing RFC and RAF pilots elevated to such senior rank as Captain or Major. Conversely, the RAF was the only branch of the military in which the officers did almost all of the fighting.

McClintock was awarded the Military Cross, which was gazetted on 22 June 1918 (albeit with a misreporting of his middle name):

> Lt (T./Capt.) Ronald Sinclair McClintock, RFA and RFC

> For conspicuous gallantry and devotion to duty. On one occasion he shot down two enemy machines, and on the following day he attacked and shot down a hostile two-seater machine at a height of 100 feet. He has led upwards of forty patrols and has performed much valuable work on low-flying reconnaissance and bombing patrols. As a Flight Commander he has been untiring in his care of personnel and machines, and as a patrol leader he has displayed the greatest courage and resource.[9]

McClintock's time in charge of No. 3 Squadron produced one or two interesting occurrences. The squadron was tasked with ground-strafing operations, which was costly, dangerous work. One character who joined them in September that year was 2nd Lieutenant Roy Victor Curtis, a brother of the great Canadian naval ace Wilfred Austin Curtis. In early November 1918, just days before the Armistice, Roy Curtis, after a few drinks, decided to expound his honest views of the disparaging assessment of his limited schooling by McClintock and a couple of young American pilots, 2nd Lieutenants Paul Lemay, Dexter David Ashley, and James Edward Mutty. Curtis bloodied a few noses and did not spare the CO in the fisticuffs. To

McClintock's credit, he did not file any disciplinary proceedings against Curtis.[10] Good-natured joshing between Americans and Canadians of similar rank and age could easily descend into bullying behaviour, and McClintock could literally expect to take the matter on the chin.

McClintock continued to serve in the RAF following the armistice. In August 1919 he was promoted to Captain (Aeroplane).[11] I do not have a reference to cite as to when McClintock's period as Acting Major and Acting Captain came to an end, but *Flight* magazine of 10 March 1921 reported that 'Flight Lieutenant' McClintock was in attendance at the King's Levée of 7 March 1921 at St James' Palace.

On 22 June 1922, while serving as a Flight Lieutenant with No. 1 School of Technical Training, in Middlesex, McClintock was killed in a crash involving a Sopwith Snipe (F2409). The aircraft, which had previously been used by No. 24 Squadron's relay team, would appear to have disintegrated, and McClintock fell from a considerable height to his death. The RAF casualty card states that he had been training for the RAF Pageant. Although it notes that the machine did not catch fire in the air, and claims that McClintock probably didn't fasten his safety belt properly, it notes that the weather conditions were exceptionally bumpy and that McClintock may have been thrown from the aircraft in severe turbulence. It was a difficult time for his widow, as his death came less than four months after the birth of their daughter, Pamela. Their elder child, John, born on 30 April 1920, was barely two years of age when he lost his father.

John became a Pilot Officer (91064) with the RAF, serving with No. 615 Squadron before the war as a teenager and then as a pilot in the Battle of Britain. On 12 August 1940 he damaged a Bf 109 E-1 (W.Nr.3367), forcing it down east of Lewes. The pilot, Unteroffizier Leo Zaunbrecher of JG52, survived; there are several photos of his 'Red 14' aircraft, replete with 2 Staffel's red-painted 'little devil' emblem. Zaunbrecher was no novice, with two kills to his name, a French Potez Po.63 on 13 March 1940 and an RAF Fairey Battle on 14 May 1940. On 24 August McClintock shared in the destruction of a Heinkel 111. On 26 August, following a scrap with a Bf 109, he was shot down in Hurricane Mk.I (R4121), baled out, and was rescued from the sea off Sheerness without suffering injury. John McClintock did not die facing the enemy but in an air crash, just like his father. On 25 November 1940 he was piloting a Magister when it suffered catastrophic wing failure, about 200 feet off the ground. McClintock and Petty Officer Anthony John Jamieson Truran (91019) were both killed instantly. McClintock was only twenty years of age.

19

McCORMACK,
George
(5 aerial victories)

Born: 11 February 1896, Belfast
Died: 28 March 1928, Amman, British Trans-Jordan
Commemorated: Ramleh War Cemetery, Israel

George McCormack was born in Belfast in 1896. The War Office and Air Ministry official records used both 'McCormack' and 'McCormick', and much of his service records were destroyed in 1932, while other parts of his files have gone missing.[1] Consequently he has been the subject of much confusion and mistaken identity.

George McCormack joined the colours with the 17th (Reserve) Battalion of the Royal Irish Rifles on 7 June 1915. He enlisted at the Old Town Hall in Belfast as a rifleman (cadet) and was assigned the service number 17/1067. He was a draper from 14 Dufferin Terrace, Ormeau Rd, Belfast. Following the initial medical examination he was vaccinated against typhoid in July 1915, with the second inoculation taking place at Newcastle, Co. Down. His father Samuel was manager of J. R. Noble Coal Importers. George is therefore sometimes mistaken for being the son of Noble McCormack, an elderly veteran who died in the war.

On 27 September McCormack applied for a commission as a 2nd lieutenant, which was granted in October 1915. On 26 February 1916 he applied for a transfer to the cavalry, and was assigned to the 10th Reserve Cavalry Regiment, which was based at Curragh Camp. He reported for duty on 8 April 1916.

Within days of joining McCormack suffered severe injuries, falling from a horse. In many secondary publications—including his obituary—it is stated that McCormack was wounded in the fighting in the 1916 Easter Rising. However, this is not the case—his injuries arose in the Curragh Camp. They were severe, however, as McCormack's right clavicle was broken in such a manner that his back was also affected. A medical board examination of 28 July at Yorkhill War Hospital, Glasgow, found McCormack unfit for general service for six weeks. It noted that the fracture had united but that there were a considerable number of fragments. A subsequent medical board examination on 28 August found McCormack unfit for three months, noting that an operation would probably be necessary. Irish Command granted leave until 27 October, upon which date a medical examination in Belfast noted that McCormack was recovering from an operation on his clavicle and that there was still loss of power in his right arm.

On 3 November McCormack applied for a transfer back to the infantry. His application was commendably blunt, honest and forthright.

> My reasons for wishing to transfer are that I have a good knowledge of infantry training, and that owing to an accident, which will prevent my performing any active mounted work, I am unlikely to make an efficient cavalry officer; I am anxious to go to the Front as soon as possible.

A medical board examination at the Curragh on 27 November found him unfit for a further month. In the interim McCormack's transfer from the 10th Reserve Cavalry Regiment back to the 17th (Reserve) Battalion of the Royal Irish Rifles was granted in November. The CO of the 10th Reserve Cavalry Regiment wrote to the Brigade Major of the 3rd Reserve Cavalry Brigade, 'I am of the opinion that this officer will never make a cavalry officer as he possesses none of the necessary qualifications and is an indifferent horseman,' so they certainly weren't fighting to keep him. On 4 December 1916 the War Office announced McCormack's promotion to Temporary 2nd Lieutenant dated to 22 November 1916, to take effect from 4 October 1915.[2]

On 16 December McCormack was found fit to return to duty. He had good reason to declare himself fighting fit, for he had two brothers serving in France at the time. Furthermore, active service was a prerequisite for admission to the Indian Army, which he had set his sights on.

McCormack was granted a transfer to the 10th Battalion of the Royal Irish Rifles. They suffered severe losses at Thiepval Wood in July 1916, losing their CO, Colonel H. C. Bernard, and most of their officers. McCormack was promoted to Lieutenant in July 1917, and he applied for a transfer to the RFC and to the Indian Army around that time. At the commencement of the attack on the Messines Ridge, the battalion lost sixty killed, wounded, or missing on 7 June alone. On 29 August McCormack was wounded during the heavy fighting at Messines. He was evacuated on 7 September to Rouen and arrived on the HMHS *Western Australia* at Southampton the next day. However, the 10th Battalion survived, and took 213 other ranks from the remnants of the amalgamated 8/9th Battalion to recover to near-full strength. McCormack does not feature in the Battalion War Diary.[3] Unfortunately for him, in the interim between his application to transfer to the RFC and his wounding and during his hospitalisation, the RFC had arranged an examination before its Officers Invaliding Board in Hampstead in December, unaware that he was still under Army medical reporting arrangements.

On 12 September 1917 an Army medical board examination found McCormack unfit for six weeks, and a subsequent examination at Tidworth in October found him unfit for a further seven weeks. He was transferred to the Countess of Radnor's Hospital, Longford Castle, Salisbury, leaving on 25 October with three weeks' sick leave. He returned home instead of travelling to the Royal Irish Rifles, who were stationed at Ayr in Scotland. McCormack began reporting to the military barracks at Belfast on a daily basis, awaiting news of his next move. However, on 27 November he sought to withdraw his application for a transfer to the RFC, as his father was unhappy with it.

Inter-departmental correspondence was still slowly working its way through the system at this time—the term 'juggernaut' springs to mind. On 19 October the Indian Army wrote to the RFC to see if they wished to accept McCormack's application, and exchanges wrangled on for several months. Although McCormack had applied in the first instance for a permanent commission in the Indian Army, with the RFC being cited as an alternative, it is clear that the Indian Army did not wish to accept McCormack. The India Office had made inquiries and found that although his application received the recommendation of a former CO and a report from his brigadier, the actual covering letter of his present CO stated that he had not seen McCormack and so could not recommend him. It unclear whether McCormack was innocent or delusional, but he wrote again in December 1917, enclosing a letter of support from the Model School, Belfast. The headmaster duly wrote, 'during his time he passed with credit through Fifth and Sixth Standards, and his conduct was good.' But it was hardly Eton or Harrow, and unlikely to impress those adjudicating on his application, and a commission in the Indian Army was prestigious and, relative to British Army pay, quite lucrative.

McCormack called in personally to the India Office in January 1918 to adduce further support for his application. He followed up in writing on 6 January to explain that he already understood that Lieuteant-Colinel Norman George Burnand DSO could not recommend him on the basis that McCormack had no family connections and knew nothing of the languages. However, this should not be taken as *ad misericordiam*: McCormack actually asked that they contact Lieutenant-Colonel H. T. Lyle DSO, with whom McCormack had also served; 'I am sure he would sign them for me.' Lyle was a Boer War veteran, formerly with the 8th Service Battalion (East Belfast Volunteers) of the Royal Irish Rifles and Ulster Volunteer Force (UVF). But McCormack's pleas were to no avail.

Although not yet passed fit, McCormack was ordered to join at Reading for instruction in the RFC. Upon issuance of that correspondence the India Office then wrote on 30 January to reject McCormack's application, stating that they would not depart from the 'rule' that applications for permanent commissions could only be considered on the recommendation of the applicant's CO and Brigade Commander. (This was nonsense: discretion existed and influence was regularly exerted, but McCormack was an outsider who did not have any influence that could be brought to bear.) McCormack was still resident at 14 Dufferin Terrace, Ormeau Road, Belfast, when the news came through from both the India Office and the RFC. He replied on 10 February to the RFC, to state that he would travel that evening on the ferry crossing.

After initial training, McCormack was assigned to No. 22 Squadron as an observer. It was a multi-functional unit which flew the Bristol F2.b two-seater fighter. McCormack scored his first aerial victory on 3 September 1918, destroying a Pfalz D.XII in a Bristol F2.b (F5820) piloted by an American, Lieutenant Chester William McKinley Thompson. That same aircraft was brought down by anti-aircraft fire just two days later, with the crew severely wounded. McCormack and Thompson were to achieve ace status together: over the course of a three-week period in September they accounted for five enemy aircraft. Their fifth victory came on 24 September 1918 in Bristol F2.b (C1035) over Cambrai, which left McCormack wounded.[4]

Thompson did not fare too well afterwards: although he scored further victories in September—including one with Irishman Lieutenant William Tyrrell as his observer—and shared a further kill with an aircraft in which Tyrrell was an observer, he was shot down east of Cambrai on 29 September 1918 and taken prisoner of war. There is a suggestion that McCormack was wounded again in October and/ or November 1918, but I cannot find a matching record. *Flight* magazine of 17 October carried a notice of his being taken prisoner dated 11 October, but an *Irish Times* article many years later claims that McCormack was wounded several days before the Armistice.[5]

McCormack survived his wounds and continued to serve with the RAF after the war. On 1 August 1919 his permanent commission in the RAF, at the rank of Lieutenant, was granted. He served with No. 20 Squadron on the North-West Frontier. He was one of the squadron's original complement of men to set sail from Marseilles to India on the SS *Malwa* and SS *Syria*. Their machines did not arrive until later, on the SS *Clan Striart*. According to the squadron's ORB, on 13 September 1919 Captain C. E. W. Foster and Lieutenant McCormack, in B.F.4 (1549), conducted No. 20 Squadron's first-ever bombing operation in India. They dropped two 112-lb bombs on Chora Fort, in the Bazaar Valley.[6]

Given his unfortunate record of being wounded on land, on horse and in the air it is no surprise that McCormack had no luck in his post-war RAF career either: when serving on the North-West Frontier in 1919 he was forced to land with a bullet in his fuel tank. He was taken prisoner and ransomed. According to an *Irish Times* article, 'his safe return excited such interest that he was specially presented to the Viceroy, and, on his return to England, was presented to the King.' *Flight* reported that McCormack had attended the King's Levée on 10 February 1922 and was 'presented to the King,' so there is probably some truth to the story.[7] Two other remarkable Irishman, Robert Francis Casey and John Charles Quinnell, were also presented to the King on this occasion, so perhaps there was a long list of crashes and rescues warranting a royal handshake or nod of appreciation.

On 12 April 1921, the War Office wrote to McCormack refusing him a wounds gratuity. The rationale for refusal was that the injury was not of a 'severe and permanent nature.' McCormack's address at this time was 20 Stranmills Road, Belfast.

On 12 July 1921—the Glorious Twelfth, he would have hoped—McCormack applied to the RAF School of Photography at Farnborough for a wounds gratuity in respect of his wartime service during the Easter Rising. Having been informed of the need for severity and permanence by his War Office application, McCormack explained the circumstances surrounding his injuries in greater detail, and the consequent medical procedures necessary to redress the matter.

> During the Dublin Rebellion in 1916 I was stationed ... in Ireland as an officer with the 10th Res. Regt of Cavalry ... I was thrown off and received a broken collar bone (right); this was set rather badly by the Medical Officer at the Curragh Hospital, causing an overlap and after some time had an operation and the overlap removed. I am still very weak on this shoulder. I have had four operations during the war, including wounds etc. and I never received any gratuity.[8]

Nevertheless, his application was rejected.

McCormack's promotion from 2nd Lieutenant (Honorary Lieutenant) to Lieutenant with effect from 23 August 1918 was gazetted in March 1922.[9] This may appear to be quite late, but in reality a simple validation of McCormack's actual status.

Flying Officer McCormack was transferred to No. 111 Squadron, Duxford, with effect from 12 December 1923. This was a fighter squadron, under the command of Galway man Tom Falcon Hazell. McCormack remained a Flying Officer for many years, though transferred from fighters to other roles. On 1 January 1927 McCormack's promotion from Flying Officer to Flight Lieutenant was announced. By December that year, he had transferred to No. 14 Squadron, in the Middle East. Another Irish ace, Henry George Crowe, was one of the Flight Commanders of that squadron.

On 28 March 1928 McCormack and Leading Aircraftman J. Kimberly (as passenger) were killed when a D.H.9A of No. 14 Squadron crashed near Amman. Both men are buried in Ramleh War Cemetery. The squadron records the D.H.9A as having crashed while on the mail flight to Ramleh.[10] It barely receives a mention and is one of a litany of crashes that year. The next most significant entry in the ORB relates to His Majesty the Emir Abdullah presenting the prizes at the squadron sports on 21 April 1928, but that the occasion was somewhat interfered with by low-flying clouds of locusts.

McCormack's death was reported in *The Irish Times* of 31 March 1928 and *The Weekly Irish Times* of Saturday 7 April 1918 in a brief obituary. He was undecorated for his wartime service, and remains one of Ireland's forgotten aces.

20

McELROY,
George Edward Henry
(47 aerial victories)

Born: 14 May 1893, Co. Dublin
Died: 31 July 1918
Awards: Military Cross and Two Bars, Distinguished Flying Cross and Bar
Commemorated: Laventie Military Cemetery, La Gorgue, France; War Memorial
Cross, St Mary's Church, Donnybrook, Dublin

Captain George McElroy was one of the Allies' highest-scoring aces of the war. Not only was he the highest-scoring pilot with No. 40 Squadron—being credited with at least thirty aerial victories there—but also one of the most successful pilots of No. 24 Squadron, with at least sixteen aerial victories during his short period of service with that unit.

McElroy was born in Donnybrook, Dublin, to Samuel and Ellen McElroy (née Synnott). In 1901 the family are recorded as resident in Beaver Row, Donnybrook. George was the eldest of the children. At this stage he had one brother, Robert, and three sisters, Eileen, Louisa, and Elizabeth. Both of McElroy's parents were from the Irish Midlands—his father was a primary school teacher from Co. Roscommon, and his mother was a 'work-mistress' (a teaching assistant) from Co. Westmeath. Samuel McElroy used to enter a school choir to the *Feis Ceoileanna* Irish cultural festivals, which was quite unusual for a Church of Ireland school, but he used also to teach French and other non-curricular subjects to the children. His interest in choir-singing extended to his participation in the choir of St Mary's Church, Donnybrook, for many decades.

McElroy was, of course, initially educated at Donnybrook School, Beaver Row, from 1897 to 1906. He then attended the Educational Institute, Dundalk, Co. Louth, from 1906 to 1909, after which he became a student at the Mountjoy in Dublin. McElroy passed his Senior Grade Examinations in 1910. The Intermediate Education Board for Ireland recorded passes in a wide range of subjects—English, Natural Philosophy, Latin, French, Trigonometry, Chemistry, and Mechanics—and passes with honours in Arithmetic and Algebra, and Geometry. In the Irish census of 1911 McElroy was a boarder at the Mountjoy School in Dublin. (This school later merged with the Hibernian Marine and the Bertrand & Rutland School to form Mount Temple Comprehensive—a school with a reputation for developing original talent, for instance Irish musicians such as Cactus World News, Damien Dempsey, and U2.) McElroy was one of only a handful of Dublin students at Mountjoy, which seemed to cater to those from rural areas which would not have independently had the population threshold to support a Protestant school.

McElroy's parents were still living beside the school on Beaver Row, with five children in 1911. Although George and his sister Eileen had moved out, Louisa, Elizabeth, and Robert were still there, since joined by Olivia, William, and John. As may be noted, McElroy came from a family of modest means, the eldest children receiving their post-primary education from a special Protestant-funded resource that largely relied on rental income from estates bequeathed to it. Several of McElroy's uncles emigrated from Ireland to the USA, as did those on his mother's side, so there were a substantial number of American-born McElroy and Synnott descendants.

In 1912 McElroy briefly studied at Rosse College Dublin, possibly to prepare for civil service entrance exams.[1] Some sources suggest that he was a student at Trinity College Dublin from 1913 to 1914. However, TCD does not include him on the rolls of honour in the 1937 Reading Room of Trinity College, which commemorates the 3,529 members of TCD, the Dublin University OTC, and both their employees who served in the war. By 1914 McElroy had succeeded in passing a civil service admission examination and was working as a second division clerk.

McElroy's early military service career is often the subject of much confusion, as he transferred between multiple service branches. He actually enlisted with the Motor Cyclist Section of the Royal Engineers on 13 September 1914 (service number 28292) as a corporal. He served on Home Establishment duties until 29 September 1914, joining the BEF on 30 September, and so was eligible for the 'Mons Star' on that basis. He joined GHQ of Signals Company in October 1914 and was assigned to the 4th Signals Company on 24 October. On 8 April 1915 McElroy was attached to Cadet School, Ballieul. On 8 May he obtained a commission as a Temporary 2nd Lieutenant in the 1st Battalion of the Royal Irish Regiment. Although he is not specifically mentioned in the Battalion War Diary, McElroy would appear to have suffered badly from a mustard gas attack in the battles for Ypres.[2] McElroy attended a medical board examination in Dublin on 26 October 1915, which found him unfit and extended his leave until 16 November. Surgery was performed on the inferior turbinate bone on the right side of his nose to cure his chronic hypertrophy and nose-bleeds. This took place in Dublin and entailed simple cauterisation. McElroy was notionally on the establishment of the 4th Battalion from 18 November to 9 December 1915, when he formally transferred to the 3rd Battalion. Further medical board examinations took place in November and December 1915 at the King George V Hospital in Dublin; an examination on 17 December 1915 found him fit to resume duties.

Allegedly, McElroy was recuperating at home in Dublin at the outbreak of the Easter Rising in 1916 but refused to fire on his countrymen and was sent to a southern garrison for the duration of the summer as punishment. Numerous sources make reference to this claim. However, I have not found a single corresponding regimental record to confirm any disciplinary proceedings against McElroy. On the other hand, the records of the Bureau of Military History include an account by Provisional Government Minister and Treaty signatory Robert Barton (WS0979), which state that he was permitted to go home on the dubious pretext of having no uniform. (It was at a tailor's shop in Dame St, which was under siege.) Barton, serving with the 10th Battalion of the Royal Dublin Fusiliers, returned a week later from the family estate in Co. Wicklow to help manage the ownership of prisoners' effects, prevent further looting by British troops, and engage in routine duties to bring civilian life in the city back to some level of normalcy. It is therefore quite possible that McElroy was given some pretext for not having to fire on fellow Irishmen and was then assigned non-combat military duties without a disciplinary issue arising.

In January 1916 McElroy was temporarily with the 4th Battalion of the Royal Irish Regiment in Ireland when he applied for admission to the Royal Military Academy at Woolwich. The CO of the 4th Royal Irish Regiment, who was at the time based in Fermoy, Co. Cork, provided the certification of McElroy's good moral character, on 14 January, in support of the application. Similarly, the CO of the 3rd Reserve Battalion of the Royal Irish Regiment, who was based at Richmond Barracks in Dublin, provided a character reference on 18 January in support of McElroy's application.

The Royal Military Academy at Woolwich states that George Edward Henry McElroy enrolled as Cadet No. 10089 in 1916. He sat the Army entrance examination in February 1916, coming 69th in the order of merit, and prior to travelling to Woolwich was the subject of a medical board examination on 2 March 1916. An order to join was issued to him in April 1916. McElroy was twenty-three, his DOB recorded as 14 May 1893, while his religion was misrecorded as 'RC' in the enrolment ledger. HE came 55th in the order of merit on joining, which would suggest that not all candidates who succeeded at the exam were in a position to take up their enrolment in the academy. McElroy was ranked 41st in the order of merit on leaving Woolwich, graduating on 26 February 1917. His commission to the Royal Garrison Artillery was granted on the 28th, while his previous temporary commission was relinquished. The Royal Regiment of Artillery had evolved from a series of mergers but it retained three sub-branches— the Royal Horse Artillery, the Royal Field Artillery, and the Royal Garrison Artillery (which, as the name implies, had its origins in manning the guns of coastal artillery batteries, and those of the forts and fortresses of the Empire). It was this last branch that was McElroy's route to a permanent commission.

On 12 March 1917 McElroy transferred to the RFC and was posted to the No. 1 School of Military Aeronautics.[3] There are an elaborate series of designations for training squadrons—RS (known as such from January 1916) and TS (known as such from May 1917)—in McElroy's service records; initially, these training squadrons were called reserve aeroplane squadrons. On 31 March 1917 McElroy was transferred to No. 14 RS, and thereafter to No. 6 RS (later re-designated No. 6 TS). On 28 June he was appointed Flying Officer while at No. 6 TS, and briefly posted to No. 54 TS from 2 to 15 July. On 20 July 2nd Lieutenant G. E. H. McElroy was confirmed in his rank while seconded to the RFC, with effect from 28 June 1917; and on 27 July the War Office announced that he was promoted to 2nd Lieutenant with effect from 9 February 1916.[4, 5] To explain this as briefly as possible, and so hopefully to quash stories of him being stripped of rank and then having his commission restored as the Irish political circumstances changed, McElroy would have been eligible for promotion to a permanent commission in December 1915 under the older regulations had he not accepted a cadetship at Woolwich. The amended date of his commission merely follows the general principles applied to promotions in changing circumstances.

McElroy arrived in France on 16 August 1917, posted to No. 40 Squadron, and on the 23rd he was assigned to Mannock's 'A' Flight. On 3 September he crashed a Nieuport (B1693) when returning from an advanced landing ground. However, the crash was not due to rough terrain but to McElroy getting into a spin upon attempting to climb and turn—an elementary error. On the same day McElroy accounted for another Nieuport (B1558) on return from an offensive patrol, once again being unable to align an approach for landing without entering a spin. McElroy then proceeded to crash a Nieuport 23 (A6774) on 19 September. It was not quite McElroy's fault on this occasion, as there was a strong crosswind and he simply overturned, something Mannock had done himself on occasion. He was almost sent home for further training, but Mannock persuaded Major Tilney to retain McElroy, who he had nicknamed 'McIrish' to differentiate him from William MacLanachan 'McScotch'. McElroy would not be considered a competent pilot on the Nieuport 17 or Nieuport 23, but he was to prove a major success with the S.E.5a, scoring some spectacular victories and becoming the highest-scoring pilot on that type.

RFC Communiqué No. 108 of 1917 reports on one of McElroy's early unconfirmed claims:

> Lt G. E. H. McElroy, 40 Squadron, attacked a hostile balloon south-east of Lens and saw it smoking, but owing to anti-aircraft fire could not see further result. Anti-aircraft observers report that at this time a hostile balloon was seen to break loose.[6]

This claim, on 7 October 1917, was not awarded. McElroy had still not quite repaid Mannock's faith in him, and on 4 December managed to crash one of the squadron's new mounts, S.E.5 A8913, but it was not a serious crash, merely a case of overturning on landing. Superficially one might conclude that McElroy was quite useless at landing, but in reality the ground was quite soft at this time of year and so no matter how careful the approach, or how well the speed and descent might have been judged, there was always the prospect of an aircraft going on its back.

On 28 December 1917 McElroy obtained his first aerial victory, though many accounts attribute this to Mannock riddling the LVG aircraft and setting up the crippled two-seater for McElroy to administer the *coup de grâce*. These sorts of claims should always be made with caution, as they usually were part of a larger agenda to talk up Mannock's total victories. From McElroy's actual 'Combats in the Air' report it would appear that the German two-seater was 'very dark coloured, light coloured underneath,' and that McElroy fired 100 rounds at just 50 yards. However, he actually *over*shot the falling LVG, such was the angle of his dive, and upon turning could see the German crash. MacLanachan 'McScotch' witnessed the encounter and confirmed McElroy's victory. (Actually, McElroy's dive had scattered a formation of German aircraft, losing the other S.E.5s the opportunity to use their positional and height advantage to inflict greater losses: Mannock is reported to have criticised rather than praised McElroy for his first victory, calling him a *spailpín*, but McScotch disclosed to McElroy that Mannock was in fact happy with the outcome.)

Given his spectacular ineptitude in his early career, it is hardly any wonder that McElroy's tally of forty-seven aerial victories over a seven-month period was treated with skepticism. But, if anything, it is understated: there was a tendency towards caution by Major Tilney and Captain Napier with McElroy's early claims of January 1918. For example, No. 40 Squadron's 'Combats in the Air' files for 13 January 1918 report on McElroy's victory over a two-seater Rumpler when flying S.E.5A B598.[7] McElroy followed the British anti-aircraft artillery to locate the target and got underneath an enemy aircraft, firing two long bursts of 100 rounds each at 100-150 yards' distance. He suffered broken landing wires in the encounter and so was unable to follow his victim down. However, there is a note on the record to the effect that 'C' Battery AA had seen the fight but was also unable to see the final result due to haze. This suggests that McElroy's claims were being made the subject of external validation. Similarly a report of 19 January 1918 records McElroy, in S.E.5a (B598), attacking a blue- and white-camouflaged DFW over Vitry. McElroy fired 60 rounds from just 10 yards' distance, which is practically point-blank range. The German was followed down to 2,000 feet, McElroy firing as the opportunity arose. However, the note to the claim states, 'this EA confirmed as crashed by observers of 'D' Battery AA,' which once again suggests that McElroy's claim required external confirmation before being declared 'destroyed'. Similarly, the same 'Combats in the Air' files for 24 January 1918 describe two separate encounters in which McElroy engages enemy aircraft at close range, flying an S.E.5A (B598). He is credited with one of the aircraft—a green DFW two-seater—between Oppy and Henin-Lietard, but is not given credit for the second aircraft, which he actually hit from above and below at very close range. In fact it would appear that McElroy was only granted the first claim on the basis that 'E' Battery had observed the encounter. It is therefore unfair on McElroy his forty-seven aerial victories should be seen as an exaggeration: if anything, this figure is an understatement, given the amount of aircraft McElroy engaged and damaged.

Throughout the month of January and mid-February 1918 McElroy was to score victories over several German two-seaters, with double victories on 5 February and 17 February 1918. RFC Communiqué No. 126 of February 1918 reports on McElroy's double-victory of 5 February 1918:

> Lt G. McElroy, 40 Squadron, singled out a DFW and when within 100 yards range fired 100 rounds. Pieces were seen to fall from the EA's tail and fuselage and it went down in a slow spin and crashed. He then observed a DFW which was pointed out to him by anti-aircraft fire; he dived, fired about 200 rounds, and the EA burst into flames.[8]

That particular communiqué also disclosed that McElroy had been awarded the Military Cross, although it was not gazetted at the time. On 31 January 1918 it was reported that G. E. H. McElroy had been promoted from Temporary 2nd Lieutenant to Temporary Lieutenant with effect from 9 August 1917 and was to remain seconded to the RFC.[9] McElroy was to finish his first spell with No. 40 Squadron with eleven confirmed victories.

A mechanic with No. 40 Squadron, F. T. Gilbert, wrote an article for *Popular Flying* in 1936, in which he outlined McElroy's apparent low expenditure rate of ammunition, noting that the armourers would find that McElroy had fired an average of 130 rounds per sortie—although Gilbert mistakenly believed that McElroy therefore fired just one or two accurate short bursts. From the combat reports it's clear that McElroy would indeed hold fire until certain of his target, but he would fire a burst of 100 rounds or so when he had his mark. Gilbert also believed that McElroy used to fire at long range to lull the opponent into believing that he was a novice, and would then settle the matter with his exceptionally accurate shooting. His account tells us more about the admiration that McElroy solicited, however, than McElroy's skill.

On 18 February 1918 McElroy transferred to No. 24 Squadron, being promoted to Flight Commander. No. 24 Squadron also flew the S.E.5a and, like No. 40 Squadron, had a significant Irish contingent. McElroy went quickly into his stride, sending down an Albatros D.V out of control south of Honnecourt on 21 February, then destroying a Fokker Dr.I east of Laon on 26 February. RFC Communiqué No. 128 of 1918 records McElroy being awarded a bar to his Military Cross, although this was not gazetted.

McElroy scored eight victories in March alone, including double victories on 8 March and 29 March 1918. RFC Communiqué No. 133 of 1918 records the following sequence of victories on 29 March.

Capt. G. E. H. McElroy, 24 Squadron, saw five EA Scouts behind their lines west of Foucaucourt. He climbed above the clouds and approached the EA through a gap, apparently unobserved, then dived on one Albatros Scout, firing 100 rounds into it at a range of from 100 to 20 yards. Pieces were seen to fall off the EA's fuselage and it went down completely out of control, crashing between Foucaucourt and the River Somme. Capt. McElroy also shot down one EA out of control.[10]

McElroy's leadership skills were developing as well as his fighting prowess. The American ace Bill Lambert recalls joining No. 24 Squadron in March and being assigned to McElroy, who he evidently came to hold in high esteem.

I was posted to 'C' Flight on 16 March 1918 with Capt. G. E. H. McElroy as Flight Commander. George McElroy was without a doubt one of the most fearless men I have ever met. He was also most considerate of the pilots under him and at all times tried to keep his pilots out of trouble. He would not allow me to go out until he felt I was ready and I think I owe my survival to his teachings. I finally did four or five patrols with him before he was transferred another squadron ... An excellent leader.[11]

Lambert's praise of McElroy and Hazell—both are 'fearless', but McElroy is also 'considerate' while Hazell is described as 'reckless'—presents something of a dichotomy. There's too much loaded into these few sentences, and we must bear in mind that Hazell was leading balloon-busting and ground-strafing operations, which in effect required a bit more recklessness than consideration. McElroy, on the other hand, was sticking to elements of his training under Mannock, i.e. preserve life and attack targets of opportunity as they present themselves. There was always a countervailing philosophy of engaging every identifiable threat. Indeed, the early CO of No. 24 Squadron, Hawker VC, reduced Nelson's instruction of 'engage the enemy more closely' to a simple 'attack everything'. Over in No. 40 Squadron, Mannock's approach was counterbalanced by 'Grid' Caldwell's exhortation to his charges to attack everything.

On 25 March 1918 McElroy's promotion to Temporary Captain while serving as a Flight Commander, with effect from 16 February was gazetted.[12] His Army regiment remained the Royal Regiment of Artillery. On 22 March 1918 *The London Gazette* reported that McElroy had been awarded the Military Cross, but did not publish the citation. This award related to his achievements with No. 40 Squadron, not No. 24 Squadron.

On 1 April 1918, the very first day of operations for the RAF, McElroy took on three enemy aircraft and crashed one north of Ignaucourt.[13] On the 4th, he was to account for another enemy aircraft, again when the odds were ridiculously stacked against him, for he took on eight German aircraft, sending one down in a spin north of Warfusee. And just three days later, he accounted for several more German aircraft:

Capt. G. E. H. McElroy, 24 Sqn, dived on three EA two-seaters and reserved his fire until under the tail of the nearest, into which he fired 70 rounds at 50 yards range. The EA fell in a nose-dive and crashed three miles east of Marcelcave. Shortly afterwards, while flying through the clouds at 3,000 feet, he saw three SE's being attacked by five enemy triplanes. Capt. McElroy got on the tail of one of the triplanes and fired 20 rounds at point-blank range into it. The EA went down in a spin and crashed north of Moreuil Wood.

There is some speculation as to whether the crashed aircraft was that of fellow Irishman, P. J. Nolan. The Indian-born, Irish-raised Nolan was awarded the DFC; he is regarded as a six-kill ace in Illingworth's history, and at least four shared aerial victories are mentioned in the RFC/RAF communiqués, but it would appear that some of his shared claims were rejected at Wing or Brigade level. I therefore do not include Nolan as an ace in this work. There is the possibility that he died in the above-cited encounter, as Bill Lambert and Illingworth's official history of the squadron inform us,

> Lt Nolan is missing after a very gallant scrap in which he followed his opponent right down onto the top of Moreuil Wood and then apparently hit a tree, or at any rate was forced to land in the wood.[14]

McElroy himself was to crash on the evening patrol of the 7th, following the above encounter. He was returning from visiting the lines when he hit a tree. His S.E.5 (C1098) was badly damaged and he himself injured. Bill Lambert recalled him hitting a treetop, crashing onto a hangar, and then just missing the CO's hut. McElroy was only slightly wounded, but was returned to Home Establishment for a rest.

Over those short few days in April, McElroy had recorded six aerial victories. His MC citation was actually gazetted on 24 August 1918, so was somewhat out of sequence with his other awards:

2nd Lt George Edward Henry McElroy, RGA and RFC

For conspicuous gallantry and devotion to duty. He has shown a splendid offensive spirit in dealing with enemy aircraft. He has destroyed at least two enemy machines, and has always set a magnificent example of courage and initiative.[15]

On 22 April 1918 the award of a bar to his Military Cross was gazetted:

2nd Lt George Edward Henry McElroy, MC, RGA, and RFC

For conspicuous gallantry and devotion to duty. When on an offensive patrol, observing a hostile scout diving on one of our aeroplanes, he opened fire, and sent down the enemy machine in an irregular spin out of control, when it finally crashed completely.

Later in the same day, he sent down another enemy machine in flames. On another occasion, when on offensive patrol, he singled one out of four enemy machines, and sent it down crashing to earth. On the same day he attacked another enemy machine, and, after firing 200 rounds, it burst into flames.

On a later occasion, he opened fire on an enemy scout at 400 yards' range, and finally sent it down in a slow spin out of control.

In addition, this officer has brought down two other enemy machines completely out of control, his skill and determination being most praiseworthy. (MC gazetted 26th March 1918.)[16]

On 12 April 1918 McElroy was hospitalised and invalided to England. A medical board examination reported that he was unfit for four weeks. He returned to service via No. 28 TS and No. 90 Squadron in May and June 1918. This last squadron would have been a fighter squadron but never saw active service in the war and was disbanded before it ended.

McElroy returned to No. 40 Squadron on 14 June 1918 and was reunited with a much changed Mick Mannock, who was at this stage nearing the end of his service with No. 74 Squadron. McElroy at this stage had twenty-six victories to his name, and was one of the highest-scoring Allied aces. His return to frontline combat was not uneventful. On 19 June the Hispano-Suiza engine of his S.E.5a (D5982) suffered a broken connector rod while he was out on offensive patrol, and he had to make a forced landing near Magnicourt. Another member of his patrol, Lieutenant Gilbert 'Ben' Strange, overturned his S.E.5a (D395) in the course of landing to assist McElroy. Strange, with whom McElroy had shared three aerial victories, was to be killed in combat just days later.

McElroy was awarded the second bar to his Military Cross. The citation was gazetted on 26 June 1918:

Lt (T./Capt.) George Edward Henry McElroy, MC, RGA, and RFC

For conspicuous gallantry and devotion to duty. While flying at a height of 2,000 feet, he observed a patrol of five enemy aircraft patrolling behind the lines. After climbing into the clouds, he dived to the attack, shot down and crashed one of them. Later, observing a two-seater, he engaged and shot it down out of control. On another occasion he shot down an enemy scout which was attacking our positions with machine gun fire. He has carried out most enterprising work in attacking enemy troops and transport and in the course of a month has shot down six enemy aircraft, which were seen to crash, and five others out of control.

(MC gazetted 26th March 1918.)
(1st Bar gazetted 22nd April 1918.)[17]

The same day McElroy re-opened his account with No. 40 Squadron, destroying a DFW two-seater just south-east of Annay. He then managed to destroy three balloons in less than a week. Balloons were well defended targets, but the RAF had been tasked with this difficult role at a time when the situation on the ground was chaotic.

McElroy scored double victories on 2, 8, 13, 15, and 25 July. Several of his victories were shared with Lieutenants Strange and Indra Roy. Indeed, McElroy seemed to have built quite a friendship with Indra Lal 'Laddie' Roy, the only Indian pilot to reach ace status in the war. Many decades later Irish newspapers and historians would receive letters from various Indian student biographers of Roy inquiring of his Irish friend McElroy. It's therefore likely that McElroy featured in Roy's correspondence to friends and family.

On 20 July McElroy's S.E.5a (D3511) experienced engine failure when engaging enemy aircraft over La Bassée. The carburettor caught fire, but he successfully landed in a field near Noeux les Mines. However, McElroy had recovered sufficient composure by that evening to attend a farewell dinner and drinks for the quiet Welshman 'Noisy' Lewis. In an interview for the Imperial War Museum in 1990, Wing Commander Gwilym Lewis recalls Mannock's admonishment of McElroy on 20 July for following down a kill too low when attempting to confirm the victory. Yet, just days later, Mannock was killed doing just that.

Gilbert also recorded his impression that both Mannock and McElroy were taking excessive risks to confirm their kills.

Each was convinced that the other was rash and took risks. Each reproached the other and issued solemn warnings. To hear them on this was amazing. But Mac was less *berserk* than Mannock, and until he caught fire in the air just before his death [20 July incident] his nerves showed little sign of being on edge, except in a new petulance when he could not get combats.[18]

On 22 July McElroy lost another friend; Indra Roy went down in flames in a dogfight between No. 40 Squadron and the Fokker DVIIs of Jasta 29.

On 31 July McElroy was shot down and killed; some sources claim by Vizefeldwebel Gullmann of Jasta 56, although the majority of sources claim he was shot down either by ground fire or by anti-aircraft fire. McElroy had gone out alone that morning in S.E.5a (E1310), a new machine with just eleven hours' flying time in its logbook. Norman Franks' *Who Downed the Aces in World War I?* examines in detail the competing accounts of what potentially transpired, but notes that the Germans took the trouble to drop a note to say that McElroy had been shot down by AA fire. Apparently McElroy shot down a two-seater—probably a Hannover CL of Schlasta 19 lost on that date. McElroy was buried at Laventie, which gave rise to all sorts of half-baked stories about him being buried next to Mick Mannock.

For such a distinguished pilot, it is difficult to understand how he was not awarded the DSO, for which RAF officers became eligible in July 1918. Neither the DSO nor the DFC can be awarded posthumously, but fortunately previous recommendations in relation to McElroy's achievements were acted on. On 3 August 1918 McElroy's DFC citation was gazetted:

Lt (T./Capt.) George Edward Henry McElroy, MC

A brilliant fighting pilot who has destroyed thirty-five machines and three kite balloons to date. He has led many offensive patrols with marked success, never hesitating to engage the enemy regardless of their being, on many occasions, in superior numbers. Under his dashing and skilful leadership his Flight has largely contributed to the excellent record obtained by the squadron.[19]

In this same edition, Edward Dawson Atkinson and Samuel Marcus Kinkead (a South African with a father from Co. Derry) were also honoured with the DFC. On 21 September 1918 McElroy's bar to the DFC was gazetted:

Lt (T./Capt.) George Edward Henry McElroy, MC, DFC (Royal G. Artillery)

In the recent battles on various army fronts this officer has carried out numerous patrols, and flying at low altitudes, has inflicted heavy casualties on massed enemy troops, transport, artillery teams, etc., both with machine gun fire and bombs. He has destroyed three enemy kite balloons and forty-three machines, accounting for eight of the latter in eight consecutive days. His brilliant achievements, keenness and dash have at all times set a fine example, and inspired all who came in contact with him.

(MC gazetted 26th March 1918,
1st Bar 22nd April 1918,
2nd Bar 26th July 1918,
DFC gazetted 3rd August 1918.)[20]

In this same edition Captain Edgar James McClaughry, an Australian with a father from Larne, Co. Antrim, also received a bar to the DFC.

McElroy's is commemorated on the War Memorial Cross at St Mary's Church, Donnybrook, Dublin. Other Irish aviators commemorated on the memorial are the aces Maurice Lea Cooper and Sidney Edward Cowan, together with Gerald Lovell Backhouse, Philip Chalmers Cowan (Sidney's brother), and Richard Patrick Hemphill.

McElroy's mother, Ellen, died in 1922. His brother, William Alfred, is also commemorated on the War Memorial Cross in St Mary's Church, Donnybrook. He was killed in the Second World War on 23 February 1945, and is buried in the

Dar es Salaam War Cemetery in Tanzania. The Royal Navy's Fleet Air Arm Station at Durban, South Africa, is usually attributed the HMS *Kongoni* designation, but it would appear that McElroy died of illness on the island of Zanzibar. He had served as pilot with No. 753 Squadron at Arbroath, Scotland, before being transferred to No. 796 Squadron at Tanga, Tanganyika. It was only in the late stages of the war that he was assigned to No. 726 Squadron, which was based at Durban.

McElroy's other two brothers were qualified doctors, one serving in East Africa, and the other a Fellow of the Royal College of Surgeons. His father, Samuel, died in 1948 according to an *Irish Times* obituary of 17 January 1948.

21

MILLS,
Alfred Stanley
(15-16 aerial victories)

Born: 26 June 1897, Belfast
Awards: Distinguished Flying Cross

Lieutenant Alfred Mills was born in Belfast, the youngest of eleven surviving children to James, a foreman carpenter, and Ana Maria Mills. In 1901 the family were living at Woodvale Road, Belfast. Both parents were born in Co. Down, but all ten of the children present at the 1901 census were Belfast-born. Two of Mills's older brothers became joiners and a younger brother an iron moulder. In the Irish census of 1911 the family were still resident at Woodvale Road. By this stage only seven of Alfred's brothers and sisters were still living at the family home.

An Alfred Mills of 50 Woodvale Road, Belfast, at Belfast City Hall signed the Ulster Covenant. He was the only Irish ace to have done so, but certainly not the only Ulster Covenanter to have served in the RFC, RNAS, or RAF. Thus far I have identified approximately fifty of them, but this is likely a gross underestimate.

Mills studied a Campbell College Belfast from 1908 to 1914. He enlisted in Belfast, changing his date of birth in order to appear eighteen years of age. Mills enlisted in the ranks as a private (No. 2535), with the 2nd/6th Black Watch (Embodied Territorial Force), from 19 November 1914 to 14 July 1915. Mills obtained a temporary commission as 2nd Lieutenant in the 11th Battalion of the Argyll & Sutherland Highlanders on 15 July 1915.

Mills embarked from Folkestone on 11 September 1916, arriving in Boulogne that day and joining No. 19 Infantry Base Depot. By 21 September he was with the 11th Battalion of the Argyll & Sutherland Highlanders. However, on 23 October he was diagnosed with trench foot. There's no indication that gangrene had set in or that there were any other complications, such as the amputation of toes being required. On 27 October Mills embarked on HMHS *St George* from Rouen to Southampton, and was received at Somerville Hospital, Oxford. A medical board assessment on 15 December 1916 at the 3rd Southern General Hospital in Oxford found Mills unfit for any service for six weeks, noting that although his feet were healing, he was unable to walk very far. A further assessment on 31 January 1917 in Belfast found Mills fit for home service duties and notified the OC of the 3rd Reserve Battalion of the Argyll & Sutherland Highlanders that Mills was capable of resuming duty. Mills joined the 3rd Battalion on 2 February 1917, reporting to Dreghorn Camp, Colinton, Edinburgh. However, it was not until 5 March that he was certified fit, the Military Hospital in Edinburgh at that time finding that his trench foot had healed.

Mills was promoted to Lieutenant on 1 July 1917. Unfortunately his second frontline spell was also short-lived, as he was wounded in action on 10 July. He was treated at a field hospital and by 11 August was back at the Front. Mills was granted leave from 22 October to 3 November, after which he transferred to the RFC in November 1917. On 22 November he was posted to Reading, then to the No. 3 School of Aerial Gunnery at New Romney, and subsequently to the No. 1 School of Aerial Gunnery at Hythe on 7 January 1918.

On 24 March 1918 Mills was an observer in a Bristol F2.b (B1122) piloted by 2nd Lieutenant Campbell, when it was brought down by machine gun fire and the engine's magneto was damaged, which necessitated a forced landing north-west of Ypres. It was a difficult induction to No. 20 Squadron. On 7 April Mills was formally posted to there on appointment as 2nd Lieutenant (Flying Observer). The squadron had a number of Irish aces, and Mills and Cowell were two of the highest-scoring observer gunners of the war.

RAF Communiqué No. 6 of 1918 describes Mills's first victory, on 9 May 1918, in a Bristol F2.b flown by Lieutenant L. M. Price, when they destroyed a Fokker Dr.I triplane in flames near Lille.[1] Communiqué No. 9 of May 1918 reports Mills's observer/gunner actions against considerable odds:

> Capt. T. P. Middleton and Lt A. Mills, 20 Sqn, while leading a patrol, attacked nine EA. Capt. Middleton fired at one Albatros Scout at close range, which fell into the Canal at Lille. He then side-slipped onto one of seven Pfalz Scouts at which Lt Mills fired. This machine broke up in the air.[2]

Mills was to obtain six further victories that month as observer gunning for Captain Thomas Percy Middleton, Lieutenant William McKenzine Thompson (a Canadian), and Lieutenant John Henry Colbert. Colbert was an interesting character, born in Columbo, Ceylon, to a plantation-owning father and Indian mother. He too had served in the ranks before obtaining a commission.

On 2 August 1918 Mills's DFC citation was gazetted:

2nd Lt (Hon. Lt) Alfred Mills

A capable and gallant observer who has been very successful in destroying enemy machines by reason of excellent marksmanship.

He has accounted for many enemy aircraft in a short period of time, and has generally fought against larger formations than his own. When on reconnaissance 8,000 yards behind the enemy lines he saw a hostile balloon on the ground; descending to 1,700 feet, he and his observer engaged and destroyed it. He then completed his reconnaissance.

On another occasion, when on photography work, he was attacked by nine hostile scouts.[3]

Note that although his medal citation specifically refers to the destruction of a balloon, it does not appear in Mills's credited list of kills.

On 6 September 1918 Mills was observer in a Bristol F2.b (E2470) piloted by Lieutenant Paul Thayer Iaccaci they were shot up badly, but neither were harmed. Iaccaci, a French-born New Yorker, also had a brother serving in No. 20 Squadron, and both were to achieve ace status. Mills and Iaccaci had already scored two aerial victories that morning in F2.b E2470, both of which against the excellent Fokker D.VII. RAF Communiqué No. 23 of 1918 reports Mills shooting down in flames one of their attackers on 6 September. Over the course of that month Mills achieved six aerial victories. Their unfortunate E2470 was to survive with a different crew until 23 October, when it was shot down.

Mills was hospitalised on 2 October 1918 and transferred to the Prince of Wales Hospital. His service record describes him as 'invalided', but this does not necessarily imply permanent disability or disfigurement. Mills was notionally assigned to the Armaments School at Uxbridge on 6 November for general duties until a further medical board examination. On 10 February 1919 he was sent to Crystal Palace for dispersal. *The London Gazette* of 1 April 1919 included a notice that Mills had been transferred to the Unemployed List with effect from 12 February, but a further notice issued on 30 September stated that the previous notice had been cancelled.

On 23 January 1920 *The London Gazette* announced that 2nd Lieutenant (Honorary Lieutenant) Mills had relinquished his commission with effect from 12 February 1919, but again a notice was issued that that of 1 April 1919 had been cancelled.

Mills had come from a large family of hard-working people. However, somewhere in the post-war unemployment crisis, the war-wounded veteran went astray: in October 1924 he was remanded at Marylebone on bail for two months on a charge of theft. He was convicted and sentenced to several months' imprisonment, although his Air Ministry service record does not make any formal mention of proceedings other than a reference to an extract from the *Daily Express* of 10 October 1924.[4] Mills was nevertheless deprived of his DFC.

In July 1937 he sought a statement of service from the War Office rather than the Air Ministry. On 29 July he called in on their records office in person:

It is urgently necessary that I should have some official confirmation of the fact that I was wounded while serving in France. I was wounded twice—during the

Somme battle of 1916—invalided to Somerville College Hospital, Oxford, and later, sent for treatment to the Duchess of Westminster Hospital, Le Touquet, both occasions serving with 11th A&SH, 45 Bgde, 15 Div.

The urgency is as follows: I am plaintiff in litigation over copyright. My funds have been exhausted through protracted delays. On 26th inst. I was informed by solicitors that another firm of lawyers (who administer the 'Nash Fund', Messrs Peachey & Co.) would help me immediately if I had proof I was wounded on service. It is essential that I should lodge some affidavits etc. before the High Court closes.[5]

The Army Council duly wrote to Mills in August 1937, but although it included the much-needed sentence, 'I am to state that his record and services shown above were satisfactory,' it also included a disclaimer:

I am to add that any application for particulars of the above-mentioned officer's service with the RAF should be addressed to the Secretary, Air Ministry, Adastral House, Kingsway.

In effect Mills was back to square one, trying to distance himself from his flying career and any consequent mention of the gain and loss of a DFC. However, perhaps unknown to Mills, there had been a telephone enquiry from Messrs Peachey & Co., and there's an indication that the War Office disclosed that Mills had been wounded on 10 July 1917 in France.

Mills's address at the time was 23 Duke Street, Manchester Square, W1, but it is unclear as to how long he resided in London at that address, as he does not appear on the electoral register there. Note that he was the Plaintiff and not the Defendant in the action, for Mills initiated the litigation. Presumably the 'Nash Fund' was a creation of the aircraft and armaments company founded by Captain Frazer-Nash (the manufacturers of the Nash & Thompson gun turret).

On 16 July 1938 Mills wrote again to the War Office, seeking an additional copy of his statement of service. 'I forwarded the original in applying for a lectureship; it was not returned and has since been misplaced,' Mills ruefully noted, though realistically it could have been used for anything, for instance an application for housing or disability benefit. Mills was living at 139 Grays Inn Road, WC1, at the time, but once again he does not appear to have resided there for any length of time.

22

MOLESWORTH,
William Earle 'Moley'
(18-19 aerial victories)

Born: 14 March 1894, Andaman Islands
Died: 22 October 1955
Awards: Military Cross with Bar, Medaglia d'Oro al Valore Militare (Italy)

Lieutenant-Colonel William Earle Molesworth is one of the four Indian-born Irish aces of the First World War. He was born on the Andaman Islands in the Indian Ocean, the son of Winifred Anne Weekes and Colonel Molesworth, CIE, CBE, of the Indian Army Medical Service. William's grandfather was Lieutenant-Colonel Anthony Oliver Molesworth. William was a descendant of Viscount Molesworth of Swords, Co. Dublin. (Molesworth Street in Dublin is named after Richard, 3rd Viscount Molesworth.) William's mother's family, the Weekes of Hazeldeane, Monkstown, Co. Cork, were a prominent Anglo-Irish family; his grandfather, Thomas Earle Weekes, was a Justice of the Peace for Co. Cork. Unlike the Molesworths, his maternal family did not have a long-standing connection to Ireland, having only arrived there in the previous century. William's sister, Kathleen Winifred Molesworth, married Alfred Alyson Fennell Minchin, who—contrary to some accounts—was not actually related to the Anglo-Irish aviator Frederick Frank Reilly Minchin.

Molesworth was educated at Marlborough College from 1908 to 1911, by which time he was living at the college's Preshute House in Wiltshire, as a boarder (or, in their parlance, '*in static pupillari*'). Molesworth spent two years at the Royal Military College at Sandhurst, from 1912 to 1914. Cadet Molesworth's promotion to 2nd Lieutenant upon graduation from Sandhurst was gazetted on 7 August 1914.[1]

Molesworth served on the Western Front from October 1914 with the 2nd Battalion of the Royal Munster Fusiliers. The heavy casualties suffered by the battalion in August and December 1914 would lead some to question the continuity of any unit carrying the 2nd Battalion's name from 1915 onwards. Indeed, it lost over 100 killed on 26–27 August alone, 90 of which were buried in Étreux British Cemetery. An attempt at maintaining a Battalion War Diary includes a private letter from Captain Gower in December 1914, explaining what happened in late August 1914 during the retreat from Mons, when the 2nd Battalion made its stand at an orchard outside Étreux. There were 444 survivors taken prisoner, 106 wounded, and 150 killed in their rearguard action to save the BEF.

There's little mention in the War Diary of individual officers other than as fatalities—even the wounded casualties aren't individually recorded, though they appear on other official casualty lists. Molesworth was wounded in December 1914—a month when fatlaities ran high, and in which the battalion's actions added over seventy names to Le Touret Memorial. On 8 December 1914 Molesworth's promotion from 2nd Lieutenant to Lieutenant in the Royal Munster Fusiliers was gazetted. Molesworth served with the 2nd Battalion until March 1916, when he was transferred from the field.

In August 1916 Molesworth transferred to the RFC.[3] He was posted to the Central Flying School on 6 October, from where he was assigned to No. 8 RS. Upon appointment as Flying Officer on 26 December, Molesworth returned to the Central Flying School.

On 21 February 1917 he was posted to No. 60 Squadron, which by this stage of the war had become a famous and highly decorated fighting unit. Although it had been commanded in its early years by two well-respected Irishmen—Robert Raymond Smith Barry and Francis Fitzgerald Waldron—it is undoubtedly most commonly associated with the great English ace Albert Ball, and the controversial but brilliant Canadian ace Billy Bishop. Unsurprisingly, this part of Molesworth's military career has been well documented. One of his letters, dated March 1917, describes his early experiences after joining the squadron:

> I don't think I told you about a Boche we brought down last week ... apparently he had lost his way in the clouds. He appeared out of them at about 3,000 feet over our heads. Of course, every available machine dashed off in pursuit, and caught him up in a few minutes ... he had to land in a ploughed field near-by. He put the machine down quite well, without crashing anything, but one of his pursuers ... turned upside down in his excitement when landing. However, he did not hurt himself, and managed to prevent the Hun from setting his machine on fire, by holding a Very pistol at his head ... Afterwards I had a chat with the prisoner in French, and found out that he was a star pilot, having a number of our machines to his credit and the inevitable Iron Cross.[4]

RFC Communiqué No. 81 of 1917 actually credits Lieutenants A. Binnie and Molesworth with a 'forced-to-land' victory each, but they were not granted these claims. The capture of aircraft was still granted in some circumstances, but by and large 'forced-to-land' aerial victories were not included in pilots' tallies even if they were often be mentioned in medal citations. In fact, it would appear that Molesworth didn't really consider capture to be an aerial victory either, as in another letter home in March he writes: 'no luck for me in the Hun line yet.' But then, Molesworth wasn't being entirely truthful, for the pilot who had overturned his aircraft on landing was, on this occasion, Molesworth himself! His Nieuport (A200) survived with only minor damage.

In another letter dated March 1917, Molesworth writes about getting lost in the clouds when observing the German retreat.

> Suddenly we were met by a perfect tornado of bursting 'archies', and so were forced to turn into a cloud. This cloud was so thick that we all promptly proceeded to lose ourselves. ... At last, after about half an hour's flying, I found myself alone in an opening in the clouds. Below me were dozens of shell-holes filled with water; round about, black clouds and sheets of driving rain. I knew I was somewhere near the lines ... Trusting to the compass I still pushed on west ... Just as my petrol was giving out I spotted some hangars. There was nothing for it, so I decided to land. Coming down to about 200 feet I did a half-circle to get into the wind, and to my utter disgust saw a large party of Germans on the ground. I therefore made up my mind that it must be a Hun aerodrome. ... I landed, jumped out of the machine, seized the Very pistol, and was just going to fire it into the grid when I saw, to my amazement, two mechanics in khaki. Evidently the party I had seen were German prisoners. When the old kite had been filled up I pushed off again, and got home after about an hour's run. ... In future I shall take jolly good care to get to know the country better before playing about in the clouds.[5]

On 22 April 1917 Molesworth scored his first confirmed aerial victory flying Nieuport B1569, driving down an Albatros D.III out of control near Vitry. RFC Communiqué No. 85 also credits him with damaging a balloon on this day, too. However, although Molesworth and 2nd Lieutenants Penny and Lloyd were awarded victories for these claims, Molesworth's letters claim his destruction of a balloon at Boiry Notre Dame alone as occurring two days later.

> We had been practising firing the Le Prieur rockets for some time ... We did not think these were much of a success ... so decided to use tracer and Buckingham bullets instead. These are filled with a compound of phosphorous and leave a long trail of smoke behind them... We all went off individually to the various balloons which had been allotted us. ... I personally crossed the trenches at about 10,000 feet, dropping all the time towards my sausage, which was five or six miles away. It was floating in company with another at about 3,000 feet ... I started a straight dive towards them, and then the fun began. Archie ... following me down to about 5,000 feet, where I was met by two or three strings of flaming onions, luckily too far off to do any damage. Then came thousands of machine gun bullets from the ground ... I zigzagged about a bit, still heading for the balloons, and when within two hundred yards opened fire. The old Huns in the basket got wind up and jumped out in their

parachute. Not bothering about them, I kept my sight on one of the balloons and saw the tracer going right into it and causing it to smoke. ... I had to now change drums. ... By this time the second balloon was almost on the floor. I gave it a burst, which I don't think did any damage. The first sausage was in flames ... On the way back a good shot from Archie exploded very near my tail, and carried away part of the elevator. Don't you think this is the limit for anyone who wants excitement? I must say I prefer it to the infantry, as one gets decent food and a comfortable bed every night, if you are lucky enough to get back.[6]

Molesworth was promoted to Temporary Captain (Flight Commander) with effect from 26 April 1917. On 2 June his secondment as Captain to the RFC was gazetted. Molesworth had an eventful May and June, destroying an Albatos D.III on 29 June 1917, but equally getting himself into a number of near-fatal encounters. In June he wrote:

Yesterday I had the narrowest shave I've ever had since I first started Boche-strafing. I was properly caught out this time, and really thought things were all up. ... Just as I was passing over Gavrelle I espied three fat Hun two-seaters making south-east.

'Here we are, my son,' say I to myself. 'We'll just hop down and put the gust up one of these Huns.'

No sooner said than done. I pushed my nose down and, when within range, opened fire. The next thing I knew there was a perfect hail of bullets pouring round me.

Molesworth's account of his thoughts have the character of a cartoon strip.

Crackle! Crackle! Crackle!
   'My cheery aunt! There's a Hun on my tail.'
   'By jove! The blighter is making my grid into a sieve. Confound him!'
   'Let's pull her up in a good climbing turn and have a look at him.'
   'Heavens! It's "The Circus".'
   ... 'Let's give him a dose and see how he likes it.'
   'Here he comes straight at me, loosing off with both guns.'
   'I hope we aren't going to collide.'
   'Missed! Bon! Everything's A1. Wish I'd hit him, though!'
   'I must pull her round quick or he will be on my tail'.
   ... 'Once again, boys, round with her. Let him have it hot.'
   'No good. Try again.'
   'Confound it! There's my beastly drum empty. I must spin and change it.'
   'Good enough! Now where's the blighter?'
   'My Harry! He has got me stiff this time; here he comes down on me from the right.'

'Crack! Crack! Crack! Bang! Zip! Zip!'

'There goes my petrol tank; now for the flames.'

... Luckily for me, my friend and his pals, who had been watching the scrap, thought I was done for. ... I managed to pull the machine out, just scraping over the trenches. The engine was still running, although the petrol was pouring out all over my legs. A few minutes afterwards the engine conked out altogether, and I had to land in a field.[7]

Molesworth had survived a reeling dogfight, with his petrol tank hit but without it igniting, i.e. the vapour trail may have given the impression of smoke and flames. Molesworth's machine had suffered extensive damage, with at least forty bullet holes, in the planes, propeller, spars, and fuselage, some missing the pilot's seat by inches.

However, it was not just enemy aircraft that were a danger—in June 1917 Molesworth survived a forced landing that would have killed many a less experienced pilot: at 12,000 feet, the engine malfunctioned and part of the cowling broke away, hitting the wings and fuselage. He managed to keep control until the aircraft reached 2,000 feet then took it down via a side-slip and making a landing into the wind. The No. 60 Squadron literature generally credits Molesworth with driving down out of control an Albatros D.III on 11 July 1917 when flying a Nieuport (B1652). However, in his own recollections, a damaged German aircraft escaped him after Molesworth's gun jammed.

Although the RFC discouraged media attempts to lionise individual pilots, propaganda had to make some concession to public demand for heroes, and No. 60 Squadron provided ideal material for the newsreel. In July 1917, Molesworth was filmed for the cinema:

Charlie Chaplin isn't in it now with us! We were cinematographed the other day. Some of us stood in a row and tried to look pleasant and unconcerned, but this was rather difficult, as everyone was making rude remarks about us. We then bundled into our new grids [the S.E.5], which we had just got, and started off on a stunt formation, nearly running down the old cinema man to put the wind up him. After we had done a circuit, my radiator began to boil, and I was forced to come down. Thank heavens it was a good landing, as the old man was still at it turning the handle. My part of the show was to be known as 'Pilot landing for more ammunition after fierce fight'.[8]

The new S.E.5a was to prove an excellent machine in the context of the endless swapping of aerial superiority between the Allies and Central Powers. In August 1917 Molesworth was to achieve two victories with the S.E.5a. Molesworth describes his victory on 5 August 1917, piloting S.E.5a (A4851) over Hendecourt when he sent an Albatros D.III down in flames.

A burning machine is a glorious but terrible sight to see—a tiny red stream of flame trickles from the petrol tank, then long tongues of blazing petrol lick the sides of the fuselage, and, finally, a sheet of white fire envelops the whole machine, and it glides steeply towards the ground in a zigzag course, leaving a long trail of black smoke behind it, until it eventually breaks up. There is no doubt that your first Hun in flames gives you a wonderful feeling of satisfaction. I can well imagine what the big-game hunter must think when he sees the dead lion in front of him. Somehow, you do not realise that you are sending a man to an awful doom, but rather your thoughts are all turned on the hateful machine which you are destroying, so fascinating to look at and yet so deadly in its attack.[9]

His other victory that month came on 9 August 1917, when he destroyed an Albatros D.V while flying S.E.5a A8392, but this aircraft was badly shot-up in the encounter, losing a large chunk of the tail plane. Molesworth had performed magnificently with No. 60 Squadron, achieving six aerial victories—usually sufficient for the awarding of the Military Cross—so it was no surprise that in August he was told of his immanent decoration in the context of being rotated to Home Establishment. Molesworth's service record indicates that the MC was awarded on 26 September 1917 and ultimately gazetted on 9 January 1918.

Notwithstanding the many secondary sources which dismiss Molesworth as nothing more than a Bishop stooge, he was an accomplished pilot who had survived 'Bloody April' and taken on the best of Manfred von Richthofen's 'Flying Circus' that summer. For any Army officer on secondment to the RFC, this would be a fine achievement. However, Molesworth's career as an aviator was not finished yet. In the winter of 1917 he was posted to No. 62 TS.

On 20 October 1917 he returned to the frontline, joining No. 29 Squadron, which was still equipped with Nieuports. Molesworth did not take long to add to his tally. On 8 November he destroyed two enemy aircraft in flames. (According to RFC Communiqué No. 113 of 1917 he took on fifteen German aircraft while securing the first of those victories.) Later that month he sent down an Albatros D.V out of control near the Houlthoulst forest area.

No. 29 Squadron was commanded by Major James McCudden, son of a Co. Carlow man, and one of three brothers to die serving with the RFC and RAF. Of the squadron's Irish aces there was Captain Sidney Edward Cowan, and of Irish parentage or Irish ancestry there was McCudden and the Canadian Henry Coyle Rath. However, the most famous Irishman to have served with the squadron would have been Galway-born William Arthur Grattan-Bellew. He already had at least three confirmed aerial victories to his name with No. 25 Squadron before he transferred to No. 29 Squadron. Grattan-Bellew is mentioned several times in McCudden's memoirs and would appear to have had at least one confirmed aerial victory with the squadron, but he did not 'make ace', and died in a crash in March 1917. However, several other prominent Irish pilots served with the squadron, namely Captain Ernest William Barrett and William Kerr Magill Britton.

As mentioned previously, Molesworth's maternal family were the Weekes of Monkstown, Co. Cork, so there is sometimes confusion as to whether he was a cousin of Lieutenant Owen Harry Weekes, Section 31, 18th Balloon Company, 3rd Balloon Wing. Weekes was shot down on 29 November 1917 by Julius Buckler of Jasta 17 but survived. However, this is a simple case of mistaking the Monkstowns in Dublin with the Monkstowns in Cork, which were two separate families. Interestingly, Buckler was to account for a number of Irishmen around that time, among them Lieutenant Donald St Patrick Prince-Smith from Co. Wicklow, of No. 16 Squadron, who was killed on 24 October in R.E.8 B5896, in which he was an observer. Co. Armagh-born Lieutenant Alexander Wilson MacLaughlin of No. 1 Squadron, in Nieuport 17 B3630, also fell prey to Buckler's guns on 26 October.

The winter of 1917–18 was particularly harsh for operational flying purposes, yet Molesworth achieved five aerial victories with No. 29 Squadron in January 1918. His Military Cross citation was gazetted on 9 January 1918:

Capt. William Earle Molesworth, R. Muns. Fus. and RFC

For conspicuous gallantry and devotion to duty on offensive patrol. He has frequently led his patrol against superior numbers of the enemy, destroying some and dispersing others. He has also brought down two balloons and has proved himself to be a dashing and fearless pilot of great skill and determination.[10]

Molesworth was only officially credited with one balloon, however, so there's a divergence between squadron, wing, and brigade records. RFC Communiqué No. 124 of 1918 records a double-victory by Molesworth on 24 January 1918, in which he sends one down in flames.[11] Molesworth scored three victories in February 1918 and one final victory in March 1918, but was transferred back to Home Establishment on 17 March 1918, St Patrick's Day. On 26 March 1918 Molesworth's award of a bar to the Military Cross was announced but the actual citation was not gazetted until 24 August 1918:

Capt. William Earle Molesworth, MC, R. Muns. Fus. and RFC

For conspicuous gallantry and devotion to duty. He has done excellent work as patrol leader, handling his formations with great skill and courage. He has destroyed four enemy machines and driven several down out of control.[12]

Molesworth returned to the Central Flying School on 27 May 1918, to serve as an instructor, so was graded as Major (Flying) for pay purposes. In June 1918

Molesworth married Dorothy Loftus Steele, daughter of Colonel St George Loftus Steele. The next-of-kin address on his service record reads as 'Kelston, Hythe, Kent' and 'Edgemont, Reigate, Surrey'.

On 4 September 1918 Molesworth transferred to No. 158 Squadron as commanding officer. This squadron had been formed in May 1918, originally envisaged as a fighter squadron but subsequently converted to a ground attack role by the time it became operational. It was equipped with the Sopwith TF.2 Salamander but did not see active service in the First World War and was disbanded on 20 November 1918. (Production of the Salamander had proven troublesome, as the armour plating had become increasingly problematic in the tempering process. The 'TF' designation stood for 'Trench Fighter' but it had no specialized ground attack equipment, merely additional armour to reduce vulnerability to ground fire. By the end of the war fewer than 50 Salamanders had been supplied, from an initial order of 500 aircraft.)

On 12 September 1918 the King's permission for Molesworth to wear the Silver Medal for Military Valour conferred by the King of Italy was announced.[13]

On 16 October 1918 Molesworth was hospitalised, not returning to No. 158 Squadron until 26 October, after which he was transferred to No. 45 Training Depot Station (TDS). On 31 January 1919 Molesworth's status as an instructor with the Central Flying School was gazetted.[14] On 18 April 1919 it was further reported that Molesworth had been promoted from Captain to Acting Major, with effect from 3 September 1918, from the time of his transfer to command of No. 158 Squadron following his service as an instructor.[15]

On 9 April 1919 it would appear that Molesworth had been scheduled for dispersal but that this was subsequently cancelled. In the end, Molesworth transferred from No. 45 TDS to No. 108 Squadron on 21 May 1919. No. 108 Squadron had been a bomber squadron during the war but was in the process of being stood down by the time Molesworth had transferred there. It was disbanded in July 1919, by which stage Molesworth had been redeployed to 8 Aircraft Acceptance Park at Lympne. It would appear that No. 120 Squadron had been given the role of providing airmail services between Lympne and Cologne but that this ended in September 1919, after which No. 120 Squadron moved from Lympne to Hawkinge. With No. 108 Squadron disbanded Lympne was transferred to the civil authorities.

On 15 October 1919 Molesworth returned to the Royal Munsters, relinquishing his RAF commission, which was confirmed in Air Ministry and War Office announcements that Captain W. E. Molesworth, Royal Munster Fusiliers, had been restored to the establishment with effect from 15 October 1919.[16]

In the medal card index Molesworth's address is '1st Bn, Royal Munster Fusiliers, Crownhill Barracks, Plymouth, Devon on 21 June 1921'. Molesworth served with the Royal Munsters prior to their disbandment, but *The London Gazette* of 12 September 1922 lists Captain W. E. Molesworth's transfer from the Royal Munster Regiment to the Royal Sussex Regiment with effect from 13 September 1922 and with seniority from 7 April 1917. Subsequently, Captain W. E. Molesworth, Royal Sussex Regiment, was granted a temporary appointment with the Royal Traffic Officers from 1 to 28 September 1922.[17]

Molesworth was appointed to the rank of Captain with the Royal Tank Corps (as it was then known) with effect from 13 February 1924. The P&O ship *Khyber* arrived in London on 11 May 1924, having travelled from Kobe, Japan, via Shanghai, and on board was Captain W. E. Molesworth, his wife Dorothy, and their young daughter Pamela. On 27 February 1931 the War Office announced that Captain W. E. Molesworth MC was promoted to Major in the Royal Tank Corps with effect from 28 February 1931.[18]

Patrick Delaforce's *Battles with Panzers* covers some of the actions of the 1st and 2nd Battalions of the Royal Tank Regiment in North Africa, and describes Molesworth as 'a dead-beat major who had been passed over for promotion for years.'[19] This would appear to be a quote from Field Marshal Michael Carver's memoirs.[20] Molesworth did indeed serve in the Second World War; his wartime service records are not publicly accessible, but it is known that Major Molesworth was promoted to Lieutenant-Colonel with effect from 1 April 1940.[21] He served with the 1st Battalion, which along with the 6th Battalion was part of the Heavy Armoured Brigade in Egypt. On 17 March 1941 (St Patrick's Day) the *Dominion Monarch* arrived in Liverpool from New Zealand via Cape Town, Mombasa, and the Middle East. In the category of First Class 'Service' (as opposed to First Class 'Civilian') passengers was a Colonel W. E. Molesworth, his wife Dorothy, and their twenty-one-year-old daughter Pamela. Their prospective address in the UK was given as Cruicksfield, Duns, Scotland, and their previous place of residence was in Egypt. Presumably Molesworth had been replaced on frontline service duties.

Molesworth served out part of the war in charge of supplies for the Royal Armoured Corps. On 30 September 1941 the War Office announced that Lieutenant-Colonel Molesworth (under the service reference number 8675) had been placed on retired pay with effect from 13 September.[22] On 15 March 1949 it announced that Molesworth had ceased to belong to the Reserve of Officers for the Royal Tank Regiment due to having reached the age limit of liability to being recalled.

Even if Molesworth's second wartime career was not particularly illustrious, this does not mean that his family escaped lightly. His sister Kathleen had married into the Minchin clan, and her eldest son Desmond was killed on 1 July 1944 in the aftermath of the Normandy landings, a lieutenant with the King's Own Scottish Borderers. Desmond is buried at Bayeux, the first major French town to be liberated. Patrick Molesworth Minchin, Kathleen's younger son, survived the war, reaching the rank of Captain in the Indian Army.

Molesworth's address was later 242 Tilehurst Road, Reading. He died in October 1955.

23

O'GRADY,
Conn Standish
(9 aerial victories)

Born: 4 October 1888, Dublin
Died: 7 May 1968
Awards: Military Cross, Air Force Cross

Squadron Leader Conn Standish O'Grady served in both the First and Second World War. A highly regarded glider pilot, O'Grady was to continue flying until late in life.

He was born in Dublin to Standish and Margaret O'Grady, both from Co. Cork. Standish James O'Grady was a writer and a friend of W. B. Yeats. In the 1890s he achieved a measure of success in translating various Celtic myths and legends into English and publishing them in modern prose, namely romantic tales shorn of their pre-Christian roots. However, his histories were disliked by his Victorian contemporaries for being too intellectually dishonest in their treatment of the Cromwellian conquest of Ireland. Standish James was sometimes mistaken for his cousin Standish Hayes O'Grady, another figure in Celtic literature (neither man to be confused with 1st Viscount Guillamore O'Grady.)

The Irish census of 1901 records the family as resident at Highfield Road, Rathmines, Dublin. Conn and his older brother Carew were both present, as were their parents and two servants. Conn's other older brother, Hugh Art O'Grady, editor of the *Cork Free Press*, was not.

Conn was initially educated at Tipperary Grammar School, which was an Erasmus Smith school. These schools were funded by the proceeds of a trust established by a Cromwellian adventurer, who donated lands and other proceeds of plunder in Ireland to educate Irish children on the estates within a 2-mile radius of the schools. The trust proved the subject of controversy throughout the centuries, whether for the treatment of tenants on the estate trust lands or the trust's abuse of its charter in the children it chose to educate, not fulfilling its child proselytism objectives while on the other hand managing to spend considerable amounts on scholarships and academic bursaries. Conn transferred from Tipperary Grammar School to the High School in Dublin. (The High School, now in Rathmines, is the only surviving school funded by the trust.) O'Grady also spent six months at L'Institut Robert in Brussels for the purpose of learning French.

In 1911 Conn was still living with his parents, on Milltown Road, Dublin. The Irish census described him as an engineer. He had by this stage recently graduated from Trinity College Dublin, with BA and BAI degrees in 1910.

In May 1911 Conn got work with the Congested Districts Board for Ireland as an assistant inspector. He came third in the competitive examination process for admission to the Board. He was involved mainly with various engineering works, such as land reclamation and drainage, before emigrating from Ireland to Canada in April 1912, where he found work with the Canadian Department of the Interior.[1] The Dominion Water Power Branch of the Canadian Department of the Interior published a 'Progress Report' in 1916, in which several references were made to O'Grady's pre-war work in conducting surveys in rough country for the water, power, and reclamation service. O'Grady established the gauging station at the mouth of the Saskatchewan River on 30 July 1912, and a similar station at Grand Rapids, Morrison's Dock, on 28 August 1912. On the Winnipeg River, O'Grady established a number of gauging stations and related hydrometric installations in 1912 and 1913, for instance from the Lake of the Woods to the Whitedog Falls. Although some installations were subsequently relocated elsewhere, overall O'Grady's judgment held up well, and his gauges were in use for taking water height and other hydrometric data.

Reflecting on O'Grady's personality and his unusual combination of the outdoor life with the academic persona, Charles C. Spence (a hill walker, rock climber, and international standard fencing competitor) recalled that O'Grady's

> ... boyish joy in life was combined with a great knowledge of history and literature, and a lively interest in everything under the sun ...
>
> He was the most charming person and a delightful companion, always cheerful and interesting company, and having the kind of vagueness that traditionally attaches to the academic.[2]

O'Grady married Mabel Ann Golloch on 4 June 1914 at Winnipeg, Manitoba, Canada. He returned to Ireland in 1916. There is some confusion as to when O'Grady was accepted into the RFC, as it would appear that there was an issue with his eyesight in one assessment, which led to the rejection of one his applications. O'Grady also turned down a role as a mechanic petty officer in the RNAS. In one of his applications for a commission, O'Grady's character reference was signed by Professor John Joly, Professor of Geology, Trinity College Dublin on 27 June 1916. It provided cautious but positive endorsement:

> Standish Conn O'Grady has been absent from Ireland for the past four years but I have, from hearsay, every reason to believe his character is unchanged during that period. Previously I knew him for many years. I cannot speak too highly of him.[3]

Professor Joly was of course best known for his work on the use of radium to date the Earth, but—unlike O'Grady—the geological interest was just one small aspect of Joly's life: he was to invent photometers, calorimeters, and the Joly colour process for photography. (There's even a crater on Mars named after him!) O'Grady's successful geological and hydrometric work might even have been a disappointment to Joly, given the high standards he set for his *protégés*.

One curious item of correspondence on behalf of O'Grady is an irreverent reference from Lieutenant-Colonel W. Davidson. It's addressed to HQ of Eastern Command at Horse Guards, Whitehall:

> I know little about him except that he married a mighty plain cousin of mine, though fairly well gilded ... He is very keen, in the event of there being a delay in getting into the RFC, to take out a course at Hendon, if that were possible. ... O'Grady's record as an engineer seems to be pretty good for a man of only 28. I believe him to be 'quiet, honest and sober'![4]

O'Grady had no military experience, but he does make a passing reference to serving in a 'volunteer capacity with Trinity College OTC during recent disturbances.' Yet he did not receive a silver commemorative cup, which was awarded to 127 of the Trinity College OTC cadets and 20 or so college staff, along with 14 soldiers, who operated from the grounds of Trinity College in the suppression of the Easter Rising. (Some of those TCD cadets were to serve with the Allied flying services in the First World War: Frederick Cyril Hoey, James Alastair Kirker, Ernest Thomas Molyneux, Theodore Conyngham Kingsmill Moore, Leslie Stuart McCullagh, Lionel Wigoder, Edward Francis Wilson, for instance.)

O'Grady joined the RFC as Temporary 2nd Lieutenant with effect from 25 July 1916.[5] O'Grady was initially sent to Reading, posted with No. 7 RS until 12 September, after which he trained with 'C' Squadron at the Central Flying School. On 17 November his position was confirmed, on appointment as 2nd Lieutenant (Flying Officer) with effect from 31 October. By this stage O'Grady had been posted to No. 8 RS, serving there from November 1916 to March 1917.

Following a short spell at the Central Flying School, O'Grady was sent to No. 23 Squadron on 4 April 1917. Of the nineteen aces who served with this squadron, the highest-scoring were the Scot William Kennedy-Cochran-Patrick, who had Irish ancestry on both sides of his family, and the American-born, English-raised Lovell Dickens Baker,who had an Irish-American father and had enlisted with the Royal Dublin Fusiliers prior to joining the RFC. But this was a hugely diverse squadron: in addition to Baker, the aces James Pearson and Clive Warman were American; Herbert Drewitt was a New Zealander; Harry Compton, Arthur Fairclough, Douglas McGregor, Alfred Eddie McKay, George Marks, and John MacRae were all Canadian.

The Squadron ORB for No. 23 Squadron has not survived, but from pilots' logbooks, memoirs, combat reports, Wing Diaries, a wealth of information on the squadron has nevertheless survived, bearing in mind that this was one of the few squadrons in the RFC to fly the French-designed SPAD VII fighter. Both No. 19 and No. 23 Squadrons had a reputation for heavy drinking; in the latter case it came right from the top, from Major Wilkinson to Flight Leaders such as Kennedy Cochran-Patrick.

On 30 April 1917 O'Grady scored his first victory in a SPAD S.VII (A262), sending down out of control an Albatros D.III over Inchy-en-Artois. However, on 6 May he experienced a forced landing near 22 Wing's advanced landing ground due to enemy fire. His SPAD (B1591) was damaged.

In one engagement, on 8 June 1917, O'Grady, Langlands, Cochran-Patrick, Gibbs, and McGregor went on a deep offensive patrol. This was the day that Messines-Wytscharte Ridge fell to the British, so not only was aerial fighting continuous but also ground attack was expected on targets of opportunity. McGregor and O'Grady attacked vehicular traffic, but McGregor then got to engage a low-flying Albatros C-type at about 1,200 feet, forcing it to make an emergency landing. According to the aviation historian Stewart K. Taylor, the success on the ground forces' advances obviated the need for further strafing operations by No. 23 Squadron. By 10 June O'Grady and McGregor led the return to Bruay from the Erquinghem advanced landing ground.[6] Taylor's description of the relationship between the Canadian ace McGregor and O'Grady is interesting:

> Since the time Mac joined 'C' Flight, Lt Standish Conn O'Grady acted as the on-again-off-again Flight deputy. Not a moderate drinker by any stretch of the imagination, he upheld that part of his fellow countrymen's tradition almost to the letter and when not up to the task the morning after, Capt. Patrick summoned McGregor to take O'Grady's place.[7]

In July 1917 O'Grady took compassionate leave. His absence coincided with some other reshuffling and machinations within the squadron's ranks. Cochran-Patrick (aka 'Capt. Pat') had been promoted to Acting Major and offered command of the elite No. 60 Squadron. The initial beneficiary would have been O'Grady's friend and rival McGregor, who got the recommendation from Cochran-Patrick as his anointed successor to command 'C' Flight. However, Major Wilkinson favoured O'Grady, which caused further friction with the Canadians McGregor and Ivan Marks. Perhaps the regular alternation of O'Grady and McGregor by Cochran-Patrick for his deputy's position in the Flight had created unrealistic expectations among these men. Ultimately, O'Grady was relegated to deputy and a new Flight Leader from outside the squadron was brought in.

Over the course of just a few months (from late April to August 1917) O'Grady had scored a total of nine victories with No. 23 Squadron, most of which were achieved in SPAD (B3556). Some were shared victories, but the majority were against the Albatros D.III and D.V fighters, several sent down in flames. For example, RFC Communiqué No. 102 describes O'Grady's actions on 20 August 1917, in which he drove one enemy aircraft off a Nieuport's tail then shot down another that was harrying a SPAD.[8]

How some of No. 23 Squadron's kills should have been shared remains up for debate—in one grim battle, on 14 August 1917, a combined 'circus' of No. 1 Squadron (flying Nieuport Scouts), No. 23 Squadron (SPADs), No. 70 Squadron (Sopwith Camels), and No. 1 Naval Squadron (Sopwith Triplanes) had a chaotic encounter with dozens of German aircraft in the 5-mile Langemarck-Poelcappelle-Zonnebeke triangle. O'Grady and Marks may have accounted for an Albatros, but in a further engagement O'Grady suffered a 'No. 3 Stoppage' in his gun (a bent cartridge), which forced him to break off an attack on a DFW, leaving Marks to continue alone. Marks's SPAD (B3539) was badly damaged by return fire from the German two-seater and had to make for La Lovie before the engine failed. Confusingly, O'Grady was credited with a DFW crashed east of St Julien when the various combat report claims were analysed in conjunction with British AA reports, even though No. 1 Squadron's Nieuports had claimed the O'Grady/Marks white-winged, yellow-fuselaged Albatros near Moorslede.

In August and September 1917 O'Grady was promoted from Lieutenant to Temporary Captain, then to Flight Commander. He returned to Home Establishment on 15 September and his leave was extended to 15 October, after which he was sent to the Northern Training Brigade and assigned to No. 81 Squadron.

O'Grady's service record indicates that he was awarded the MC on 26 September 1917, which was gazetted on that date, though the citation did not appear until 9 January 1918:

2nd Lt Conn Standish O'Grady, RFC, Spec. Res.

For conspicuous gallantry and devotion to duty in leading fighting patrols against superior numbers of enemy aircraft. He has himself brought down three enemy machines completely out of control, and others were seen to be destroyed, and his dash and determination when outnumbered by the enemy have continually won the highest praise.[9]

No. 81 Squadron had originally been formed in January 1917 as a training unit but was not mobilised for active service. It was disbanded on 4 July 1918, well before the end of the war. O'Grady was subsequently transferred to 23 Wing, and in November 1918 was serving with No. 34 TDS. On 7 November 1918 O'Grady's promotion to Captain was gazetted. His next-of-kin address for his wife was amended in 1918 from '107 Anglesea Road, Donnybrook, Dublin' to 'c/o Hill Rowan Esq, 32 Belsize Road, South Hampstead, NW'. Subsequently it became '27 Belsize Square, NW3'. On 13 March 1919 O'Grady transferred from No. 34 TDS back to 23 Wing.

O'Grady was transferred to the Unemployed List with effect from 24 May 1919. However, there is a note on his service record to the effect that on 29 August 1919 O'Grady was 'mentioned for valuable services' on the Army List. O'Grady did not return to Canada, despite the post being kept open for him by the Canadian authorities. Initially he worked with Boving & Co. (Engineers), then struck out as a consulting engineer on his own account. He became a corporate member of the Institute of Civil Engineers in 1919. His practice was known as Merall & O'Grady, but appeared to install his former employers' equipment, namely one Boving turbine at the Great Almond School in 1920s.

When joining the reserve his name was recorded as 'Standish Conn O'Grady'. A medical board examination of 30 January 1925 deemed him fit for Class 'A' Reserve. On 10 February 1925 his probation in the General Duties Branch, Reserve of Air Force Officers, Class A, with the humble rank of Flying Officer was gazetted.[10] O'Grady was required to undergo the embarrassment of a refresher course, which he attended in Renfrew in March 1925. The resulting assessment found that O'Grady was a 'very capable pilot, suited to SSF [single-seat fighter] aeroplanes— Category 1.' O'Grady's address is recorded as 'Craighleith, Edinburgh', with his wife's permanent address recorded as '13 Royal Terrace West, Kingstown, Ireland'. This would explain Renfrew as an assessment location. On 11 August 1925 he was confirmed in rank as a Flying Officer.[11]

On his second refresher course in February and March 1926, O'Grady was described as a 'very capable pilot whose general flying and landings are excellent. Suited to SSF aeroplanes—Category 1.' The course assessment became a regular opportunity to pay homage to O'Grady, for example in June and July 1926. On 31 January 1928 his promotion to Flight Lieutenant was gazetted, and later that year he had occasion to impress while flying the Armstrong Whitworth.[12] But granted a further five years in the Class 'A' Reserve from 10 February 1928, O'Grady's advancing years began to count against him. On 10 February 1933 he was granted a further five years but in the Class 'C' Reserve.[13]

In 1931 O'Grady was appointed Lecturer in Civil Engineering at Armstrong College, University of Durham. He joined the Newcastle Gliding Club in 1936, becoming their chief flying instructor, but although his chief passion was gliding he also enjoyed hill-walking and mountaineering. At the University of Durham he was a leading instructor in the Fencing Club, and chose to represent Scotland at International level, despite the infrequency of their participation in international competition.

O'Grady served as a flying instructor in the Second World War, mainly in South Africa. Initially he flew Avro Ansons and Fairey Battles with No. 5 Air Observer Navigation School, RAF Weston-Super-Mare, from May to August 1940. Subsequently, at No. 45 Air School, Oustshoorn, South Africa, he trained pilots from October 1941 to October 1943. He was awarded the Air Force Cross, which was gazetted on 1 January 1944. O'Grady resigned his commission with effect from 24 March 1944, leaving the RAF with the rank of Squadron Leader. In 1944 he returned to the University of Durham, being promoted to Senior Lecturer in hydraulic engineering. He retired in 1954.

Alas, O'Grady's flying abilities and fencing prowess did not translate well into rock climbing:

I remember nerve-wracking occasions when Conn seconded me. He was not reassuring in that capacity. He was the untidiest man I have ever met and 'rope management' was beyond him. I can still recollect very clearly gazing down upon him poised on the Napes 'Eagle's Nest' surrounded by a cocoon of alpine line, muttering curses in his soft Irish brogue.[14]

O'Grady broke both ankles in an accident on the Thearlaich Dubh Gap on the Isle of Skye, which left him partly lame for the rest of his life. Nevertheless, he served on the committee of Newcastle Gliding Club in the 1950s. His wife Mabel died in 1955, after a long illness. In October 1958 O'Grady travelled on the *Hilary*, a Booth SS cruise ship, bound for Leixões, Lisbon, Barbados, and Trinidad. Presumably this was a seventieth birthday treat. He travelled 'tourist' class; his address was '57 Bridge Park, Newcastle'.

The October 1960 edition of *Sailplane and Gliding* made a passing reference to O'Grady; he and the new Chief Flying Instructor, Allan Pratt, had shared Kite I. O'Grady was then the club's oldest flying member at the time—he would have been seventy-two. He gave up gliding three years later, but continued to ride a motorbike.

O'Grady died in on 7 May 1968, aged eighty. Warm tributes were paid to him in many obituaries, notably by the Institution of Civil Engineers.[15]

24

POPE,
Sydney Leo Gregory 'Poppy'
(6 aerial victories)

Born: 27 or 28 March 1898, Co. Dublin
Died: 5 November 1980
Awards: Military Cross (1917); Distinguished Flying Cross (28 May 1926); Air
Force Cross (1 March 1929); Knight Commander, Order of Orange-Nassau (20
October 1942); Mentioned in Despatches (8 June 1944); Commander of the
British Empire (1 January 1946).

Air Commodore Sydney Pope was born in Dublin to William and Elizabeth Pope,
one of seven children, most of whom were born in Co. Waterford. In the Irish
census of 1901 the family was resident in Co. Kilkenny, and had a governess and
two domestic servants. Sydney's father was a wine and spirit merchant, originally
from Iowa, USA. Sydney's mother was from Melbourne, Australia. It's unclear why
he was named Sydney, but 'Leo' and 'Gregory' may well have made reference to
Popes Leo XIII and Gregory XVI.

Pope's service records claim that he was initially educated by the Jesuits at
Belvedere College in Dublin, and further educated at St Mary's College, Dundalk,
Co. Louth, and St Joseph's College, London. However, Pope does not appear on the
Belvedere Great War Roll of Honour.

In the Irish census of 1911, he and his younger brother Philip were living with
their aunt and uncle, Patrick and Mary Forde, in the subdivision of a house in
Lower Baggot Street, Dublin. Sydney was a student of Marist College, Dublin,
while the rest of his family would appear to have left Ireland by this stage. His older
sister Ethel was an elementary school teacher at a convent school near East India
Dock in Poplar. Later, Pope lived at Brook House, Pinner, Middlesex during his
initial years in London.

Sydney enlisted as a private with the Inns of Court OTC on 23 August 1915,
under the service number 5781. He was later promoted to Lance Corporal on 25
January, initially on an unpaid basis, and then appointed substantively to the grade
from 23 March 1916 onwards.

Pope sought a transfer to the RFC. General Sir Bindon Blood wrote a letter of overall support, but obviously knew the recipient (and decision-maker) on applications for a commission in the RFC.

My dear Scott,

Can you help the bearer—Private Sydney Pope, OTC—about the Flying Corps.... I know some of his people and can recommend him on that score, and he seems a useful and promising sort—barely 18 years old.

I hope you are keeping fit.[1]

Blood was of the prominent Anglo-Irish family and educated at the Royal School, Banagher, Co. Offaly, and Queen's College, Galway (the predecessor of National University of Ireland). In many cases it's completely unnecessary for a young OTC cadet to bring out the heavy artillery of influence but, oddly enough, the absence of an endorsement could be taken as the applicant not having the family's approval, when there was to some extent a social expectation that he would.

However, in Pope's application the real certification of moral character was provided by Rev. John J. Caulfield, the parish priest at Hatch End, Harrow. The emergence of an Irish Catholic middle class in the suburbs is difficult to explain, but Rev. Caulfied was the driving force behind the new church of St Luke at Pinner parish in 1915, which is now a parish hall. He attested to knowing Pope for ten years, i.e. from when Pope was eight years of age. Given that Pope was not in London for that length of time, and that this certification is dated 5 May 1916, we must deduce that he knew the Pope family in Ireland.

On 3 June 1916 Pope was one of twelve OTC cadets to receive commissions as Temporary 2nd Lieutenants on the General List, being assigned to the RFC. Of those other eleven, Philip Solomon Joyce was to be killed in action with Pope's No. 60 Squadron.

Pope was 6 foot 2 inches tall, and at 140 lb he was within the weight limit for RFC pilots. Pope was awarded RAeC Certificate No. 2074 in August 1916. According to Central Flying School correspondence, Pope and fellow Irishman Desmond Herlouin de Burgh were two of the four who graduated on 29 August 1916. Pope's promotion to Temporary 2nd Lieutenant was gazetted on 23 September 1916.

However, in August 1916 Pope contracted gonorrhoea. On 8 November 1916 a medical board examination in London found that he had been cured. Pope was found fit for service at home and so was posted to No. 49 Squadron, based at Dover. At this point in time this squadron would have been training with B.E.2Cs and R.E.7s. It was not until well into 1917 that it became a bomber squadron, equipped with D.H.4s and later D.H.9s. On 15 December 1916 Pope was certified fit for general service.

He joined No. 60 Squadron in April 1917—'Bloody April'. Four Irish aces served with No. 60 Squadron—Molesworth and Pope served together in 1917, and Hegarty and Saunders in 1918. But although Molesworth does occasionally mention Pope, it is not in any specific way, more in passing when discussing the squadron as a whole. Discussing the spring months of 1917, Molesworth comments on the performance of pretty much everyone else:

> Caldwell, Daly, Whitehead, Weidon and Meintzies all did excellent work but the weather was so bad that only the experts could do much good, while some of our best pilots went 'West'. Throughout this trying time I managed to survive ... It was just about this time that Pope, now a Squadron Leader in the RAF, and [the Canadian ace] Bishop were posted to the Squadron. The latter showed great promise as a fighter shortly after he arrived ...[2]

But then, Molesworth's memoirs tend to be monopolised by Bishop, so nothing too much can be read into his lack of interest in Pope.

Bishop was certainly not a team player, but it's unlikely he ever consciously sacrificed one of his own for the sake of another kill, though the accusation lingers among his detractors. Tales regarding Bishop should be set against the absence of air-to-air communication systems and the confused nature of aerial warfare, circumstances in which someone like Bishop may well identify a target of opportunity and engage, regardless of the positional awareness of others. Pope was not a Bishop fan. According to David Bashow's *Knights of the Air*, Pope was on one occasion deployed on a photography mission with Bishop as his escort, and the latter peeled away on one of his 'lone wolf' sorties. Pope was later infuriated, as he had carried on with his mission, unaware of the absence of any protection.

On 26 May, upon return from a photography patrol, Pope experienced a hard landing, damaging the tail of his Nieuport (A6647) when a wheel came off his undercarriage during the landing. His first aerial victory did not come until 8 June 1917: while flying Nieuport B1652, he sent an Albatros down out of control near Vitry. Molesworth used that same Nieuport to destroy two Albatros D.IIIs, on 29 June and 11 July, so they could not have been strangers to one another.

On 20 June 1917 Pope achieved his second confirmed aerial victory, with Nieuport B1679, on this occasion against an Albatros D.V, which went down out of control near Equerchin. However, when No. 60 Squadron converted from Nieuports to the S.E.5 (and the S.E.5a) Pope's kill-rate improved considerably. He achieved four further aerial victories by mid-November 1917, all of which were confirmed destructions rather than out-of-control victories.

On 14 September, Pope overturned his S.E.5a (B4858) on landing. It was common enough for the Nieuport to end up on its back if it encountered the slightest bump on the grass strips, but the S.E.5 took a bit more punishment. Pope was uninjured and unaffected by the incident, destroying an Albatros D.III just two days later.

RFC Communiqué No. 113 of 1917, which covers the period 6 November 1917 to 12 November 1917, reports three of Pope's victories, including a double-victory on 8 November 1917.[3] In Scott's history of No. 60 Squadron, Pope is mentioned in the context of that day's action:

> On November 8, Pope, an old member of the squadron, who had come through the Arras battle with us, destroyed two hostile two-seaters in one day. This was a good pilot and a popular officer, who for some reason was a long time before he began to get Huns but, having once found his form, became a very useful and formidable fighter. He went home soon after this, and showed himself to be an exceptionally gifted trainer of pilots, both in flying and fighting.[4]

Pope was wounded in action, being forced down near St Julien on 18 November 1917. The propeller of his S.E.5 (B519) broke when on offensive patrol. Pope had to crash-land in a crater full of water, suffering multiple injuries but none too serious. He was transferred to Home Establishment on 24 December 1917 and re-assigned to the Central Flying School.

One curious incident relating to Pope from the transition to Home Establishment entailed a dishonoured cheque, dated 26 November 1917, for 200 Francs. Pope had submitted it to the Expeditionary Force Canteens (EFC), not some tavern or house of ill repute, so he must have known that if the cheque bounced it would be followed up with him. In March 1918 Pope wrote to explain that the EFC had presented three of his cheques within three weeks, and that the fourth was referred to drawer by Cox's Bank in the expectation of it being presented again, which had not occurred by the time he had been transferred. The War Office accepted Pope's explanation and no disciplinary proceedings arose.

By this stage Pope had been promoted to Temporary Lieutenant, in February 1918, and by August he was promoted to Temporary Captain (Aeroplane). Pope actually got to command 'A' Flight of No. 24 Squadron from 18 December 1918 to 3 February 1919, in its final stages of existence as a 'scout' squadron, being reduced to cadre strength. Pope then transferred to the Army of occupation as a Flight Commander. In August 1919 the Air Ministry announced that Pope had retained his temporary rank. Pope's appointment as Flying Officer (Aeroplane & Seaplane) was gazetted on 24 October 1919.[5] It would appear that he was awarded a short service commission at that rank and appointed Qualified Flying Instructor (QFI) at the RAF (Cadet) College, Cranwell. In May 1922 the Air Ministry announced that Pope had been granted a permanent commission in the RAF, retaining rank and seniority at the level of Flying Officer, the short service commission of 24 October 1919 being cancelled.[6]

Pope flew with No. 8 Squadron from April 1922 onwards. It had served in an Army Cooperation role for much of the war, but in the early 1920s spent time in Egypt and Mesopotamia (Iraq). However, in August 1922 it was announced that he had relinquished the rank of Captain for pay and allowance purposes, with effect from 4 August 1919.[7]

In June 1923, Pope was promoted from Flying Officer to Flight Lieutenant. Pope was posted to No. 55 Squadron, in Iraq, with effect from 24 September 1923.[8] He was subsequently transferred to RAF HQ Egypt on 24 December 1924, but nothing much can be read into the rotation of RAF personnel at this time. Galwegian Tom Hazell would have been in command of No. 55 Squadron during part of Pope's period of service there.

Pope was awarded the DFC for his service in Iraq. No. 55 Squadron had been a Bomber Squadron in the First World War, forming part of the Independent Force (the forerunner of RAF Bomber Command) from July 1918 onwards. In the post-war years it had been disbanded and re-formed in 1920. Although No. 55 Squadron flew from Mosul in the early 1920s, by May 1924 it was based at RAF Hinaidi, near Baghdad. A dispute had broken out between Assyrian recruits and the local population in Kirkuk in Sulaimaniya in May 1924, which resulted in Air Vice Marshal Higgins ordering two platoons of the Royal Inniskilling Fusiliers from Baghdad to Kirkuk to quell disturbances. This further exacerbated the situation and Sheikh Mahmud declared a full-scale Jihad against the British forces. Aircraft from several squadrons were involved in the bombing of Sulaimaniya in May 1924, and although Pope was serving with 'C' Flight of No. 55 Squadron at the time, it would appear that he was part of a deployment from Mosul to RAF Hinaidi (i.e. to Baghdad) as part of a series of related operations.

Although the province had been carved from the dismembered remnants of the Ottoman Empire under the Treaty of Sèvres—and had been granted to the British to administer as part of the League of Nations mandate—the Turks had not relinquished territorial claims to Mosul and the surrounding areas. Following the overthrow of the Sultan and the Turkish War of Independence led by Mustafa Kemal Ataturk, the Treaty of Lausanne—which came into force on 6 August 1924—had superseded the Treaty of Sèvres, but the fate of Mosul had been left to the League of Nations to resolve and this had not been concluded by the time the various revolts and uprisings were taking place. Although British troops re-occupied Sulaimaniya by late July 1924, there were still minor clashes between the British and Sheikh Mahmud's forces, and also a series of skirmishes between the British and Turkish forces over the late summer and early autumn of 1924. By late December 1924 Pope had transferred to RAF HQ Egypt.

Pope was awarded the DFC. There is no actual citation in *The London Gazette* of 28 May 1926, but it carried the following general citation for a number of officers and other ranks:

> The King has been graciously pleased to approve of the undermentioned awards in recognition of gallant and distinguished service in connection with the operations in Iraq during the period of September to November 1924.[9]

Air Ministry records note the following:

> Flight Lieutenant Pope constantly led patrols with great fearlessness and
> determination, often at low altitudes through mountain passes infested with the
> enemy, and frequently under severe fire. He carried out over 90 hours' operational
> flying in one month and at all times set a splendid example of courage and zeal.[10]

By February 1927 Pope had transferred to No. 22 Squadron. This squadron was in
effect an integral part of the Aeroplane Experimental Establishment at Martlesham
Heath, Suffolk. The purpose of the squadron was to test new aircraft prior to their
acceptance into service with the RAF.

The Investiture for Pope's DFC was held at Buckingham Palace on 15 February
1927. Pope participated in a 20-mile handicap race on Good Friday, 15 April 1927,
flying a De Havilland Moth (G-EBPG) as part of the Bournemouth Easter Meeting
series. He came second in his race.[11]

Pope became an air race regular, flying in the Bournemouth Whitsun Meeting
at Ensbury Park Racecourse on the bank holiday weekend of 4-6 June 1927.[12] He
flew a blue De Havilland Moth in a number of races, too, and was elected to the
committee of the Royal Aero Club in September 1927. In February 1928 Pope got
engaged to a Miss Pamela Young from Ipswich. Pope was one of those in attendance
at a *levée* held by the King at St James's Palace on 6 March 1928.[13]

On 24 February 1929 Pope survived the disintegration of a prototype Parnall
Pipit single-seater using a parachute—the first RAF test pilot to do so. Some decades
later, the auction catalogue of his medals states that the incident occurred a short
time after Pope's arrival at Martlesham.

> While at the Parnall factory at Yate, testing a Parnall Pippit, a single-seater fighter
> undergoing acceptance trials, Pope felt a twitch when at 800 feet. He glanced over
> his shoulder and was just in time to see the rudder and fin floating away in mid-
> air behind him. Deciding that the time had come for him and the Pippet to part
> company, Pope jerked the throttle shut, pulled the nose up and reached down to
> undo the straps of his Sutton harness.

It is suggested that Pope spent precious seconds tugging at the string of his pencil
that he had been using to record test data! Apparently, after this struggle with his
harness he only managed to bale out at 300 feet. And there was more drama—the
ripcord handle was not where it should have been:

> He had somersaulted and was falling feet-first; below him he could see a row of
> Africa Star tall oaks coming up fast. In that same split second he saw the ripcord
> ring hanging by his leg—it had slipped from its sheath. He reached down, gave
> it a despairing tug and his chute blossomed out above him with a bump. As he

reached up to grasp the lift webs his feet slashed through the top branches on to the ground.

'The people over at the aerodrome hadn't seen me get out,' Pope said. 'When they came running over they expected to find me in the wreckage. Instead I was running round the field like a madman, making sure that my back, which had received a severe jar, was in working order. The only visible injuries were two scratches on my ankle.'

It would appear that only two prototypes of the Parnall Pipit were built. One crashed in October 1928, when the tailplane spar fractured. The pilot survived, but with a broken neck. Pope flew the second prototype, with a strengthened tailplane featuring support struts, which crashed in 1929. However, the melodramatic story of surviving a bale-out at 300 feet via parachute and treetops is not supported in other contemporary reports. The squadron's ORB records the date of the incident as being 7 March 1929.[14] The squadron had already had a number of fatal or near-fatal experiences with test aircraft: on 8 December 1926, Flying Officer Wheatley had been killed when the wings came off the Gamecock during a test flight; on 23 January 1928, Flying Officer Dauncey was killed in a speed course test of a Turcock single-seater; and on 17 December 1929, Flight Lieutenant Jenkins, who had set several records in the squadron's Fairey Postal, was killed in a crash.

On 1 March 1929 Pope was awarded the Air Force Cross, which was gazetted on that date. It was awarded for his test flight work. *The Edinburgh Gazette* of 5 March 1929 also reports Pope being awarded the AFC.[15] Pope was awarded the AFC at an Investiture held by the King at Buckingham Palace on 28 March 1929.

Pope's use of an Irvin parachute and survival to tell the tale had won him membership of the 'Caterpillar Club' (conceptually the parachute was the silk, and the cockpit the cocoon). Pope would have received a gold tie-pin of caterpillar design from the Irvin Air Chute Company of Buffalo, New York. By 1930 he was one of just 47 British-based parachute survivors, among 300 Caterpillar Club members worldwide.

On 1 August 1929 Pope transferred to the Air Ministry with the Department of the Air Member for Supply and Research (AMSR) with effect from 13 July. This was a research and technical development service branch, but there would not appear to have been any prohibition of Pope flying in a private capacity. In the King's Cup Air Race to Hamworth on 5 July 1930, Pope flew an Avro V but had to retire at the Manchester leg of the race.

On 1 February 1932 Pope was promoted from Flight Lieutenant to Squadron Leader.[16] He was subsequently transferred from the Department of the AMSR to No. 54 Squadron, Hornchurch, with effect from 7 March 1932. Although his squadron's pilots had by this stage been training for two years on day and night operations, No. 54 Squadron suffered two fatalities on Pope's watch: Flying Officer L. E. P. Mahon died on 12 June 1932 and Petty Officer A. J. Draper on 8 July 1932. Pope led No. 54

(Fighter) Squadron in several mock-fighting events in June and July 1932, including an attack on an aerodrome, as part of the 'Northlands' *versus* 'Southlands' exercises. His squadron flew Bristol Bulldogs from Upavon. Pope did not stay long with No. 54 Squadron, however; on 21 January 1933 he was posted to the RAF Staff College.[17]

In September 1933 Pope transferred to command No. 801 (FF) Squadron. This was a Naval Air Squadron. (In the post-war years the Royal Navy had been granted a successor to the RNAS, but only in respect of seaborne duties not assigned to RAF Coastal Command, i.e. the Fleet Air Arm did not re-gain the former RNAS seaplane squadrons or coastal and maritime patrol aircraft.) No. 801 Squadron was formed in April 1933, flying Hawker Nimrod biplanes from HMS *Hermes*. Squadron Leader Pope was transferred to the School of Naval Co-operation, Lee-on-the-Solent, for duty as Adjutant, with effect from 27 May 1936. Pope was promoted from Squadron Leader to Wing Commander with effect from 1 April 1937.[18] Subsequently, Wing Commander Pope was appointed to RAF Station Debden to command with effect from 21 April 1937. RAF Debden had only been opened that month, and Pope's command was effectively of two grass landing strips to begin with. However, it was subjected to continuous improvement and by the outbreak of the Second World War the grass had been replaced with concrete.

In July 1938 it was reported that Wing Commander Pope led a formation of eleven Hawker Hurricanes of No. 111 (Fighter) Squadron and four Gloster Gladiators of No. 87 (Fighter) Squadron in escorting a Vickers Valentia bomber transport and two Avro Ansons from RAF Northolt in a crossing to Paris. They made the journey in sixty-six minutes, being escorted by French Amiot bombers and Dewoitine fighters. The exercises by the Hurricanes and Gladiators were well received in Paris.[19] Indeed Pope would appear to have been a minor celebrity in the late 1930s: on 14 May 1938 he gave a radio interview in Daventry for the BBC World Service, called 'Milestones in an Airman's Life', and on 17 November he narrated a London regional BBC Radio broadcast, 'The ABC of Flying', for which another version was broadcast on 12 January 1939.

In March 1939 Pope transferred to take command of No. 226 Squadron. This squadron had only been reformed in March 1937, flying the Fairey Battle light bomber. The Battle was a single-engined, three-crewed aircraft that was obsolete before the war even began—it was developed at a time when light bombers and short-range operations were prioritised, for instance bombing France from England in the event of an Anglo-French war, or Germany from France in the event that the Western Front of the First World War be resurrected in a new conflict. The Battle's development in the 1930s had not kept pace with vast improvements in fighter performance. Further, although the early Würzburg radar would hold none of the menace of the radar-directed fire control predictors of anti-aircraft batteries in the later war years, by May 1940 radar data was being relayed to flak crews.

According to the squadron's ORB, Pope commanded No. 72 Wing. This was to be part of the RAF's Advanced Air Striking Force (AASF), which was under the command of Air Vice-Marshal Patrick Henry Lyon 'Pip' Playfair, a Scottish First World War veteran who had served in both the Army and the Air Force. On 2 September 1939 Pope led No. 226 Squadron's 'air party' of fifteen Fairey Battles from Harwell to Reims. (A contingent of NCOs and other ranks travelled in civil aircraft, with ground crew arriving as a 'sea party'.) War had not yet been declared on Germany, but they were 'tooling-up' in Reims.

No. 226 Squadron undertook some photographic reconnaissance operations in September but these were hampered by bad weather. Their first offensive operations on 27 September saw no casualties, but only two of the Flight's six aircraft returned to Reims, four others having to force-land at Laon due to a shortage of petrol. Pope would not be at fault, for planning operations' estimation of range and payload is complicated by vagueness in target identification and so forth, but it would be problematic if there was any presumption that the squadron would always have the luxury of landing 70 km further north. More worryingly for Pope was the fact that two of the six Battles (K9346 and K7705) had been damaged by anti-aircraft fire, despite the cloud and fog cover. On 13 October 1939 Pope and his Squadron Leader, C. E. S. Lockett, were filmed by Paramount News. But Pope can't be accused of neglecting to prepare the squadron for what was to come: in October they actually got a loan of a French Curtiss fighter to rehearse defensive tactics, and on the 31st Pope got AASF HQ to send a Squadron Leader to advise them of defensive tactics.

Yet there was still an air of unreality about the enemy threat; Pope received a visit from King George V on 8 December 1939 at Reims, and on 12th the Chief of Air Staff inspected the squadron accompanied by Lord Londonderry. Pope took some leave in mid-January 1940, and in February his No. 72 Wing was dissolved and absorbed into No. 76 Wing, though Pope did in fact act for Group Captain H. S. Kerby as part of No. 76 Wing's reorganisation. He took No. 226 Squadron to No. 1 ATS (France) for revision to bombing training and for further work in air-to-air gunnery. The squadron returned to Reims in March 1940. They flew night reconnaissance operations in April, probing German defences.

In the Battle of France the three Battle-equipped squadrons of Pope's No. 76 Wing (Nos 12, 148, and 226) suffered grievous losses. By May 1940, their remnants only had twenty serviceable aircraft between them. Pope was relieved of his command at No. 226 Squadron, which may relate to the failure No. 76 Wing in reaching objectives with the Fairey Battle, but could equally have resulted from Pope's exasperation at the waste of human life in attempting to deploy this slow, heavy single-engined bomber against well-defended targets. Wing Commander H. C. Parker was put in command of No. 226 Squadron during its evacuation in June 1940. It eventually proceeded to Northern Ireland and was based at Hollywood, Co. Down. (The officers were put up at Redburn House, their mess being situated at Ardtullagh, Hollywood.)

Pope's career did not suffer, however, as he was promoted from Wing Commander to Group Captain with effect from 1 June 1940, and that same month was appointed in command of RAF Leuchars—the base from which No. 224 Squadron attempted to engage German flying boats and Condors in the North Sea. It would appear that over the course of 1941 and 1942, Group Captain Pope commanded various training resources, most notably the transfer of RAF No. 32 OTU from England to Patricia Bay, Victoria, Canada in July 1941. The unit used Avro Ansons and Bristol Beaufort torpedo bombers to train Australian, British, Canadian, and New Zealand crews.

Pope was then posted to command RAF Syerston in Nottinghamshire. This base had originally seen Polish-crewed Wellington bombers being replaced by Royal Canadian Air Force (RCAF) crewed Hampdens, and subsequently Lancaster heavy bombers. Pope's command of the base coincided with its transition to a station for bomber crew training. It was to become known at the Lancaster Finishing School, but there was also a Bombing and Gunnery Defence Training Flight based there in 1942 and 1943.

On 20 October 1942 Pope's permission to wear the Commander of the Order of Orange-Nassau with Swords, which had been conferred by the Queen of the Netherlands (Royal Decree No. 12 of 15 January 1942), was gazetted.[20]

It would appear that by late 1943 he had returned to command RAF Leuchars and its maritime patrol squadrons. However, by February 1944 he was in command of No. 53 Base, which was part of RAF Bomber Command, not Coastal Command. No. 53 (Operational) Base was formed in January 1943, composed of RAF Waddington, RAF Skellingthorpe, and RAF Bardney, and was part of No. 5 Group, which was based in Lincolnshire throughout the Second World War. Pope was mentioned in despatches in June 1944, at which point he was still an Acting Air Commodore.

On 1 January 1946 Pope became a Commander of the Military Division of the Most Excellent Order of the British Empire, a military CBE in the New Year Honours List.[21] According to information at the auction of Pope's medals many years later, the Air Ministry had recommended Pope as being 'a most capable and efficient base commander who has successfully organised the squadrons under his command to a high standard.'

Pope retired on 2 March 1946, after a remarkable and varied career—one in which he had survived being brought down without a parachute and yet nearly been killed when he had relied on one in his test flight years. He died in November 1980 in Worthing, West Sussex. Pope's ten medals—both his service medals and gallantry awards—were auctioned by Dix Noonan Webb on 18 June 1997.

25

PROCTOR,
Thomas
(5 aerial victories)

Born: 23 August 1888, Co. Armagh
Died: 27 September 1918
Commemorated: Arras Flying Services Memorial, Pas-de-Calais, France

Sergeant Thomas Proctor was born in Lurgan, Co. Armagh, to Elizabeth Proctor, though his next-of-kin address is recorded as '47 Lanark St, Belfast'. By 1911 he was living at Wilton Street, Woodvale, Belfast. Thomas' mother Elizabeth, a widow, is described as being a linen weaver, as is Thomas' sister Elizabeth. Thomas was a 'machine oiler in mill'.

Like several other Irish aces, Proctor served with the RNAS. However, his active service in air-to-air fighting was with the RAF, as an observer in two-seater Bristol F.2 fighters with No. 88 Squadron, and he scored all his victories with this squadron. Accordingly, Proctor is not an RNAS, but an RAF ace.

The relatively common forename and surname combination, together with the transition from RNAS to RAF, can often give rise to confusion regarding Proctor. He is neither the Thomas Augustus Pugh Proctor (DOB 25 July 1898) nor the Thomas Proctor (DOB 8 January 1900) recorded in various Air Ministry officer files.[1] There is a Thomas Proctor (DOB 7 August 1887) recorded as an Ordinary Seaman, Able Seaman, under the Service Number R/1783, and in the RN Volunteer Reserve Division ('Palace'), under the Service Number Z/2624.[2] But despite the proximity of age, neither are the Irish Thomas Proctor of No. 88 Squadron.

Proctor's date of enlistment with the RNAS under Service Number F12137 was 19 February 1916.[3] Just 5 foot 6 inches, he was tattooed and had a scar on his right forearm. He had been a town labourer before the war, and served as an air mechanic (2nd Class), receiving a 'very good' rating in all his reviews. Until 9 September 1917 he was assigned to *President II* (Dover), the first of a series of shore establishments where he would be posted. On 10 September Proctor transferred to *Daedalus* (Eastchurch), serving there until 31 December, whereupon he was reassigned to *President II* (Dover). He was transferred to *President II* (Dunkirk) on 15 January

1918, then subsequently to *Daedalus* (Dunkirk) from 1 February 1918 until the merger of the RNAS with the RFC into the RAF.

Upon the merger, former RNAS personnel numbers had their letter removed and 200,000 added, i.e. Proctor's F2137 became 212137. Similarly, each Wing had 60 added to its number, and squadrons had 200 added, i.e. No. 3 (Naval) Squadron became No. 203 Squadron RAF.

Upon transfer to the RAF on 1 April 1918, Proctor was given the rank of Private (2nd Class), so he was still part of groundcrew rather than aircrew. His notional establishment was changed to 'Guston, Dover'. The Guston Road airfield was one of three in and around Dover during the war, including the RNAS seaplane station. Proctor was then assigned to No. 218 Squadron upon its foundation on 24 April. The squadron was equipped with the D.H.9 bomber, and although composed of ex-RNAS personnel, its lineage was relatively straightforward compared to others whose names had been through several confusing alterations—not least because at one stage in the war the RNAS used the term 'Squadron' for what the RFC would have called a 'Flight', and the term 'Wing' for what the RFC would have called a 'Squadron'.

In an unexplained development, Proctor transferred from No. 218 Squadron the week before it was due to leave Dover for Petit Synthe in France. On 11 May 1918 he was assigned to No. 88 Squadron—quite a contrast, for No. 88 flew Bristol F2.b fighters. Furthermore, there's nothing in the RNAS or RAF records to suggest Proctor trained as an observer (none of the ledgers for the schools of aerial gunnery show a return for 'Proctor'). The squadron itself is an interesting one: although No. 88 Squadron conducted bomber escort duties, it also conducted reconnaissance, in addition to bombing operations of its own. Proctor had no training in aerial photography, but somewhere in the chaos of the German advance he found himself serving as an observer not long after the squadron had moved to France.

His first victory came on 31 May 1918, when his Bristol F2.b (C821), which was piloted by Allan Hepburn, sent an Albatros D.V down out of control over Ostend. On 2 June 1918 the same pairing in the same aircraft sent an Albatros D.V down in flames between Middlekerke and Ostende.

Proctor's next recorded victories did not come until August 1918, scoring three victories with two different pilots. He was the only Irish ace to have served with No. 88 Squadron, but it was a diverse group: the highest-scoring aces were Kenneth Conn, a Canadian, and Edgar Johnston and Allan Hepburn, both Australian. Of the squadron's claimed 147 victories, Proctor was the only Irish contributor, although the mother (Elizabeth) of Coventry-born ace William Wheeler was from Derry and the mother (Mary Jane, née Cuthbert) of Kent-born ace Robert James Cullen from Kerry. Irish casualties with No. 88 Squadron included 2nd Lieutenant Stephen Griffin from Ennis, Co. Clare, who was killed on 18 May 1918.

Proctor was promoted to Sergeant on 1 September 1918.[4] According to the most authoritative source, he was killed in action on the 27th when his Bristol F2.b (E2153) was shot down by the German ace Vizefeldwebel Friedrich 'Fritz' Classen of Jasta 26, the latter's ninth of his eleven victories.[5] Proctor's pilot, Lieutenant Cuthbert Foster, was also killed. They had been engaged in an escort role for aircraft of No. 103 Squadron, who were on a bombing mission. During the flight they were attacked by a number of enemy aircraft and Cuthbert was seen to perform a double loop in an attempt to outmanoeuvre a German aircraft that was on their tail. According to the British accounts, they were seen flying low and heading for the British lines. However, in the immediate aftermath of combat it is often difficult to gage whether an aircraft has engine trouble or has been badly shot up. According to *Above the War Fronts*, they were shot down near Abancourt.

Regardless of the exact sequence of events, Proctor has no known grave. They had met a formidable enemy: Royal Prussian Jasta 26 scored 177 aerial victories for the loss of fewer than 30 casualties in the course of the war.

Proctor's mother was living at 26 Argyle Street, Belfast, at the time of his death. A war gratuity was paid on 30 January 1920.

26

SAUNDERS,
Alfred William
(12 aerial victories)

Born: 16 January 1888, Dublin
Died: 22 May 1930
Awards: Distinguished Flying Cross

Captain Alfred William Saunders was born in Dublin to Amelia Adelaide Saunders, a hospital nurse from London, and Matthew Johnston Saunders, a contractor, from Co. Wicklow.

In 1901 Saunders was living at 14 Leinster Street, Dublin, with his mother, his older sister Margaret, and his brothers Arthur and William. Their London-born grandmother was also resident with them. Other baptismal data, however, suggests that the family lived at 14 York Street for a number of years and that elder siblings Letitia and Matthew had moved on by 1901. In 1911 Saunders was no longer living with his mother, while his father had become an inmate at Northbrook Road, Dublin, an old man's asylum. The building itself still stands, a Gothic Revival pile complete with spire, tiny cell-like windows, and a peculiar asymmetrical design.

Saunders's brother William was to become the sketch artist Paddy Drew. There are numerous Pathé newsreels of the 1930s and 1940s in which he sketches caricatures Chamberlain, Hitler, and so forth for the cameras.

Saunders originally joined the colours with the Royal Field Artillery, under the service number 1455. He enlisted in the ranks on 11 September 1914, as a Bombardier in the 1st City of London Brigade, RFA. He served with the Second Battery, which was stationed at Blyth when he originally applied for a commission in April 1915, but had moved down to Ipswich by the time his application was assessed. Saunders's good character certification was signed by Dr Cowe of St Stephen's Green, Dublin. His education was certified by Mr Sharpe, a tutor at Tallaght School, Co. Dublin. A letter of support was also issued from a former Grenadier Guard who was living in Ballymore Eustace, Co. Kildare; he stated that Saunders had been working in Canada for seven years, engaged in bridge building and other works on the Canadian Pacific. Saunders was granted a temporary commission as a 2nd Lieutenant.

He was attached to 'D' Howitzer Battery, 69th Brigade, RFA, 13th (Western) Division, which landed at Gallipoli in July 1915. In August and September the Division lost 6,000 killed, wounded, missing, or taken prisoner, from an original strength of just over 10,000. The photographic images taken of 'D' Battery by Sergeant James Cornelius Read are reminiscent of an artillery unit from a previous era, with their pith helmets and limited sandbag defences.

Saunders was evacuated from Gallipoli on 23 October 1915, aboard the HMHS *Formosa*, which arrived at Southampton on 9 November. A medical board examination in London on 17 February 1916 found him to be still suffering from dysentery, and that there were several complications. It recommended two months' further rest. On 29 March he attended a medical board examination at King George V Hospital in Dublin, which found that he had now recovered from dysentery. On 4 April he was posted to the 5th 'A' Reserve Brigade, RFA, in Athlone, Co. Westmeath. He passed a further medical board examination in Dublin on the 15th, a week before the Easter Rising broke out. Yet Saunders does not appear to have taken part in the RFA's operations there. The 5th ('A' Reserve) Brigade consisted of the 25th, 26th, and 27th Battery, which were based at Athlone, Co. Westmeath. In Easter 1916 they were deployed to Dublin, but as they only had four artillery pieces available it is unclear which personnel from which unit were actually assigned to the operations.

Saunders transferred to the RFC in the summer of 1916. He obtained his Royal Aero Club certificate on 20 July, flying a Maurice Farman biplane at the Military School, Catterick Bridge. He was at the time living at 9B Kelfield Gardens, North Kensington, London. In August Saunders was appointed 2nd Lieutenant in the RFC, but in October he contracted syphilis.[1] Not until December was he passed fit again.

Saunders was assigned to No. 17 TS at Yatesbury. On 7 January 1917 Saunders survived a bad crash on landing at Croydon Aerodrome. He broke his nose and jaw, lost several teeth, and was severely concussed. He had been undertaking tests on an Avro (499), and after six successful take-off and landing sequences, the control wires snapped; the joystick became useless, and Saunders was helpless as the machine nosedived from 150 feet. The CO of No. 17 TS wrote to the Air Board to state that Saunders was in no way to blame for the accident. In the aftermath of hospitalisation and several medical board examinations, the note to file includes an order to cease the issuance of Flying Pay while invalided from his injuries, despite this being a case of mechanical failure, not pilot error.

As part of the gradual recovery process toward operational flying, Saunders was posted to the School of Aerial Gunnery at Loch Doon in Scotland. However, he did require a period of hospitalisation at Palace Green in May 1917, but this suggests psychosomatic issues in addition to the physical suffering. Nevertheless, on 4 October he was promoted from 2nd Lieutenant to Temporary Lieutenant.[2] He was assigned to No. 60 Squadron the following January.

Saunders's service is only briefly mentioned in Scott's history of No. 60 Squadron, but he joined long after marquee names such as Molesworth and Pope had passed through. Saunders did have a significant overlapping period of service with Galway-born ace Herbert George Hegarty, and they appeared to swap command of 'A' Flight at various stages in the summer of 1918. In several accounts he is called 'Pat' Saunders, so the Dublin accent must still have been discernible, even after his years in London and Canada.

RAF Communiqué No. 6 of 1918, which covers the period 6–12 May 1918, reports Lieutenant A. W. Saunders having achieved at least one aerial victory. The various No. 60 Squadron histories generally record Saunders as destroying two Albatros D.V fighters on 10 May. However, Captain James Dacre Belgrave includes Lieutenants Saunders and Lewis in the capture of a Rumpler, which was forced to land east of Albert. (This aerial victory was not credited to Saunders, however.) RAF Communiqué No. 7 of 1918 reports that on 16 May 1918 Saunders drove down a damaged German aircraft, but it survived a spin, and that he destroyed another, which crashed near Beaulencourt.[3] Hegarty also destroyed a German aircraft on that day. On 19 May, Saunders's S.E.5a (C9536) struck a ridge when landing in fading light following an offensive patrol. It did not shake his confidence, however. On 4 June Captain Belgrave led Saunders and Lewis on a balloon-busting mission. They forced down two kite balloons near Mametz Wood, but they were not ignited and so no aerial victories were credited to the patrol.

On 2 July Saunders really showed his rate of improvement, being awarded a triple-victory in respect of the following claim of destructions and collisions:

Five machines of 60 Sqn, led by Lt A. W. Saunders, saw a formation of six Pfalz Scouts 7,000 feet below flying over Villers Bretonneux. The patrol went down and attacked the EA at the tail end of the left-hand side of the formation. A drum of Lewis and a long burst of Vickers were fired at it by Lt Saunders, whereupon it went down vertically and was seen to crash by an AA battery. The second EA on the left of the leader suddenly turned to the right and collided into the EA leader, both machines collapsing and crashing into the Bois de Pierret. ... Lt Saunders then became separated from his patrol and saw three Pfalz Scouts, which he attacked and chased east. On coming home he saw an EA attacking an S.E.5 and joined in, whereupon this EA also flew east. Lt Saunders was fighting altogether 45 minutes.[4]

Saunders was almost immediately awarded the DFC, which suggests that he may have been recommended for a higher award. On that day his patrol had had an unusual flying companion—Major Joseph 'Casey' Cruess Callaghan in his Sopwith Dolphin. Callaghan, the CO of No. 87 Squadron, was on one of his 'lone wolf' actions when he tagged along with No. 60 Squadron for a while, and then was caught out on his own when he took on twenty-five German aircraft. A patrol from

No. 56 Squadron spotted him in the distance, but he had turned to take on his opponents instead of running for cover, and the No. 56 Squadron patrol could not help. (In fact, they lost Lieutenant Francis Read, who was wounded in the skirmishes afterwards.)

On 3 August Saunders led an operation against enemy kite balloons. He drove one down near Martinpuich but once again it was not considered decisive, as the balloon had not been ignited.

Saunders's DFC citation was gazetted on 3 August 1918:

Lt Alfred William Saunders

A gallant and determined officer whose fighting spirit and enthusiasm has been a splendid example to his squadron. On one occasion while leading his formation of six machines, he attacked six enemy aeroplanes. Diving from 11,000 to 3,000 feet, he singled out a group of three, and shot down one. He then engaged the other two, which in their endeavour to get away collided and crashed.[5]

Saunders was promoted to Temporary Captain (Aeroplane) in August 1918, and took command of 'B' Flight on a permanent basis.[6] RAF Communiqué No. 19 of 1918 reports Saunders taking on targets of opportunity on 8 August:

Capt. A. W. Saunders, 60 Sqn, dived on a Fokker biplane, which he observed to go down in a spin and crash. Soon afterwards he attacked another enemy machine, which fell through the clouds out of control, and on following it down he saw a train, into which he fired from 50 feet, circling twice round the engine. Though heavily fired at from the ground and shot in the seat of his machine, and having fired all his ammunition away, Capt. Saunders returned.[7]

Saunders would appear to have done well as a Flight Commander, his patrol accounting for four enemy aircraft on 9 August 1918. Saunders was required to attend a medical board examination at Wimereux on the 15th. He was posted to Home Establishment, with his next medical board examination taking place on 21 August.

Saunders's post-war career took many twists and turns, some of which are not fully explained. He served briefly with the short-lived Lithuanian Air Force of the interwar years. Saunders was notionally transferred to the Unemployed List on 31 October 1919, which was gazetted on 13 January 1920.[8] He had been subjected to a medical board examination on 28 October 1919 at No. 38 TDS, which was based at Tadcaster. Apparently he joined the Lithuanian Air Force on 31 October 1919, and was released on 17 January 1920. Indeed, the RAF had provided a range of advisory and training roles to enable Lithuania hold its ground in the conflicts between Poland and the USSR and their neighbours. Saunders was one of a number of 'civilian volunteer' advisors to the Lithuanians. While farmed out to Lithuania it would appear that Saunders was promoted to Flying Officer, which was gazetted on 12 December 1919.[9] He was subsequently promoted from Temporary 2nd Lieutenant to Temporary Lieutenant in the Royal Army Service Corps, with effect from 10 December 1919.[10] He also had to attend a further medical board examination, at Arkwright Lodge, Hampstead, on 18 December 1919.

It may be noted that the abovementioned sequence of appointments appear contradictory, but whether as a civilian or under military service, Saunders did serve alongside Pranas 'Frank' Hiska, a Lithuanian with RAF training, and a small number of RAF pilots. He was lucky to have got out in January 1920, as the Polish-Lithuanian situation deteriorated severely thereafter. Saunders had to attend a further medical board examination on 18 February at Cheltenham Terrace, so the release date was probably agreed in consideration of this appointment. This particular medical board examination was for the purposes of assessing Saunders for a wounds gratuity.

Saunders accepted a short service commission in the RAF in April 1920, which led to his temporary retired pay lapsing due to abatement rules on emoluments from Exchequer funds. Saunders initial application for a wound gratuity in September 1920 was rejected in December 1920 on the basis that it was not 'very severe'. Saunders' address at the time was No. 1 Squadron, Bangalore, Mysore. The RAF had disbanded several squadrons and recycled their numbers. The venerable No. 1 Squadron of Atkinson and Hazell had become an Indian-based unit, with an assortment of men and material. Squadron Leader J. O. Andrews described the situation thus:

> The personnel, both officers and men, was in part drawn from existing squadrons in India. Since 'P' Staff had little or no knowledge of the RAF officers or units it was a heaven sent opportunity for Squadrons to unload undesirables, and to refuse to part with experienced scout pilots who were desirous of coming to the squadron.[11]

This unhappy situation was not helped with the Indian Wing falling under the command of Air Commodore T. I. Webb-Bowen. He reduced officers' pay and allowances, which further impacted on morale. No. 1 Squadron moved to Bangalore in May 1920. Perhaps Saunders's initiation of correspondence with the War Office was the beginning of his own attempt at exiting the unit. No. 1 Squadron's reputation recovered substantially when it was transferred to Iraq in April 1921, but Saunders would appear to have transferred out by that stage.

Saunders served with No. 20 Squadron at Quetta, India. He returned to the UK in late January 1923 for demobilisation. On 6 February the Air Ministry announced that Flying Officer Alfred William Saunders DFC had been transferred to the Class 'A' Reserve with effect from 5 February.[12]

During much of March and April 1923 the War Office and Air Ministry exchanged correspondence on whether Saunders was eligible for a wounds pension or a wounds gratuity. He had been the subject of a medical board examination on 8 March 1923, which resulted in Saunders having to remain in London pending any further follow-up examinations. The prevailing bureaucratic view was that, although the injuries Saunders sustained in January 1917 were serious and had rendered him unfit for general service for a twelve-month period, the effects of the wounds were not permanent, even though he was left scarred and crooked-jawed. The interdepartmental wrangling over this issue was such that even the Ministry of Pensions at one stage became involved. Finally, in April 1923 the report of the medical board examination of March came to Saunders's rescue: it found that his nose had been fractured and recognised that bone and cartilage had been removed at the time of the accident. Although Saunders was exaggerating his reactions to some of the tests, the maxilla bones of his skull (those which form the upper jaw and palate of the mouth) had been displaced upwards, being shortened vertically and driven in a little. Several teeth were lost, others chipped or reduced to damaged stumps. The board overturned the original decision of 27 January 1917, substituting its own finding—that the injuries should have been categorised as 'very severe' and that this diagnosis should have remained in place for two years from the date of injury. Eventually, in April 1923 the War Office wrote to Saunders to state that he was ineligible for a wounds pension but did pay him a gratuity of £250 to cover the period from 7 January 1917 to 6 January 1918.

On 16 December 1924 the Air Ministry announced that Saunders was one of a number of officers transferred from Class 'A' Reserve to Class 'C' Reserve, with effect from that date.[13] By 25 February 1927 he had relinquished his commission upon completion of his service.[14]

Saunders died in an air crash involving a de Havilland Gipsy Moth over Auckland, New Zealand, on 22 May 1930. According to the press, Saunders attempted to spin too close to the ground. An Alfred W. Minchin was also killed in the crash.

27

TIDMARSH,
David Mary
(7 aerial victories)

Born: 28 January 1892, Co. Limerick
Died: 27 November 1944
Awards: Military Cross

Captain David Mary Tidmarsh was born in Co. Limerick to David Aloysius and Elizabeth 'Lillie' Tidmarsh, of Lota, North Circular Road, Limerick. David's father was from Kilkenny City, and his mother from Nenagh, Co. Tipperary. The Tidmarshes were a well-known drapers in Limerick, James Moriarty Tidmarsh having acquired the department store Cannock & Co. in 1869 from Peter Tait and George Cannock. James's son, David James Tidmarsh, succeeded him in January 1877, and David Aloysius succeeded him in September 1896.[1]

In 1901, neither he nor his brothers John and Gerard were present at the Limerick family home, but his sisters Ethel, Lillie, and Mary all resided there, as did a governess, a servant, a coachman, and a nurse. All three brothers were boarders at Baylis House in Eton, Berkshire. Superficially this would appear to be quite surprising given the Tidmarshes' religious background: Ampleforth, Downside, or Stonyhurst would have been more appropriate for a wealthy Catholic family. However, Baylis was a Roman Catholic school owned and run by the Butt family until they went bankrupt in 1907. Among the staff present in 1901 was an Irish priest, Rev. James Shore, and among the scholars twelve Irish, three Spanish, one Bolivian and one French. By 1911 Tidmarsh and the family were living on Circular Road, Limerick City, along with his cousin, Mary Hamilton, a housemaid, and a cook. His older brother Gerard and his three sisters were no longer living at the family home, while he was working as a draper with his father.

Tidmarsh joined the colours with the Royal Irish Regiment. He was promoted from 2nd Lieutenant to Lieutenant on 23 April 1915.[2] He transferred to the RFC in August and was initially posted to Shoreham for training, then to South Harrow on the 27th.[3] He was awarded Royal Aero Club Aviator's Certificate No. 1833, qualifying on a Maurice Farman biplane at the Military School, Ruislip, on

7 October. This was only three days after Joseph Cruess Callaghan had obtained Certificate No. 1829 at Norwich, so the Irish were well represented among the early aviators of the war.

In December 1915 Tidmarsh trained with No. 4 RAS (Reserve Aircraft Squadron) and subsequently No.11 RAS, before being posted to No. 24 Squadron upon appointment as Flying Officer in January 1916, possibly on the 13th.[4] He was a founding member of No. 24 Squadron, assigned to 'B' Flight. There were only twelve pilots in the original squadron, and only four pilots to each Flight. The squadron was under the command of VC-winner Lanoe Hawker and was one of the first 'scout' (fighter) squadrons of the RFC. Hawker encouraged the pilots to experiment and innovate, and led by example, designing 'fug' boots and gun sighting mechanisms himself. Tidmarsh is often mentioned in the context of attempting to get the D.H.2 'pusher' to carry two Lewis guns; the experiment was not entirely satisfactory, but the factory issue only contained a single Lewis gun, with an ammunition drum that could only hold forty-seven rounds. The additional weapon was also an attempt to match the increasing firepower of the German aircraft, for the Fokker Eindecker E.III had been retrofitted to carry two Spandau *luftgekühlte Maschinengewehre* (LMG-08 machine guns), with 500 rounds of ammunition. Unfortunately for Hawker and Tidmarsh, the brigade commander forbade any further attempts at *ad hoc* innovation in the field.

In several studies of the early war aces Tidmarsh is credited with victories in which the enemy casualty is specifically identified.[5] I try not to follow the 'who got who' rounds of speculation, but for the early years of the war it is easier to reconcile competing claims. On 2 April 1916, Tidmarsh opened up No. 24 Squadron's account when he shot down an Albatros between Grandcourt and Albert, killing Unteroffizier Paul Wein and Leutnant Karl Oskar Breibisch-Guthmann of FFA32. RFC Communiqué No. 34 of 1916 records that Tidmarsh survived a close call on 21 April when an anti-aircraft shell went through the nacelle of his D.H.2 (5924) without exploding or causing any injury. The squadron only had seven serviceable aircraft available to its twelve pilots, but they had some considerable impact. Two of those, Cowan and Tidmarsh, were Irish.

On 29 April 1916, Tidmarsh in D.H.2 5956 had a difficult encounter with a German two-seater due to problems with the new fixed gun mounting and the new German tactic of dodging instead of diving away from an attack.[6] The next day he engaged a Fokker Eindecker over Péronne, which was being flown by Leutnant Otto Schmedes of *Kampfeinsitzer Kommando* (KEK) Bertincourt, attached to FFA32. Tidmarsh dived from 4,000 feet on the Eindecker, but the German aircraft disintegrated in the course of trying to evade Tidmarsh, who didn't actually open fire in the during his manoeuvre. The Germans recorded that their man was lost when his control wires were shot away!

In May 1916 the squadron's strength increased to eighteen pilots. Of the new arrivals, fellow Irishman Patrick Anthony Langan Byrne was to become a hugely important member of Tidmarsh's 'B' Flight, and was to eventually succeed him. On the 20th Tidmarsh scored his third victory, which is described in RFC Communiqué No. 37 of 1916:

> An Albatros was attacked by three of our machines over Pozières; a Martinsyde of No. 22 Sqn, pilot, Capt. Summers, and two De Havillands of No. 24 Sqn, pilots Lt Wilson and 2nd Lt Tidmarsh. Lt Wilson attacked first, opening fire at 50 yards range, and turned aside owing to his gun jamming. Capt. Summers on the Martinsyde then attacked, firing half a drum at 30 yards range, apparently without effect. Second Lt Tidmarsh then dived on to the hostile machine from above and fired a drum at 40 yards from behind it. The hostile machine burst into flames and fell between Pozières and Contalmaison.[7]

According to many sources, those killed were Franz Patzig and Georg Loenholdt.[8]

The Irish Times of 24 May 1916 reported that Tidmarsh's parents 'had received official intelligence' that their second son, 2nd Lieutenant David M. Tidmarsh, 4th Battalion, Royal Irish Regiment and RFC, had been awarded the Military Cross 'for gallant and distinguished service at the Front.' It was an open secret, however, and on 31 May 1916 Tidmarsh's MC citation was gazetted:

> 2nd Lt David Mary Tidmarsh, 4th Bn, R. Ir. R. (Spec. Res.) and RFC

> For conspicuous gallantry and skill when attacking hostile aircraft on several occasions, notably on one occasion when he dived at an enemy machine and drove it down wrecked to the ground.[9]

Also gazetted on that day was Robert Verschoyle Walker, a Donegal man who had served with the Connaught Rangers before joining the RFC. Note the use of the phase 'drove it down wrecked'—over time such descriptions would be reserved for use in the context of indecisive aerial victories, as opposed to 'destroyed' or 'driven down out of control'. It is sometimes the case that researchers disregard many early aerial victories on the basis of overly-rigorously classification of certain terminology, which was still only loosely defined at the time.

Tidmarsh was promoted from 2nd Lieutenant to Temporary Lieutenant with effect from 1 July 1916.[10] Hawker's memoirs credit Tidmarsh and Chapman with driving down three German aircraft on 19 July, but these were not decisive victories. Later that day Tidmarsh and Chapman attacked five LVGs and six Rolands, breaking up the German formation and forcing them to retire.

Tidmarsh was subsequently appointed Flight Commander with effect from 16 August, commanding 'B' Flight as a Temporary Captain.[11] It was not uncommon for pilots to serve at several grades above their home grade without actually being promoted up the intermediate grades. The arrival of the Albatros D.I and

D.II Scouts in September 1916 saw the D.H.2 hopelessly outclassed. This was compounded by the reorganisation of German units into Jastas. Oswald Boelcke's Jasta 2 soon became a regular opponent of No. 24 Squadron. On 24 September Tidmarsh helped drive away some Albatrosses which had shot up Byrne, and Byrne survived crashing near the Allied trenches.

In October 1916 the character of No. 24 Squadron changed completely: Tidmarsh—the 'grand and gallant Irishman'—was released from frontline duties, and replaced as 'B' Flight commander by Langan Byrne. Worse for Hawker, he also lost another Irishman, Cowan, who was promoted to Flight Commander on transfer to No. 29 Squadron.

On 14 October 1916 Tidmarsh was returned to Home Establishment, and assigned to the School of Aerial Gunnery on 3 November 1916, where he served as Wing Commander. Tidmarsh was an instructor there, as part of 6th Wing, until 4 March 1917, when he was assigned to No. 48 Squadron. According to Hawker's biography, the return to Home Establishment of Wilkinson and Tidmarsh was specifically to train them on the Bristol F2a two-seater fighter, which showed good promise.[12]

Tidmarsh became a Flight Commander in No. 48 Squadron, which was the first squadron to fly the Bristol F.2a fighter in combat. Tidmarsh achieved four victories in April 1917, and was generally known for killing the twenty-victory German ace Wilhelm Frankl of Jasta 4 on the 8th.[13] It would appear that Frankl's aircraft suffered structural failure when trying to manoeuvre clear of Tidmarsh's attack. Tidmarsh's squadron, however, had got off to a shaky start: on 5 April 1917 one of its Flight commanders, Captain William Leefe Robinson VC, was shot down, together with three other aircraft from his Flight. Jasta 11 claimed all scalps.

Just days later, on 11 April, another Flight commander—Tidmarsh himself—was shot down by Leutnant Kurt Wolff of Jasta 11. The problem was that the Bristol F.2 was being incorrectly deployed as a standard two-seater, when it was best deployed in the manner of an orthodox single-seat scout, i.e. with the pilot on the front gun and the rear gunner an added bonus for deterring or following up an attack. Robinson had won his VC on home defence duties, destroying a Zeppelin, but had no experience of the Western Front. He would have been reliant upon Wilkinson and Tidmarsh. Unfortunately it took the heavy losses of the squadron in these early days to reassess the manner in which the 'Brisfit' was to be best deployed.

There are several accounts of Tidmarsh going to the rescue of a companion in distress and consequently being shot down while facing hopeless odds. However, it would appear that three Bristol F.2s from Tidmarsh's patrol were lost: 2nd Lieutenants G. N. Brockhurst and C. B. Boughton in A3323, Captain Tidmarsh and 2nd Lieutenant C. B. Holland in A3338, and 2nd Lieutenants Robert Edward Adeney and Leslie Graham Lovell in A3318 (both killed).

Tidmarsh's sister Maureen, Sister Mary Fidelis, a nun in the Priory of Our Lady of Good Counsel, Hassocks, West Sussex, shared her memories of his experiences as a PoW in Germany.[14] Her version of events is somewhat different from the heroic melodrama of the RAF pilots' memoirs:

> After the War I asked him what happened ... he told me that he was pursuing a German trying to escape back to his base, and as he got near the aerodrome, their ground fire was intensified. His right wing was hit and immediately burst into flames; knowing that he couldn't return home and that he and his companion were soon to be burnt to death, like a flash he let the plane do a dead drop from a great height, hoping that this might extinguish the fire, and just when the watching Germans expected it to crash to the ground in flames, David ... flattened out and just managed to land safely—the Germans rushed forward and helped them out of the now blazing wing, and apart from some nasty burns they were both alive. The Germans did all they could to help them because a living English pilot could give them information, or might have useful papers on him, whereas a dead body wasn't much use!

Tidmarsh spent the rest of the war in a PoW camp in Germany. The following account of his treatment is the typical mix of fact and fiction that most PoWs provided to their friends and families.

> David said that they were quite decent to their prisoners, but they were not given nearly enough to eat, so were nearly starving until his letters home arrived ... He and the others always received the many parcels or food and clothing sent through the Red Cross by their relations. David said that we must not blame the Germans for the scant rations of the prisoners, because it was nearly the end of the war and Germany being blockaded on all sides was herself desperately short of food.
>
> The prisoners amused themselves getting up concerts, giving lectures, learning French and German, sketching and of course sports. In a letter home dated 28 May 1918 he said that two prisoners were shot dead for trying to escape. Because David twice drew pictures of an English pilot shooting down several German planes he was told that he would be shot at dawn. They made him stand before a wall while 5 Germans pointed guns at him, but at the command 'fire', only empty cartridges doing no harm. He said it was a 'nasty experience'.[15]

However, Tidmarsh was notionally kept on secondment from the Royal Irish Regiment to the RFC, being promoted from 2nd Lieutenant to Lieutenant with effect from 1 July 1917, which was gazetted on 4 March 1918.[16] His younger brother John, a lieutenant with the Duke of Wellington's Regiment, transferred to the RAF, but John never got to avenge his brother, as he died in a training accident on 3 September 1918. The funeral took place at St Munchin's Parish Church, with burial at Mount St Lawrence Cemetery.

Following the armistice, Tidmarsh arrived at Hull on 30 December 1918, returning to serve with the RAF. In March 1919 he was assessed and deemed fit for light flying duties. On 13 July he was assigned to No. 33 TS, and was attached to RAF Witney. On 9 August it would appear that he was assigned to an RAF sub-station at Weston-on-the-Green in Oxfordshire. Several months after rejoining the RAF, Tidmarsh was transferred to the Unemployed List with effect from 28 October 1919.[17] Tidmarsh relinquished his commission on 1 April 1920, retaining the rank of Lieutenant.[18]

Tidmarsh was one of the few Irish aces to return to Ireland after the war. According to Thomas Toomey's *War of Independence in Limerick*, this decision nearly cost Tidmarsh his life: on the night of 2/3 December 1920 he was caught in an IRA ambush intended for Colonel Michael Williamson, the local magistrate. There are two separate IRA accounts of the wounding of 'Tidmarch'. The first is by Volunteer Thomas Moynihan, Ahane Company, 3rd Battalion, Mid-Limerick Brigade, regarding the ambush at Ballinacourtney, near Castleconnell:

We had been informed that a District Inspector of the RIC was to be entertained to dinner one day by Sir Stephen Quinn. ... we again waited in ambush. When dinner was over a motorcar which had been observed to leave Quinn's residence was attacked by our party; one occupant in the car was wounded and the car put out of action. The wounded man turned out to be a man named Tidmarch. The DI was not in the car, but had returned to Limerick by a different route from that in which he came to dinner. The man Tidmarch had been mistaken for the DI. Eight members of the IRA took part in this attack.[19]

Company Captain Seán Ó Ceallaigh discloses more in his version of events:

Sean Carroll, with a number of his men, waited in ambush positions to attack a district Inspector of the RIC. They opened fire on a private motorcar in which they thought he was travelling, but it appears that the DI had travelled in a different car. The occupant of the car was wounded he was a man named Tidmarch.[20]

Tidmarsh's father died on 21 December 1920, just weeks after the incident.

Tidmarsh re-joined the RAF to serve in the Second World War. Initially he was commissioned as a Pilot Officer on probation on 16 May 1939.[21] He was subsequently promoted to Flying Officer on 31 August 1939, under the service number 73434, then from Flight Lieutenant to Temporary Squadron Leader on 1 September 1942.[22, 23] Tidmarsh retired on ill-health grounds on 20 January 1944, retaining the rank of Squadron Leader, which was gazetted on 1 February 1944.[24]

His brother, Major Gerard David Tidmarsh, Royal Artillery, died on 9 November 1944. (Gerard had married Elizabeth Mary Shiffner on 20 March 1915 in Steyning, Sussex, into a minor baronetcy. This was not the family's only link to Sussex: as previously mentioned, their sister was a nun there.) Tidmarsh only outlived his brother by eighteen days: he died in a Dublin nursing home on 27 November 1944.

28

TYRRELL,
Walter Alexander
(17 aerial victories)

Born: 23 August 1898, Belfast
Died: 9 June 1918
Awards: Military Cross
Commemorated: Beauvais Communal Cemetery, Oise, France;
Great War Memorial, Bangor, Co. Down

Captain Walter Alexander Tyrrell was one of two brothers to serve with the RFC and RAF. Another brother was to serve with the RAF in the Second World War.

His father was John Tyrrell, an alderman and justice of the peace, and his mother Jeanie Tyrrell (née Todd). They had nine children and in 1901 lived on the Crumlin Road, in the Court Ward of Belfast. Also living with the family were a seamstress, a domestic nurse, and a servant. Walter was the second youngest in the family. One of their sisters, Jennie Ethel Tyrrell, died on 26 May 1910, aged sixteen. By 1911 the family had moved to the Antrim Road in the Clifton ward of Belfast. Walter had another brother by this stage, Charles Frederick Gerard Tyrrell. His eldest brother, William, was a medical student at Queen's University Belfast, while Herbert was helping out in the father's business. He attended the Royal Belfast Academical Institution ('Inst.') and the adjacent Belfast Municipal Technical Institution.

Tyrrell enlisted with the RNAS but did not see aerial service with them, as he fought in France with the Armoured Car Section as a petty officer (motor mechanic). According to some sources, he was injured when an armoured car crushed his foot. Tyrrell's naval service record in respect of the RNAS, however, does not indicate that he was discharged on account of his injuries.[1] It states that he was 5 foot 11 inches and had signed up on 30 December 1914 for the duration of the hostilities. His initial posting was to *Pembroke III*, a shore establishment, from 30 December 1914 to 31 March 1915. He was then placed on the notional strength of another shore establishment (*President II*), from 1 April to 14 December 1915, by which stage the RNAS Armoured Car units on the Western Front were disbanded for being unsuitable in the context of static trench warfare. Tyrrell was stationed in

France from 28 April to 29 October 1915. However, there is a note to the effect that on 7 December 1915 approval was granted for the discharge of Tyrrell from the RNAS Armoured Car Division.

Tyrrell joined the RFC on 9 April 1917. He had been a member of the Queen's University Belfast OTC and was working as an apprentice motor engineer when commissioned. Initially he was posted to the No. 2 School of Aeronautics at Oxford, but was subsequently transferred to No. 7 RS at Netheravon in June 1917. On 6 July Tyrrell's promotion to Temporary 2nd Lieutenant on probation was gazetted. On 1 August 1917 Tyrrell was posted to No. 43 TS, which was based at Tern Hill. On 30 August he was appointed Flying Officer (2nd Lieutenant). The No. 43 TS had metamorphosed into No. 13 TDS, and was to form the nucleus of No. 95 Squadron at Ternhill, but Tyrrell's service records indicate that the was flying the Airco D.H.5 at the time of his posting to the Front on 3 October 1917.

Tyrrell was appointed to No. 32 Squadron, which had once been commanded by Thomas Agar Elliott Cairnes, the brother of the Irish ace, William Jameson Cairnes. Despite the many failings of the D.H.5 and its deep unpopularity with pilots, Tyrrell scored five victories on the type between 30 October and 5 December 1917, flying the same D.H.5 (B4916). On 5 December 1917 a patrol of four D.H.5s were on Southern Offensive patrol at 4,000 feet when they encountered two German AGO two-seaters:

> Captain Pearson attacked EA, firing a burst of 100 rounds at close range, and then he had to pull out to clear a No. 3 stoppage. Lt Tyrrell got on the tail of this EA, which had turned south after Captain Pearson's dive, and fired 100 rounds at very close range. He then saw the observer throw up his arms, and collapse in the cockpit. EA fell down out of control, patrol getting good bursts into it. Meanwhile the second EA attacked Lt Howson, who attacked EA, firing a long burst into him. EA was last seen still diving, very low down over K3 Central (Sh.28).
>
> 770 rounds were fired by patrol in the two combats.

However, despite the ammunition expended, only the Tyrrell combat was awarded to the patrol as a decisive 'out of control' aerial victory, the other AGO being counted as 'driven down'.

No. 32 Squadron re-equipped with the S.E.5a. Although disliked by some (such as Mannock), and highly praised by others (such as Molesworth), it's clear that Tyrrell became one of its premier experts. That said, the initial transition was not smooth: on 10 March 1918 Tyrrell's S.E.5a (B4882) struck a pathway and overturned on landing— though he was unhurt—and on the 29th his S.E.5a (C9625) was forced to land north of Amiens, with the petrol tank shot through, following an offensive patrol.

On 7 April Tyrrell scored 'three in a day', destroying a Fokker Dr.I and an Albatros D.V north-east of Lamotte and sending another Albatros D.V down out of control. He went on to score two further victories in April, including an AGO in flames. RAF Communiqué No. 1 of 1918, which covers the period from 1 to 7 April 1918, describes his first victory flying the S.E.5a:

> 2nd Lt W. A. Tyrrell, 32 Sqn, fired 150 rounds into an EA triplane which was attacking one of our machines; the EA went down in a fast spin, pulling out at 2,000 feet. 2nd Lt Tyrrell, who followed the EA down, got onto its tail again and fired 100 rounds at close range; the EA then fell vertically and crashed into the ground north-east of La Motte.[2]

The corresponding 'Combats in the Air' report states that Tyrrell's patrol encountered ten Fokker Dr.I Triplanes over Villers-Brettonneux at 10,000 feet. Tyrrell managed to shake off a triplane and then get onto its tail when it attacked Captain Simpson; he followed it down to 2,000 feet and finished it off, and then attacked four Albatros D.Vs which were shooting up British troops in the neighbourhood of Thiennes-Hangard. Tyrrell sent one down at 200 feet. RAF Communiqué No. 2 of 1918 describes a victory of his on 11 April, in which the German went down in flames, following a series of attacks by Tyrrell in which 500 rounds were fired into it, eventually setting it ablaze.[3] The 'Combats in the Air' report indicates that his victim was identified as an AGO two-seater, and that Tyrrell 'followed, sitting on tail of EA,' which it went down in a steep dive 'with flames gushing from fuselage.'

On 3 May 1918 Tyrrell achieved his second three-in-a-day victory sequence, sending down two Fokker Dr.I triplanes down out of control over Frelinghem and bringing down an LVG, which was captured near Poperinghe. The forcing down and capturing of the German LVG is described in RAF Communiqué No. 5 of 1918:

> Lt W. A. Tyrrell, 32 Sqn, was attacked by two EA two-seaters. He maneuvered onto the tail of one EA and fired 50 rounds into it at point blank range. The EA turned west, followed by Lt Tyrrell, who prevented it from turning east again by firing short bursts, and the EA was finally forced to land in our lines about a mile WSW of Poperinghe.[4]

The crew, Unteroffizier Nievitecki and Unteroffizier Priehs of FAA 266, were both captured alive and taken PoW.

Tyrrell was to obtain one further victory that month, on 8 May, destroying a Pfalz DIII into which he fired 100 rounds at point-blank range. It went into a steep spiral then a vertical nosedive, and was seen to crash in the neighbourhood of Sailly-en-Ostrevent. On 18 May he was appointed Temporary Captain (Flying). On 6 June he managed the almost unprecedented: he scored another 'three in a day'—a double victory in the evening following a dawn patrol victory. In fact, two of his victims went down in flames that day. The 'Combats in the Air' report for the first of these states that Captain W. A. Tyrrell was on offensive patrol duties with Lieutenant J. W. Trusler at 5.50 a.m. Tyrrell was in S.E.5a B8374 at 10,000 feet when they sighted two Pfalz Scouts, one at 10,000 feet and the other at 17,000 feet. They attacked from the sun, each getting in a burst of 100 rounds at close range and sending it down in flames. At 18.45 Tyrrell was on the evening offensive patrol duties, flying his S.E.5a (B8374) at 9,000 feet over Montdidier, when the aircraft of No. 32 Squadron were attacked by seven Fokker biplanes. The 'Combats in the Air' report states the following:

> Pilot attacked EA which was attacking Lt Hooper, firing a burst of 100 rounds into EA at point blank range, whereupon EA burst into flames and went down.
> Pilot was then attacked by two other EA, and turning he opened fire at close range, firing a burst of 150 rounds into EA, whereupon EA went down in a spin, out of control, being last seen still out of control at 6,000 feet.
> Two more EA attacked pilot. No results were observed.

Major Russell of No. 32 Squadron counter-signed the claim, with the Lieutenant-Colonel of 9th Wing confirming a double victory for Tyrrell, one of the aircraft being described as 'out of control', the other as 'destroyed in flames'.

Tyrrell was awarded the Military Cross on 19 May 1918, which was gazetted on 16 September 1918:

> T./2nd Lt Walter Alexander Tyrrell, Gen. list, attd RAF

> For conspicuous gallantry and devotion to duty. On one day this officer attacked two enemy triplanes, destroying one and driving down the other out of control. After this he was attacked by two other machines, one of which he forced to land, taking the occupants prisoners. On various other occasions he has destroyed or driven down out of control enemy machines.[5]

Tyrrell was dead by the time the citation was gazetted, killed on 9 June by ground fire. According to one source, he was shot in the chest but managed to get back behind his own lines before crashing.[6] Others suggest that his S.E.5a (B8391) dived into the ground from 1,000 feet near Maignelay on account of him fainting from loss of blood after being hit by ground fire. Another S.E.5a (D6867) crash-landed following the same ground strafing operation at Montdidier-Lassigny, but the pilot, Lieutenant S. W. Graham, survived. Tyrrell was only nineteen when he was killed but remained No. 32 Squadron's highest-scoring ace for the duration of the war. His brother, Captain John Marcus Tyrrell, was killed on 20 June 1918.

Flight magazine of 20 June and 4 July 1918 contained a brief obituary for the two brothers, but also made reference to the fact that their eldest brother, Lieutenant-Colonel William Tyrrell, DSO, MC, MB, RAMC, had been on active service on the Western Front since the commencement of the war. He had been a former Irish rugby international player—becoming President of the IRFU in the 1950s—and was to develop into a highly respected Principal Medical Officer in the RAF, a significant contributor to the 1920 War Office Committee of Inquiry into 'shell shock', and later an Air Vice-Marshal.

From the information to hand it would appear that Tyrrell's brother William was a member of Richmond Masonic Lodge No. 262 in Belfast. Their father, John, was chosen by Belfast Lodge No. 977 to unfurl a memorial banner to the 36th (Ulster) Division. However, I have not identified a Freemason membership record in respect of Tyrrell himself.

29

TYRRELL,
William Upton
(6 aerial victories)

Born: 3 May 1896, Co. Kildare
Died: 1979

Colonel William Upton Tyrrell was born in Co. Kildare to Elizabeth and William Jonathan Haughton Tyrrell. He is often confused with William Tyrrell, the brother of John Marcus and Walter Alexander Tyrrell. In 1901, he, his sister, and his parents were living in the townland of Ballindoolin in the district electoral division of Carrick, Co. Kildare. Two visitors and three servants were also present at the time of the census. Tyrrell's father was a 'farmer and land agent'; his mother was Canadian. He was boarding in England, Ireland, or Canada by 1911, but I have been unable to identify exactly where.

Tyrrell joined the colours with the 3rd Reserve Battalion of the Royal Irish Rifles. He entered the Royal Military College (Sandhurst) on 15 April 1915 and by 10 August his appointment from Gentleman Cadet of the RMC to 2nd Lieutenant was gazetted.[1] He was promoted from 2nd Lieutenant to Lieutenant with effect from 10 December 1916, which was later antedated to 24 November.[2] Tyrrell's service history with the Royal Irish Rifles is unclear—he transferred from the reserve battalion to a service battalion, but its War Diaries do not record his entry to the Western Front. He did not receive the 1914–1915 Star.

Tyrrell transferred to the RAF and, on 19 May 1918, was returned to Home Establishment for training. Initially posted to the school of aerial gunnery, he was subsequently transferred to the No. 1 Flight School Tunberry on 3 August. By the 22nd he was completing his wireless training at WT School, Chattis Hill. Tyrrell was posted to the BEF on 1 September 1918 as a fighter reconnaissance observer. On the 17th his appointment as Temporary 2nd Lieutenant (Honorary Lieutenant), observer, was gazetted, with the promotion being dated as the 29th.

Tyrrell served with No. 22 Squadron. Another Irish ace, George McCormack, had also served with the squadron, and there were plenty of other pilots there with an Irish connection—the American-born, English-raised Owen Tudor Hart had married in Ireland, in 1911, to Anne Cecilia Stoney, daughter of Bindon Blood Stoney (scion of two very prominent Irish families) and Susanna Frances Walker (of Grangemore, Raheny, Dublin), and the father of Yorkshireman Frederick Williams, killed on 2 April 1918, had worked with Gallahers in Belfast. One of No. 22 Squadron's earliest casualties was Irishman Gilbert Watson Webb, killed on 1 July 1916.

Tyrrell's first victory came on 5 September 1918, just days after joining the squadron. In a Bristol F2.b (D7998) he and pilot Lieutenant Herbert Beddow drove down a Fokker D.VII out of control over Douai. Throughout September 1918 he was observer to a succession of pilots, achieving two double victories. His final aerial victory came on the 27th in a Bristol F2.b (E2517) piloted by Lieutenant L. C. Rowney; they shared in the destruction of a Fokker D.VII with Lieutenants Chester William McKinley Thompson and R. James.

RAF Communiqué No. 26 of 1918 records the following with regard to Thompson and Tyrrell's actions of 26 September 1918:

> Lts C. W. M. Thomson and W. U. Tyrrell, 22 Sqn, when returning from escort duty to the above raid [an attack on Lieu St Amand Aerodrome by No. 203 Squadron] became engaged with a number of Fokker biplanes, two of which they shot down out of control and were observed to crash by other pilots.[3]

Tyrrell was re-graded as Honorary Lieutenant in the RAF as an observer officer, with effect from 29 August 1918.[4] In common with many late-war observer aces, Tyrrell did not win the Military Cross or Distinguished Flying Cross.

Tyrrell was briefly posted to No. 205 Squadron. This was the former No. 5 (Naval) Squadron and had evolved from the RNAS role of bombing Belgian port installations and German airfields to more of an Army cooperation function using aerial photography, but essentially it continued with its previous activities in bombing railways, bridges, and other strategic targets. The squadron's ORB does not make any specific reference to Tyrrell, but it would appear to have been a short-lived posting in December 1918.[5] Tyrrell had returned to No. 22 Squadron by the end of the month, and was transferred to Home Establishment on 14 March 1919. On 18 April he was transferred to No. 11 (Irish) Group.

On 24 June 1919 Tyrrell relinquished his RAF commission, which was gazetted on 11 July.[6] Tyrrell's forename initials were misrecorded as 'W. V.' instead of 'W. U.', which can give rise to confusion. He reported to the 3rd Battalion of the Royal Irish Rifles at Ruxley. On 7 October the Air Ministry announced that he had been promoted to Lieutenant, which was backdated to 30 August 1918, and once again he was mistakenly gazetted as 'W. V. Tyrrell'.[7]

Tyrrell married Alice Helen Ennice Tyrrell in the parish of St Mary the Virgin, Twickenham, on 10 April 1920. Unusually they both had the same surname pre-marriage, Helen being the daughter of a Joseph Henry Tyrrell of Cumberland and

Alice Tyrrell of Guernsey, Channel Islands. They had two children. Desirée Helen Tyrrell was born on 11 February 1921 and died on 2 April 1974.

Tyrrell was not directly affected by the disbandment of the Irish regiments of the British Army recruited in the geographical area of what had since become the Irish Free State, for the Royal Irish Rifles simply became the Royal Ulster Rifles. But, throughout the 1920s, Tyrrell was to transfer through a number of regiments. At the time of his application for war medals in November 1922, his correspondence address was '1st Division Signals, McGregor Barracks, Aldershot'.

On 11 March 1924 Lieutenant Tyrrell was seconded from the Royal Ulster Rifles to the Royal Corps of Signals.[8] On 8 April he relinquished the appointment of Adjutant of 10 October 1923.[9] On 12 July 1924 he transferred from the Royal Ulster Rifles to the Royal Corps of Signals. On 5 August the War Office announced that Tyrrell's date of transfer was effective from 27 February and that he had been promoted to Captain from the same date.[10] Given the sheer number of adjutant and staff appointments, I do not propose to traverse them all in detail. Captain Tyrrell was seconded for employment as Temporary Adjutant from 14 August 1925, which was gazetted on 18 September 1925. He served with Anti-Aircraft Signals (Artillery Zones) as Adjutant, to which he was seconded on 3 October. He vacated this position on 1 November 1926.[11] On 29 October 1926 he was granted regimental seniority from 11 January 1920, but this did not count for Army seniority, nor for pay, allowances, or his pension upon retirement. On 11 January 1927 Captain Tyrrell was restored to the establishment with effect from 23 December 1926.[12]

Tyrrell seems to have been irrepressible. He was seconded to be a student at the Staff College from 21 January 1930.[13] However, he and his wife Helen appear on the electoral registers of Farnham, Surrey, in 1930, and at Parva, Grange Road, Frimley, in 1931.

Following his training, on 4 May 1934, Tyrrell was appointed Staff Captain, Eastern Command, with effect from 28 April, on which day he had been seconded for service on the Staff of the Royal Corps of Signals. He was serving at the rank of Captain at the time, so a staff officer position would have been an appropriate move for a man of his age. This appointment was also gazetted on 22 May 1934.[14]

On 20 March 1936, Major W. U. Tyrrell, Royal Signals, was promoted from Staff Captain in Eastern Command to General Staff Officer, 3rd Grade, at the War Office. This promotion was dated to 16 March. But he only occupied the position for a year: on 2 July 1937 it was announced that he had relinquished his appointment as General Staff Officer at the War Office with effect from 1 March, which had also been gazetted on 2 March 1937.[15]

The Army List of 1944 includes Major Tyrrell in the Royal Corps of Signals, acting as Temporary Colonel with effect from 1 May 1943. However, I have been unable to identify an associated service history. In 1948, having exceeded the age limit for retirement, he was placed on retired pay on 27 May, and granted the honorary rank of Colonel.[16] On 18 March 1955 2nd Lieutenant William Upton Tyrrell (under the service number 13536) was promoted to Captain in the Territorial Army with effect from 12 February 1955. He was still described as Major (Honorary Colonel) of the Royal Signals (retired).

His wife died in 1967 in Cleethorpes, Lincolnshire. I can find no record of a will, but, intriguingly, on 26 September that year Tyrrell is supposed to have made a claim on the estate of Harry Abraham of 'Oakdene', Walesby, Lincolnshire, a retired farmer who had died on 3 September 1967.[17]

Tyrrell himself died in Lincolnshire in 1979. Most who knew him would have undoubtedly associated Tyrrell with the Army rather than the flying services, given his lengthy career with the former, as opposed to his short but glorious one with the latter.

Endnotes

1. ATKINSON, Edward Dawson 'Spider'

1   Swanzy, *The Families of French of Belturbet and Nixon of Fermanagh and Their Descendants* (1908), p. 125.
2   TNA, WO 95/3927/3.
3   *Flight*, 17 December 1915.
4   Franks and O'Connor, *Number One in War and Peace* (2000), p. 18.
5   *The London Gazette*, 17 February 1917.
6   Christopher Shores, Norman Franks, and Russell Guest, *Above the Trenches* (1990).
7   Franks and O'Connor, *Number One in War and Peace*, p. 26.
8   *The London Gazette*, 24 July 1917.
9   *Flight*, 25 July 1918, 22 August 1918.
10 *The London Gazette*, 3 August 1918.
11 *Ibid.*, 1 January 1919.
12 Sturtivant and Page, *The D.H.4/D.H.9 File* (1999), p. 302.
13 *Flight*, 28 July 1927.
14 *The London Gazette*, 18 November 1930, and 9 December 1930.
15 *The London Gazette*, 31 March 1931.
16 *Ibid.*, 19 January 1932.

2. BLENNERHASSETT, Giles Noble

1   TNA, AIR 76/42.
2   RFC Communiqué, 15–21 April 1917. Quoted in Bowyer, ed., *RFC Communiqués 1917–1918* (1998), p. 39.
3   *The London Gazette*, 16 April 1917.
4   *Ibid.*, 26 July 1917.
5   *Ibid.*, 21 January 1921.
6   *Ibid.*, 23 December 1921.

3. BYRNE, Patrick Anthony Langan

1   *The London Gazette*, 9 October 1914.
2   *Ibid.*, 17 February 1916.
3   TNA, AIR 76/71.

4   Hawker, *Hawker VC RFC Ace—the Life of Major Lanoe Hawker VC DSO* (2013; 1965), pp. 204-205.
5   Cole, ed., *RFC Communiqués 1915–1916* (1990), p. 242.
6   *Ibid.*, p. 258
7   Hawker, p. 212.
8   Hirsch, trans., *An Aviator's Field Book—Being the Field Reports of Oswald Boelcke, from August 1, 1914 to October 29, 1916* (1919).
9   Hawker, p. 219.
10   *The London Gazette*, 14 November 1916.
11   TNA, WO 339/25256.
12   *Ibid.*

4. CAIRNES, William Jameson

1   TNA, WO 339/26752.
    2   *The London Gazette*, 21 April 1915.
3   TNA, AIR 76/72.
4   Jones, *Tiger Squadron* (1954), p. 72.
5   *Ibid.*, p. 80.
6   *Ibid.*, p. 107.
7   *Ibid.*, p. 136.

5. CALLAGHAN, Joseph Cruess

1   O'Connor, *Consuelo Remembers* (2000), p. 12.
2   TNA, WO 339/5349.
3   TNA, AIR/1/1219/204/5/2634.
4   Franks, *Sharks Among Minnows* (1995), pp. 83-84.
5   *Flight*, 10 August 1916; this carried the relevant notice from the War Office in which Cruess Callaghan is cited among the wounded.
6   Hart, *Somme Success* (2012), p. 124.
7   Irwin, *Stonyhurst War Record* (1927), p. 32.
8   Hart, p. 196.
9   *Ibid.*, p. 213.
10   TNA, AIR 76/73 and WO 339/5349.
11   *The London Gazette*, 13 February 1917.
12   Franks, *Dolphin and Snipe Aces of World War I* (2002), p. 51.
13   O'Connor, *Airfields & Airmen: Somme* (2002), pp. 103-104.
14   Irwin, *Stonyhurst War Record* (1927), p. 34.
15   Kinsella, *Out of the Dark* (2014), p. 191.
16   O'Connor, *Consuelo Remembers*, pp. 54-57.

6. COWAN, Sidney Edward

1   Institute of Civil Engineers (OCE), Minutes of Proceedings, Vol. 231, Issue 1931, 1 January 1931, p. 372. Citation: E-ISSN: 1753-7843.
2   Guttman, *Pusher Aces of World War I* (2009), p. 34.
3   Raleigh, *War in the Air*, Vol. 1 (1922), pp. 427-428.
4   Grey *et al.*, 'The Anatomy of an Aeroplane', in *Cross & Cockade (International)*, Vol. 21, No. 3 (Autumn 1990), p. 128.
5   *The London Gazette*, 31 May 1916.
6   Illingworth, *A History of 24 Squadron* (1920), p. 81.

7   Shores, Franks, and Guest, *Above The Trenches* (1990), p. 122.
8   Hart, p. 92.
9   Cole, pp. 208-209.
10   Hawker, p. 211.
11   *Ibid.*, p. 215.
12   *The London Gazette*, 20 October 1916.
13   *Ibid.*, 14 November 1916.
14   O'Connor, *Airfields & Airmen: Cambrai* (2003), p. 175.
15   TNA, WO 339/88608.

7. COWELL, John J.

1   TNA, WO 95/1599/1.
2   *The London Gazette*, 27 October 1916.
3   TNA, AIR 27/258.
4   Bowyer, p. 63.
5   *The London Gazette*, 18 July 1917.
6   *The Edinburgh Gazette*, 19 September 1917.
7   TNA, AIR 76/109, JJ Cowell.

8. CROWE, Henry George 'Hal'

1   TNA, WO 95/1970/3
2   Leslie, 'Henry George Crowe', *Cross & Cockade (International)*, Vol. 19, No. 2 (1988), p. 48.
3   *Ibid.*, p. 51.
4   *The London Gazette*, 26 July 1918.
5   Leslie, p. 55.
6   *Ibid.*, pp. 55-56.
7   *Ibid.*, p. 56.
8   *The London Gazette*, 13 January 1922.
9   Leslie, p. 63.
10   TNA, AIR 1/2390/228/11/134.
11   *Flight*, 24 September 1936.
12   Turner, *The Bader Wing* (2007), p. 108.
13   Brown, *Flying for Freedom* (2000), p. 163.
14   *The London Gazette*, 25 June 1946.

9. GREGORY, Robert William

1   Smythe, ed., *Robert Gregory 1881–1918: a centenary tribute with a foreword by his children* (1981).
2   Hill, *Lady Gregory, An Irish Life* (2005), p. 136.
3   Foster, *W. B. Yeats, A Life, I: The Apprentice Mage* (1998), p. 264.
4   *Ibid.*, pp. 350-351.
5   *Ibid.*, p. 363.
6   Ross, *Critical Companion to William Butler Yeats: A Literary Reference to His Life* (2009), p. 479.
7   Hill, pp. 155-156.
8   Pethica, 'Yeats's "Perfect Man"', *The Dublin Review*, (Issue No. 35 Summer 2009).
9   Gordon, *W. B. Yeats: Images of a Poet; My Permanent or Impermanent Images* (1970), p. 30.

10 TNA, WO 339/42377.

11 Smythe, p. 5.

12 Larson, *Shaw and History—the Annual of G.B. Shaw Studies* (1999), p. 91, also p. 96 *passim*.

13 Liggera, *The Life of Robert Lorraine: The Stage, the Sky and George Bernard Shaw* (2013), pp. 140-141.

14 TNA, AIR/1/1222/204/5/2634.

15 Franks, Giblin, and McCrery, *Under the Guns of the Red Baron* (1995), pp. 82-83.

16 *Cross & Cockade (Great Britain)*, Vol. 4, No. 4 (1973), and Vol. 5, No. 1 (1974).

17 Bond, *My Airman Over There* (1918), p. 19.

18 *Ibid.*, pp. 70-71.

19 *Ibid.*, pp. 118-119.

20 *Flight*, 26 July 1917.

21 TNA, WO 339/42377.

22 *Flight*, 21 February 1918.

23 Gordon, p. 31.

24 Warner, *Harrow War Memorials of the Great War*, Vol. 5 (1920).

25 Hill, p. 295, quoting a letter of Lady Gregory to John Quinn; also referenced in Yeats's appreciation of 17 February 1918 in *The Observer*.

26 The Bureau of Military History has made the witness statements by IRA volunteers Daniel Ryan, Thomas Keely, Joseph Stanford, Patrick Glynn, and Michael Reilly available to the public.

27 Hill, p. 300.

10. GRIBBEN, Edward

1 TNA, AIR 76/196.

2 *The London Gazette*, 1 September 1914. Also Supplement of 23 April 1915, in which appointment dates are revised.

3 *Ibid.*, 12 January 1917.

4 Bowyer, p. 99.

5 *The London Gazette*, 8 January 1918.

6 *Ibid.*, 14 February 1919.

7 Sturtivant and Page, p. 193.

8 *The London Gazette*, 13 February 1920.

9 *Ibid.*, 22 February 1921.

10 TNA, AIR 76/196, E. Gribben.

11 *The London Gazette*, 14 March 1930.

12 *Ibid.*, 13 November 1934.

11. HAZELL, Tom Falcon

1 TNA, WO 372/9.

2 *The London Gazette*, 28 June 1916.

3 Franks and O'Connor, *Number One in War and Peace*, p. 30.

4 *The London Gazette*, 26 July 1917.

5 Lambert, *Combat Report* (1973), pp. 202-205.

6 Illingworth, p. 46.

7 Udet, *Ace of the Black Cross* (1970), pp. 119-120; variation of translation in Mike O'Connor, *Airfields & Airmen: Somme* (2001); also quoted in Guttman, *Balloon-Busting Aces of World War I* (2005), pp. 27-28.

8 *The London Gazette*, 2 November 1918.

9   *Ibid.*, 2 November 1918.
10 Rochford, *I Chose the Sky* (1977), p. 195.
11 *The London Gazette*, 8 February 1919.
12 *Ibid.*, 13 May 1919; 1 August 1919.
13 Embry, *Mission Completed* (1958), pp. 23-24.
14 *Flight*, 29 November 1923.
15 TNA, AIR 27/865/1.

12. HEGARTY, Herbert George

1   'List of Officers and Men Serving in the First Canadian Contingent of the British Expeditionary Force, 1914'. Compiled by the Pay and Record Office, Canadian Contingent, 36 Victoria St, London, SW.
2   TNA, AIR 76/220.
3   WO 339/108686.
4   *The London Gazette*, 30 June 1917.
5   Bowyer, p. 248.
6   Cole, pp. 76-78.
7   *Cross & Cockade (International)*, Vol. 11, No. 4 (Winter 1980), p. 125.
8   *The Edinburgh Gazette*, 18 September 1918.

13. HERON, Oscar Aloysius Patrick

1   *The London Gazette*, 20 December 1917.
2   Cole, p. 213.
3   *The London Gazette*, 8 February 1919.
4   *Ibid.*, 15 July 1919.
5   *Ibid.*, 5 September 1919.
6   *Ibid.*, 24 October 1919.
7   TNA, AIR 76/223.
8   Heron, 'Ireland and Aviation', *An t-Oglach*, October 1929, pp. 6-12.
9   O'Malley, *Military Aviation in Ireland, 1921–1945* (2010).

14. HUSTON, Victor Henry

1   The Irish census of 1911 reports that Eileen was born in the Cape Colony, whereas Dorothy was born in Cape Town.
2   'List of Officers and Men Serving in the First Canadian Contingent of the British Expeditionary Force, 1914'. Compiled by the Pay and Record Office, Canadian Contingent, 36 Victoria St, London, SW.
3   *The London Gazette*, 1 October 1915.
4   TNA, AIR 76/246.
5   *The London Gazette*, 28 December 1916.
6   TNA, AIR/1/1219/20452634, ref.363.
7   *The London Gazette*, 18 June 1917.
8   *Ibid.*, 7 January 1918.
9   *Ibid.*, 22 June 1918.
10 'Efemérides de la Aviación: una Publicación del Museo Nacional Aeronáutico Y del Espacio Dirección General de Aeronáutica Civil', (Santiago de Chile: *Museo Nacional Aeronáutico Y Del Espacio*, November 2010), p. 90.
11 *Flight*, 19 December 1918.
12 *Ibid.*, 9 January 1919.

13   *The London Gazette*, 21 November 1919.
14   *Ibid.*, 20 February 1920.

15. KELLY, Edward Caulfield

1   TNA, AIR 76/270.
2   TNA, WO 339/43892.
3   *The London Gazette*, 2 August 1918.
4   *Ibid.*, 17 January 1919.
5   *Ibid.*, 12 September 1919.
6   *Ibid.*, 17 February 1920.

16. KIRK, Walter Alister

1   Guttman, *Bristol F2 Fighter Aces of World War I* (2007), p. 80.
2   Cutlack, *The Official History of Australia in the War of 1914–1918. Volume VIII: the Australian Flying Corps* (1933), pp. 99-100.
3   *Ibid.*, pp. 119-120.
4   Molkentin, *Fire in the Sky: The Australian Flying Corps in the First World War* (2013). Kindle edition is unpaginated.
5   *Ibid.*
6   Cutlack, pp. 129-130.
7   ibid, pp.137-138.
8   Molkentin.
9   *The London Gazette*, 8 February 1919.

17. MANNOCK, Edward 'Mick'

1   Smith, *Mick Mannock Fighter Pilot: Myth, Life and Politics* (2001), pp. 25-38.
2   TNA WO 339/66665.
3   McCudden, *Five Years in the RFC* (1922), unpaginated Kindle version.
4   Oughton, ed.,*The Personal Diary of 'Mick' Mannock VC, DSO (2 Bars, MC (1 Bar)*, (1966), pp. 153-154.
5   *Ibid.*, p. 154.
6   Jones, *King of Airfighters* (1934), p. 99.
7   Oughton, pp. 74-75.
8   Smith, p. 74.
9   Bond, p. 230.
10 Oughton, pp. 118-119.
11 Smith, p. 79.
12 Oughton, pp.124-125.
13 *Ibid.*, pp. 128-129.
14 *Ibid.*, pp. 141-145.
15 *The London Gazette*, 17 September 1917.
16 McScotch, *Fighter Pilot* (1936), pp. 84-85 indicate Mannock's concern was with honouring Lt Begbie, who went down in flames and addressing the toast to the right person.
17 Dudgeon, *Mick* (1981), p. 125; also quoted in Smith, p. 107.
18 Jones, *King of Airfighters*, p. 235.
19 Dudgeon, *Mick* (1981), p. 154, quoting Jim Eyles. See also Smith, pp. 119-120, which also contains references to his sister-in-law Dorothy Mannock's impressions of Mick's mental state and survival prospects.

20   TNA, WO 339/66665.
21   *The London Gazette*, 3 August 1918.
22   *Ibid.*, 16 September 1918.
23   *Ibid.*, 18 July 1919.
24   Franks and Saunders, *Mannock: The Life and Death of Major Edward Mannock VC, DSO, MC, RAF* (2008).
25   Jones, *King of Airfighters*, pp. 102-103.

18. McCLINTOCK, Ronald St Clair

1   Fox-Davies, *Armorial Families: A Directory of Gentlemen of Coat-Armour*, Vol. 2 (1905), p. 1247.
2   TNA, WO 372/12.
3   *The London Gazette*, 6 September 1915.
4   TNA, AIR 1/1216.
5   Cole, p. 130.
6   *The London Gazette*, 28 June 1917.
7   Cole, p. 20.
8   *The London Gazette*, 7 May 1918.
9   *Ibid.*, 22 June 1918.
10   *Cross & Cockade (International)*, Vol. 38, No. 4 (2007), p. 235.
11   *Flight*, 7 August 1919.

19. McCORMACK, George

1   TNA, WO 339/45665, contains Part 9 only.
2   *The London Gazette*, 4 December 1916.
3   TNA, WO 95/2503-4.
4   Harvey, *'Pi' in the Sky: A History of No. 22 Squadron* (1971), p. 49.
5   *The Irish Times*, 7 April 1928, p. 20; *Flight*, 17 October 1918.
6   TNA, AIR 27/258.
7   *Flight*, 16 February 1922.
8   TNA, WO 339/45665.
9   *The London Gazette*, 4 March 1922.
10   TNA, AIR 27/191.

20. McELROY, George Edward Henry

1   WO 339/11067, in McElroy's RMA Admission Form.
2   One problem with tracing McElroy's Army service history (i.e. pre-RFC) is that a Pte G. H. McElroy from the Coldstream Guards was commissioned as a T. 2Lt in the King's Own Scottish Borderers in October 1915.
3   TNA, AIR 76/317.
4   *The London Gazette*, 20 July 1917.
5   *Ibid.*, 27 July 1917.
6   Bowyer, p. 148.
7   TNA, AIR/1/1222/204/5/2634.
8   Bowyer, p. 212.
9   *The London Gazette*, 31 January 1918.
10   Bowyer, p. 247.
11   Lambert, p. 44.
12   *The London Gazette*, 25 March 1918.

13   Cole, p. 17.
14   Illingworth, p. 39.
15   *The London Gazette*, 24 August 1918.
16   *Ibid.*, 22 April 1918.
17   *Ibid.*, 26 July 1918.
18   Gilbert, 'McElroy of Forty', *Popular Flying*, June 1936, p. 160.
19   *The London Gazette*, 3 August 1918.
20   *Ibid.*, 21 September 1918.

21. MILLS, Alfred Stanley

1   Cole, p. 67.
2   *Ibid.*, p.102.
3   *The London Gazette*, 3 August 1918.
4   TNA, AIR 76/348.
5   TNA, WO 339/3449.

22. MOLESWORTH, William Earle 'Moley'

1   *The London Gazette*, 7 August 1914.
2   *Ibid.*, 8 December 1914.
3   TNA, AIR 76/352.
4   Scott, *Sixty Squadron RAF—A History of the Squadron from its Formation* (1920), pp. 25-28.
5   *Ibid.*, pp. 33-35.
6   *Ibid.*, pp. 50-53.
7   *Ibid.*, pp. 66-69.
8   *Ibid.*, p. 101.
9   *Ibid.*, pp. 101-103.
10   *The London Gazette*, 9 January 1918.
11   Bowyer, p. 204.
12   *The London Gazette*, 24 August 1918. Previously *The London Gazette*, 26 March 1918.
13   *Ibid.*, 12 September 1918.
14   *Ibid.*, 31 January 1919.
15   *Ibid.*, 18 April 1919.
16   *Ibid.*, 2 December 1919.
17   *Ibid.*, 20 October 1922.
18   *Ibid.*, 27 February 1931.
19   Delaforce, *Battles with Panzers* (2003), p. 31.
20   Carver, *Out of Step: Memoirs of a Field Marshal* (1989), p. 49.
21   *The London Gazette*, 2 April 1940.
22   *Ibid.*, 30 September 1941.

23. O'GRADY, Conn Standish

1   TNA, AIR 76/379.
2   Spence, obituary and appreciation, *The Fell and Rock Journal*, Vol. 21, No. 61 (1969), p. 171.
3   TNA, WO 339/66781.
4   *Ibid.*
5   *The London Gazette*, 7 August 1916.
6   Taylor, *Cross & Cockade (International)*, Vol. 37, No. 4 (2009), p. 253.

7   *Ibid.*, p. 257.
8   Bowyer, p. 114.
9   *The London Gazette*, 26 September 1917; 9 January 1918.
10 *Ibid.*, 10 February 1925.
11 *Ibid.*, 11 August 1925.
12 *Ibid.*, 31 January 1928.
13 *Ibid.*, 2 May 1933.
14 Spence, obituary and appreciation, p. 171.
15 ICE Proceedings, Vol. 42, Issue 2, 1 February 1969, pp.323-324.

24. POPE, Sydney Leo Gregory 'Poppy'

1   TNA, WO 339/61975.
2   Molesworth, 'Memories of 60 Squadron', *Popular Flying*, August 1936, p. 250.
3   Bowyer, p. 167.
4   Scott, p. 79.
5   *The London Gazette*, 24 October 1919.
6   *Ibid.*, 2 May 1922.
7   *Ibid.*, 22 August 1922.
8   *Flight*, 25 October 1923.
9   *The London Gazette*, 28 May 1926.
10 Dix Noonan Webb Medal Auction Catalogue, 1997.
11 *Flight*, 14 April 1927.
12 *Ibid.*, 2 June 1927.
13 *Ibid.*, 15 March 1928.
14 TNA, AIR 27/278.
15 The *Edinburgh Gazette*, 5 March 1929.
16 *The London Gazette*, 2 February 1932.
17 TNA, AIR 27/511.
18 *The London Gazette*, 2 April 1937.
19 *Flight*, 14 July 1938.
20 *The London Gazette*, 20 October 1942.
21 *Ibid.*, 28 December 1945.

25. PROCTOR, Thomas

1   TNA, AIR 76/413.
2   TNA, ADM 339/1; TNA, ADM 337/66.
3   TNA, ADM 188/584.
4   TNA, AIR 79/212137.
5   Guttman, *Bristol F2 Fighters of World War I*, p.67.

26. SAUNDERS, Alfred William

1   *The London Gazette*, 20 September 1916.
2   *Ibid.*, 2 October 1917.
3   Cole, p. 82.
4   *Ibid.*, p. 126.
5   *The London Gazette*, 3 August 1918.
6   *Ibid.*, 9 August 1918.
7   Cole, p. 154.
8   *The London Gazette*, 13 January 1920.

9   *Ibid.*, 12 December 1919.
10   *Ibid.*, 30 December 1919.
11   Franks and O'Connor, *Number One in War and Peace* (2000), p. 59.
12   *The London Gazette*, 6 February 1923.
13   *Ibid.*, 16 December 1924.
14   *Ibid.*, 25 February 1927.

27. TIDMARSH, David Mary

1   Limerick City Council have retained extensive records of Cannocks.
2   *The London Gazette*, 22 April 1915.
3   TNA, AIR 76/507.
4   *The London Gazette*, 22 February 1916.
5   Guttman, *Bristol F2 Fighter Aces of World War I*, pp. 10-11; Guttman, *Pusher Aces of World War I*, p. 32.
6   *Cross & Cockade (International)*, Vol. 21, pp. 129-130.
7   Cole, p. 151.
8   Guttman, *Pusher Aces of World War I*, p. 33.
9   *The London Gazette*, 31 May 1916.
10   *Ibid.*, 10 August 1916.
11   *Ibid.*, 1 September 1916.
12   Hawker, pp. 216-217.
13   Frankl, Fritz Beckhardt, Berthold Guthmann, and Willi Rosenstein were Jewish aces who won numerous honours but were expunged from history by the Nazis.
14   Twomey, 'Cannocks—a Social and Economic History of the Limerick Company from 1840 to 1930' (1982).
15   Letter dated 1 September 1979 from Sister Mary Fidelis to Frances Twomey. Special thanks to Limerick City Archives for making Frances' research material available.
16   *The London Gazette*, 4 March 1918.
17   *Ibid.*, 18 November 1919.
18   *Ibid.*, 20 December 1920.
19   Bureau of Military History 1913–1921, No. WS 1452, 7 July 1956, File No. S.2785.
20   *Ibid.*, No. WS 1476, 28 August 1956, File No. S.2805.
21   *The London Gazette*, 23 May 1939.
22   *Ibid.*, 26 September 1939. Further clarification on 6 February 1940.
23   *Ibid.*, 13 November 1942.
24   *Ibid.*, 1 February 1944.

28. TYRRELL, Walter Alexander

1   TNA, ADM 188/565.
2   Cole, p. 25.
3   *Ibid.*, pp. 31-32.
4   *Ibid.*, p. 57.
5   *The London Gazette*, 16 September 1918.
6   Barrett, *Casualty Figures: How Five Men Survived the First World War* (2007), pp. 109-111.

29. TYRRELL, William Upton

1   *The London Gazette*, 10 August 1915.
2   *Ibid.*, 27 December 1916; 5 January 1917.

3   Cole, p. 200.
4   *The London Gazette*, 17 September 1918.
5   TNA, AIR 27/1217.
6   *The London Gazette*, 11 July 1919.
7   *Ibid.*, 7 October 1919.
8   *Ibid.*, 11 March 1924.
9   *Ibid.*, 8 April 1924.
10   *Ibid.*, 11 July 1924; 5 August 1924.
11   *Ibid.*, 18 September 1925; 2 October 1925; 19 November 1926.
12   *Ibid.*, 29 October 1926; 11 January 1927.
13   *Ibid.*, 31 January 1930.
14   *Ibid.*, 4 May 1934; 22 May 1934.
15   *Ibid.*, 20 March 1936; 2 March 1937; 2 July 1937.
16   *Ibid.*, 28 May 1948.
17   *Ibid.*, 26 September 1967.

Bibliography

Books

Barrett, Michele, *Casualty Figures: How Five Men Survived the First World War* (London and New York: Verso, 2007)

Boff, Jonathan, *Winning and Losing on the Western Front: the British Third Army and the Defeat of Germany in 1918* (Cambridge: Cambridge University Press, 2012)

Bond, Aimée, *My Airman Over There* (New York: Moffat, Yard & Co., 1918)

Bowyer, Chaz, ed., *RFC Communiqués 1917–1918* (London: Grub Street, 1998)

Brown, Alan, *Flying for Freedom* (Stroud: History Press, 2000)

Carver, Michael, *Out of Step: Memoirs of a Field Marshal* (London: Hutchinson, 1989)

Cole, Christopher, ed., *RFC Communiqués 1915–1916* (London: Tom Donovan Publishing, 1990)

Cole, Christopher, ed., *RAF Communiqués 1918* (London: Tom Donovan Publishing, 1990)

Committee of the Irish National War Memorial, *Ireland's Memorial Records, World War I 1914–1918*, Vols. 1-8 (1923; republished by Eneclann, 2005)

Cutlack, Frederick Morely, *The Official History of Australia in the War of 1914–1918, Volume VIII: the Australian Flying Corps* (sydner: Angus & Robertson, 1933)

Delaforce, Patrick, *Battles with Panzers* (Stroud: Sutton, 2003)

Dudgeon, James M., *Mick* (London: Hale, 1981)

Dungan, Myles, *Distant Drums* (Belfast: Appletree Press, 1993)

Embry, Sir Basil, *Mission Completed* (London: Four Square Books, 1958)

Foster, W. B. *Yeats, A Life, I: The Apprentice Mage* (Oxford: Oxford University Press, 1998)

Fox-Davies, Arthur Charles, *Armorial Families: A Directory of Gentlemen of Coat-Armour*, Vol. 2 (Edinburgh: T. C. & E. C. Jack, 1905)

Franks, Norman, *SE 5/5a Aces of World War I* (London: Osprey, 2007)

—*Sopwith Pup Aces of World War I* (London: Osprey, 2005)

—*Sopwith Camel Aces of World War I* (London: Osprey, 2003)

—*Dolphin and Snipe Aces of World War I* (London: Osprey, 2002)

—*Sharks Among Minnows* (London: Grub Street, 2001)

—*Nieuport Aces of World War I* (London: Osprey, 2000)

—*Who Downed the Aces in World War I?* (London: Grub Street, 1996)

Norman Franks, Hal Giblin, and Nigel McCrery, *Under the Guns of the Red Baron* (London: Grub Street, 1995)

Norman Franks, Russell Guest, and Gregory Alegi, *Above the War Fronts* (London: Grub Street, 1997)

Norman Franks and Mike O'Connor, *Number One in War and Peace* (London: Grub Street, 2000)

Norman Franks and Andy Saunders, *Mannock: The Life and Death of Major Edward Mannock VC, DSO, MC, RAF* (London: Grub Street, 2008)

Gordon, Donal James, *W. B. Yeats: Images of a Poet; My Permanent or Impermanent Images* (Manchester University Press, 1970)

Gregory, Lady, ed., *Mr Gregory's Letter-Box 1813–1830* (London: Smith, Elder & Co., 1898)

Guinness, Arthur, and son, *Roll of Employees who served in His Majesty's Naval, Military and Air Forces, 1914–1918* (Dublin: Guinness, 1920; Reprint by Naval & Military Press)

Guttman, Jon, *SPAD VII vs Albatros DIII: 1917–1918* (London: Osprey, 2011)

—*Pusher Aces of World War I* (London: Osprey, 2009)

—*Bristol F2 Fighter Aces of World War I* (London: Osprey, 2007)

—*Balloon-Busting Aces of World War I* (London: Osprey, 2005)

—*SPAD VII Aces of World War I* (London: Osprey, 2001)

Hart, Peter, *Somme Success* (Barnsley: Leo Cooper, 2001; reprinted in 2012)

Harvey, William Frederick James, *'Pi' in the Sky: A History of No. 22 Squadron* (Leicester: Colin Huston, 1971)

Hawker, Tyrrell, *Hawker VC RFC Ace—the Life of Major Lanoe Hawker VC DSO* (Barnsley: Pen & Sword, 2013; reprint of Mitre Press, 1965)

Hennessy, Thomas, *The Great War 1914–1918, Bank of Ireland Staff Service Record* (Dublin: Alex Thom, 1920; reprint by Naval & Military Press, 2009)

Henshaw, Trevor, *The Sky Their Battlefield II* (London: Fetubi Books, 2014)

Hill, Judith, *Lady Gregory: An Irish Life* (London: Sutton, 2005)

Hirsch, Robert Reynold, trans., *An Aviator's Field Book—Being the Field Reports of Oswald Boelcke, from August 1, 1914 to October 29, 1916* (New York: National Military Publishing Co., 1919)

Illingworth, Captain A. E., *A History of 24 Squadron* (London: The Aeroplane & General Publishing Co., 1920; reprint by Naval & Military Press, 2004)

Irwin, Rev, Francis, *Stonyhurst War Record—A Memorial of the part taken by Stonyhurst men in the Great War* (Lancashire: Stonyhurst, 1927)

Jones, Ira 'Taffy', *Tiger Squadron* (London: W. H. Allen, 1954)

—*King of Airfighters* (London: Ivor Nicholson & Watson, 1934)

Kinsella, Ken, *Out of the Dark* (Dublin: Merrion, 2014)

Lambert, Bill, *Combat Report* (London: Corgi, 1973)

Larson, Gale, *Shaw and History—the Annual of G.B. Shaw Studies* (Pennsylvania: Penn State Press, 1999)

Liggera, Lanayre D., *The Life of Robert Lorraine: The Stage, the Sky and George Bernard Shaw* (Newarl, DE: University of Delaware Press, 2013)

MacCarron, Donal, *A View from Above: 200 Years of Aviation in Ireland* (Dublin: O'Brien Press, 2000)

McCudden, James, *Five Years in the RFC* (London: J. Hamilton, 1922), unpaginated Kindle version

McScotch, *Fighter Pilot* (London: Routledge, 1936)

Molkentin, Michael, *Fire in the Sky: The Australian Flying Corps in the First World War* (Sydney: Allen & Unwin, 2013)

O'Connor, Consuelo, *Consuelo Remembers* (Dublin: Privately Published, 2000)

O'Connor, Mike, *Airfields & Airmen: Arras* (Barnsley: Pen & Sword Military, 2004)

—*Airfields & Airmen: Cambrai* (Barnsley: Pen & Sword, 2003)

—*Airfields & Airmen: Somme* (Barnsley: Pen & Sword, 2002)

—*Airfields & Airmen: Ypres* (Barnsley: Pen & Sword, 2001)

—*Airfields & Airmen of the Channel Coast* (Barnsley: Pen & Sword Aviation, 2005)

O'Malley, Michael, *Military Aviation in Ireland, 1921–45* (Dublin: UCD Press, 2010)

Oughton, Frederick, ed., *The Personal Diary of 'Mick' Mannock VC, DSO (2 bars, MC 1 bar)* (London: Spearman, 1966)

Quinn, Anthony, *Wigs & Guns, Irish Barristers in the Great War* (Dublin: Four Courts Press, 2006)

Raleigh, *War in the Air*, Vol. 1 (Oxford: Clarendon Press, 1922)

Revell, Alex, *British Single-Seater Fighter Squadrons in World War I* (Pennslyvania: Schiffer, 2006)

—*No. 60 Squadron RFC/RAF* (London: Osprey, 2011)

Rochford, Leonard, *I Chose the Sky* (London: William Kimber & Co., 1977)

Ross, David, *A Critical Companion to William Butler Yeats: A Literary Reference to His Life* (New York: Infobase Publishing, 2009)

Scott, A. J. L., *Sixty Squadron RAF—A History of the Squadron from its Formation* (London: William Heinemann, 1920)

Christopher Shores, Norman Franks, and Russell Guest, *Above The Trenches* (London: Grub Street, 1990)

—*Above The Trenches Supplement* (London: Grub Street, 1996)

Smith, Adrian, *Mick Mannock Fighter Pilot: Myth, Life and Politics* (London: Palgrave, 2001)

Smythe, Colin, ed., *Robert Gregory 1881–1918: a centenary tribute with a foreword by his children* (London: Colin Smythe Ltd, 1981)

Swanzy, Rev. Henry Biddal, *The Families of French of Belturbet and Nixon of Fermanagh and their Descendants* (Dublin: Alex Thom, 1908)

Ray Sturtivant and Gordon Page, *The D.H.4/D.H.9 File* (Tunbridge Wells: Air-Britain Ltd, 1999)

Turner, John Frayn, *The Bader Wing* (Barnsley: Pen & Sword, 2007)

Udet, Ernst, *Ace of the Black Cross* (New York: Doubleday, 1970)

Van Wyngarden, Greg, *Jasta 18 the Red Noses* (Oxford: Osprey, 2011)

Warner, Philip Lee, *Harrow War Memorials of the Great War*, Vol. 5 (London: The Medici Society, 1920)

Journals, Periodicals, Newspapers, Dissertations

An t-Oglach
Cross & Cockade
The Dublin Review
The Fell and Rock Journal
Flight/Flightglobal (especially their digitised online archive)
History Ireland
Institute of Civil Engineers (OCE), Minutes of Proceedings
Irish Sword—Journal of the Military History Society of Ireland
The Irish Times (including *Weekly*)
The London Gazette
The Observer
Over the Front
Popular Flying

Miscellaneous

'Efemérides de la Aviación: una Publicación del Museo Nacional Aeronáutico Y del Espacio Dirección General de Aeronáutica Civil', (Santiago de Chile: *Museo Nacional Aeronáutico Y Del Espacio*, November 2010)

Twomey, Frances, 'Cannocks—a Social and Economic History of the Limerick Company from 1840 to 1930' (dissertation, NIHE, University of Limerick, 1982)

National Archives and Imperial War Museum

I have examined several hundred service records and squadron operations record books from the UK National Archives. It would be wholly impractical to list them all here: references are cited in respect of individual aviators in their biographies. AIR 27 refers to a Squadron ORB; AIR 76 to those records generated in respect of RFC officers and those who transferred to the RAF in April 1918; AIR 79 to a file on one of the first 329,000 people of 'other ranks' who served in the RAF from April 1918 onwards, many of whom served in the interwar years and World War II; ADM to a file of the Admiralty, of which the RNAS officers' records are generally in the ADM 273 category, with the 'other ranks' or 'lower deck' being in the ADM 188 series. WO files are War Office files, of which WO 339 relates to officers and WO 95 to Battalion War Diaries.

The Imperial War Museum also has an extensive publicly accessible collection of audio recordings, including many conducted with former RFC, RNAS, and RAF personnel. References are cited in the biographies of individual aviators.

Websites

Of the numerous genealogy websites with particular relevance to Ireland, www.irishgenealogy.ie is an excellent resource for Church of Ireland records. Similarly, www.census.nationalarchives. ie is a good starting point for tracing the early years of many Irish servicemen via the 1901 and 1911 census returns.

While cross-checking the records of the Earl of Ypres's commission and/or squadron histories, I found the following site invaluable for identifying the memorials for fallen Irishmen: www.irishmemorials.ie.

For many searches of the UK census, travel records, passport application details, and so forth, I used ancestry.co.uk and findmypast.co.uk.

For military history and aviation history I found the following sites to be particularly useful:

www.theaerodrome.com
www.1914-1918.invisionzone.com/forums/index.php
www.rafweb.org

None of the foregoing information should be taken to imply that the owners of those sites endorse in any way or form the views expressed by this author.

Index